Science fiction, social conflict and war

edited by Philip John Davies

MANCHESTER UNIVERSITY PRESS
MANCHESTER and NEW YORK

distributed exclusively in the USA and Canada by ST. MARTIN'S PRESS

Published by Manchester University Press
Oxford Road, Manchester M13 9PL, UK
and Room 400, 175 Fifth Avenue,
New York, NY 10010, USA

Distributed exclusively in the USA and Canada
by St. Martin's Press Inc.,
175 Fifth Avenue, New York, NY 10010, USA

British Library cataloguing in publication data
Science fiction, social conflict, and war. — (Cultural politics).
    1. Science fiction — critical studies
    I. Davies, Philip John. II. Series
    809.38762

Library of Congress cataloging in publication data
Science fiction, social conflict, and war / edited by Philip John
    Davies
            p.   cm. — (Cultural politics)
        ISBN 0-7190-3288-1 — ISBN 0-7190 3451-5 (pbk.)
        1. Science fiction — History and criticism. 2. Social conflict in
    literature. 3. War in literature.
    I. Davies, Philip. 1948- II. Series.
    PN3433.5.835 1990
    809.3'8782—dc20   90-6302

ISBN 0 7190 3288 1 hardback
    0 7190 3451 5 paperback

Typeset in Joanna
by Koinonia Limited, Manchester
Printed in Great Britain
by Bell & Bain Limited, Glasgow

Contents

Acknowledgements

The successful completion of a collection of this kind depends on the complex collaboration of many participants. Things rarely proceed quite according to plan, and progress requires the complict tolerance, good will and hard work of all concerned. My thanks, therefore, to the authors for responding with such good humour to my requests, explanations, persuasion, and occasional threats to stamp my feet and hold my breath. At Manchester University Press John Banks and the reviewer of the original proposal both offered valuable and welcome advice.

Special thanks to Rosamund Sarah Davies who copy-edited the volume with care, and without ever pointing out that this was not included in the marriage vows. With their parents so engaged the children took themselves daily to junior school, and used the undisturbed hours at home to become better acquainted with their computer, and to re-read *Alice in Wonderland*, as well as filling the house with unrelenting good cheer. For all these contributions Andrew and Carolyn deserve the dedication of this volume.

Science fiction and conflict

Philip John Davies

When a president who had been trained in Hollywood, and who was famous for his use of film references, proposed the expenditure of billions of dollars of United States taxpayers' money on space technology and weaponry to protect America from the 'evil empire', he called the project the Strategic Defence Initiative. The taxpayers, also referring to Hollywood, preferred to call it 'Star Wars'. The science fictional reference was used by the opposition to deride what they saw as the fantastic in the Reagan administration's visions, though the programme may have gained some approbation by association with a financially successful film featuring the victory of a clean-cut Western-style hero against the forces of an evil empire. As the debate continued, lobbying groups formed to support, and to oppose, the SDI. One group known as the Coalition for SDI raised funds to promote the cause, some of which were spent on a television advertisement in which a little girl says:

I asked my Daddy what this Star Wars stuff was all about. He said that right now we can't protect ourselves from nuclear weapons. And that's why the President wants to build the Peace Shield. It would stop missiles in outer space so they couldn't hit our house. Then nobody could win a war, and if nobody could win a war there's no reason to start one. My Daddy's smart.

This voice-over, including a childish mispronunciation of 'nuclear', accompanies an animation apparently based on a child's drawing. A family of stick people stand in the garden by their house under a melancholy sun until the curve of a protective dome appears above them. Red rockets pop harmlessly against this force shield until the rockets cease, the shield turns to a rainbow, the sun smiles, and everyone seems set to live happily ever after. The Coalition for SDI apparently felt it had a winning case with this self-consciously childish science fiction. It is uncommon for the icons of science fiction to become so closely involved with the conflicts of policy debate, but it is not so rare for science fiction to provide commentary on the politics of conflict and war. It is perhaps fortunate that science fiction does not meet politics this closely very often, since while the SF literature aims to stimulate thought, these hijacked misrepresentations appear more aimed to limit it.

If direct connections with the politics of confrontation can serve to bring science fiction into disrepute, it may nevertheless be that SF is a literary form particularly suited to the analysis of conflict and war. Some science fiction takes within its remit the hardware of science and, political priorities being as they are, much of the hardware of science is war- or, if you like, defence-related. A genre that gives centre stage to scientific advance is set fair to become entangled with that which President Eisenhower called the 'military-industrial complex'. A fiction that takes as its natural subject exploration, and the problems of dealing with different times, places, and beings, is inevitably dealing with the stuff of confrontation. This is bound to include the examination of how confrontation leads to conflict, and the discussion of how conflict may be resolved through mediation and accommodation, or institutionalised by bigotry and societal inflexibility, or even lead to war. These kinds of concerns have helped science fiction to become one of the most saleable of popular literary genres. About 10 per cent of all fiction sold in the United Kingdom is science fiction, and according to Frederick Pohl 'in the United States ... nearly one novel in four was science-fiction or fantasy by the 1980s (Pohl, 1989, p. 53), but in spite of (or perhaps because of) this popularity, SF remains in a kind of literary ghetto, perceived by many as one of the less respectable, less worthy, and less serious cousins of established literature.

Kurt Vonnegut is one writer who has complained about the prejudice suffered by those identified as science fiction writers. He commented in a piece published by the *New York Times Book Review*:

I wrote a novel [*Player Piano*] about people and machines, and machines often got the best of it, as machines will ... And I learned from the reviewers that I was a science-fiction writer ... I have been a soreheaded occupant of a file drawer labeled 'science fiction' ever since, and I would like out, particularly since so many serious critics regularly mistake the drawer for a urinal. (Vonnegut, 1976, p. 25.)

Willis McNelly shares Vonnegut's opinion, and claims that the science fiction label subverted the reception of *Slaughterhouse five*. 'Why, [reviewers] ask, did Vonnegut choose science fiction as his medium? ... His message, they imply, has been lost in his medium.' (McNelly, p. 194.)

Vonnegut himself became concerned that the cultural prejudice against science fiction was threatening to limit the reach of his work. 'I objected finally to this label because I thought it was narrowing my readership. People regard science-fiction writers as interchangeable with comic-strip writers.' (Allen, p. 4.) And on the same lines, in a 1971 interview,

science-fiction writers have been beneath the attention of any serious critic. That is, far above you are the people dealing with the really important, beautiful issues and using great skills and so forth. It used to be that if you were a science-fiction writer you really didn't belong in the arts at all, and other artists wouldn't talk to you. You just had this scruffy little gang of your own. (Allen, p. 51.)

However, there can be security and comfort in a 'scruffy little gang of your own', and some analysts and practitioners in the science fiction field do not attribute the separatism entirely to prejudice guided by the priests of high culture. Samuel Delany has expressed the opinion that the commercialism of science fiction has underpinned the development of an exculpatory self-justification of low literary standards which responds to criticism along these lines: 'Basically we are writing adventure fiction. We are writing it very fast. We do not have the time to be concerned about any but the grosser errors. More important, you are talking about subtleties too refined for the vast majority of our readers who are basically neither literary nor sophisticated', an attitude which, in Delany's opinion, leads to 'true anti-literature.' (Delany, pp. 138-9.) While Judith Merril has spoken of the success of the genre in becoming 'a recognized and accepted part of American culture in the mid-forties', and its parallel failure in that 'it just wasn't a respectable part – not something a serious American writer would do' she still refers to SF's 'self-made ghetto' (Merril, pp. 78-9). This ghetto is at least partly sustained by the loyalty of SF fans, a group that appear to emerge to the full with the 1930s development of American science fiction, and who continue to give fervent support to their literary team, and its players. According to Frederick Pohl: 'It is very difficult to explain science-fiction fandom to anyone who has never experienced it. The closest analogy, perhaps, might be to the "cellar Christians" of pagan Rome, small, furtive groups of believers, meeting in secret, shunned or even attacked by outsiders or, as fans came to call them, the "mundanes".' (Pohl, p. 45.) The actions of the establishment, and the reactions of SF loyalists, have shifted science fiction into a parallel universe. The inhabitants of this universe comfort and support each other, and feel able to contemplate the vagaries of the 'real' world more clearly from their dislocated vantage point.

Dismissal by the gatekeepers of high culture may nurture hurt and resentment, but there are times and places where such disregard can be an advantage. Darko Suvin identifies the work of H. G. Wells, 'embracing a whole dimension of radical doubt and questioning', as a turning-point for all subsequent significant SF, which Wells's influences 'endowed ... with a basically materialist look back at human life and a rebelliousness against its entropic closure' (Suvin, pp. 220-1). SF, committed to examination of the alternative, and isolated by its commitment, appears able to accommodate radical doubt and questioning, whether this be of literary form, of scientific possibility, or of social convention, and from any one of many political directions. Exclusive, or excluded, the feeling and reality of separateness create an environment where thought and invention may be liberated from normal confines. At the same time, seen (often entirely justifiably) as harmless, low-brow escapism, it can remain disregarded by the more politically oriented definers of public acceptability. Judith Merril has spoken of 'the height of the McCarthy era, when science fiction became, for a time, virtually the only vehicle of political dissent ...' (Merril, p. 74.) Patrick Parrinder, citing the work of T. A. Shippey, also claims that 'during the McCarthy years in America [SF magazines] voice[d] embattled liberal attitudes which could hardly get a hearing elsewhere' (Parrinder, p. 43). However, the lowly status of SF does not guarantee immunity from oversight. Someone in government was reading *Astounding* magazine closely enough in 1944 to prompt a raid on the offices when a story came too close to the secret truths of nuclear fission (Parrinder, p. 43; Olander *et al.*, p. 3). Mack Reynolds, for many years an active member of the US Socialist Labor party, and a leading exponent of SF with political and social content, tells a story of editorial self-censorship when a story of his called 'Russkies Go Home' was first accepted, then rejected by Horace Gold, editor of *Galaxy* on the grounds that 'it had "become a victim of the Cold War" ... it had become a taboo to treat the Russians with sympathy, even in humor' (Reynolds, pp. 138-9). The editor of the *Magazine of fantasy and science fiction* was either more daring, or less politically aware, since the story eventually appeared in its pages.

If American SF of the 1950s provided an arena for anti-establishment thought, this did not come out of a broadly-held sympathy for left-wing or progressive ideas in the science fiction world. Certainly some of the most noticed SF has been from writers claimed by the left as theirs. Edward Bellamy's Looking backward vision may not have been socialism, but it inspired thousands of Americans to join Nationalist clubs aiming to guide the nation to Utopia. One person joining the New York Nationalists was Daniel De Leon, who soon went on to be the guiding light of the Socialist Labor Party (Coleman, pp. 13-14). H. G. Wells and George Orwell also figure in the list of left-wing SF greats, albeit their writing contained grave misgivings about the possible solutions, as well as analysis of the current problems. However, the American SF clientele of the twentieth century has probably leaned to the right, and certainly the literature has encompassed authors and work of many different political shades. But in dealing with a subject matter that confronts the problems of technological and social change, which poses the possibility of alternatives, and which is not limited to the orthodoxies of the known universe, the literature regularly deals with political questions, directly or tangentially. In so doing it is inevitable that some unorthodox ideas will be expressed, regardless of the colour of the regime. While in America and Britain this challenge and examination comes from an SF world often comfortable in its isolation, the SF writers of other countries, for example in Eastern Europe and the Soviet Union, have had to rely on the ghettoisation of their literature to allow their messages a medium, while being unable to rely on the paraphernalia of western fandom and SF self-consciousness for moral support.

Writers in western countries, meanwhile, have had the luxury of being able to indulge in an orgy of debates over definition, form, and politics. The 1960s and 70s brought with them a wide range of challenges, change, conflict and politicisation. Within the SF world a New Wave of writing was announced in its own Manifesto, a shift initially 'regarded within the SF field as one of defection' (Pohl, p. 53; Parrinder, p. 18). At the same time there was a feeling that the novel was failing the intellectual challenges of the 1970s, and that SF might provide the required 'new literary form' (Greenberg and Warrick, p. 2). As Godfrey Kearns explains, 'novelists like Philip Roth and John Barth ... wonder[ed] whether the novel was redundant as a literary form. Hence Kurt Vonnegut creates his own "space oddity" in order to make sense of the horrors and hopelessness of a world which, as he points out in Jailbird (1979), has wilfully denied the moral of the Sermon on the Mount' (Kearns, p. 38). In these years everything was subject to challenge, including the definition of what was the mainstream. If this gave a window of opportunity for SF, it certainly has not led to major changes in the genre's image.

Entering the 1990s, articles have appeared in the USA and Britain bemoaning the continued unacceptability of SF. An article in the *Guardian* accused Britain's television stations of ignoring science fiction, claiming that on the whole 'TV networks have assumed that the science fiction audience is made up solely of children and have battered the air waves with a succession of cheap and tacky American cartoons with low-grade animation and lower-grade stories'. (Rayner, p. 23.) Hollywood has had some SF blockbusters, but this has not spun off into any substantial filming of the genre's classics, or use of the field's fine authors. According to Robert Moss, writing in the *New York Times*,

Among the most common reasons cited by members of the film industry ... [are] the cerebral and imaginative nature of the work itself and the lack of any real familiarity with it among the small power elite who can get a movie made. The writers themselves are often looked on as only slightly less alien than the creatures they write about. (Moss, p. H13.)

In the *New York Times Book Review* Noel Perrin reflects on fourteen years of teaching a college-level science fiction course. When the course was introduced, 'Not all my colleagues in the English department were embarrassed by the new course, just most. Say, 25 out of 30.' But, argues Perrin, 'science fiction writers continue to suppose that questions of value can be meaningfully discussed ... In fact, science fiction has become the chief refuge for metaphysics.' The argument has not convinced all of his colleagues: 'In 1989 I don't suppose that more than half the department is embarrassed by the existence of the course ... some of my colleagues' literary misgivings have been justified. Not about the books, but about me. I have found the metaphysics too tempting.' (Perrin, pp. 38-9.) Perrin appears to have something in common with the Vonnegut character, Eliot P. Rosewater when, in *God bless you, Mr Rosewater* he tells a science fiction writers' convention

You're the only ones who'll talk about the really terrific changes going on, the only ones crazy enough to know that life is a space voyage, and not a short one either, but one that will last for billions of years. You're the only ones with guts enough to really care about the future, who really know what machines do to us, what cities do to us, what big, simple ideas do to us, what tremendous mistakes, accidents, and catastrophes do to us. You're the only ones zany enough to agonize ... over the fact that we are right now determining whether the space voyage for the next billion years or so is going to Heaven or Hell. (Vonnegut, 1972, pp. 21-2.)

SF, often in conflict with the literary establishment, but bolstered by its isolation, has proved an excellent laboratory for some 'big, simple ideas', especially the ideas to do with alienation, conflict and war that are examined by the authors in this volume.

References

Allen William Rodney (ed.), *Conversations with Kurt Vonnegut* (Jackson, Miss. and London, 1988).

Bellamy, Edward, *Looking backward, 2000-1887* (many editions, first published 1888).

Coleman, Stephen, *Daniel De Leon* (Manchester and New York, 1990).

Delany, Samuel R., 'About five thousand one hundred and seventy five words' in *SF: the other side of realism* (Bowling Green, Ohio, 1971), ed. Thomas Clareson, pp. 130-46.

Greenberg Martin Harry and Warrick, Patricia S. (eds.), *Political science fiction* (Englewood Cliffs, NJ, 1974).

Kearns, Godfrey, 'United States of America' in *Literature of Europe and America in the 1960s* (Manchester and New York, 1989), eds. Spencer Pearce and Don Piper, pp. 10-43.

McNelly, Willis E., 'Science fiction, the modern mythology (Vonnegut's *Slaughterhouse Five*)' in *SF: the other side of realism* (Bowling Green, Ohio, 1971), ed. Thomas Clareson, pp. 193-8.

Merril, Judith, 'What do you mean: Science? Fiction?' in *SF: the other side of realism* (Bowling Green, Ohio, 1971), ed. Thomas Clareson, pp. 53-95.

Moss, Robert F., 'To sci-fi writers Hollywood is mostly alien', *New York Times*, 4 June 1989, pp. H13, H18.

Olander, Joseph D., Greenberg, Martin H., and Warrick, Patricia (eds.), *American government through science fiction* (Chicago, 1974).

Parrinder, Patrick, *Science fiction: its criticism and teaching* (London and New York 1980).

Perrin, Noel, 'Science fiction: imaginary worlds and real-life questions', *New York Times Book Review*, 9 April 1989, pp. 37-8.

Pohl, Frederick, 'Astounding Story', *American heritage*, Vol. 40, No. 6 (September/October 1989), pp. 42-54.

Rayner, Jay, 'Voyage into a black hole', *Guardian*, 15 June 1989, p. 23.

Reynolds, Mack, 'Science fiction and socioeconomics', in *Fantastic lives: autobiographical essays by notable science fiction writers* (Carbondale, Ill. 1981), ed. Martin H. Greenberg, pp. 118-43.

Suvin, Darko, *Metamorphoses of science fiction* (New Haven, CT, and London, 1979).

Vonnegut, Kurt, *Player piano* (New York, 1952).

—, *God bless you, Mr Rosewater* (London, 1972; first published 1965).

—, *Slaughterhouse-five* (New York, 1969).

—, *Wampeters foma & granfalloons* (London, 1976; first published 1974).

—, *Jailbird* (New York, 1979).

2

Where no man has gone before: sexual politics and women's science fiction

Jacqueline Pearson

When in recent years female writers sought to introduce new and explicitly feminist images of women, many turned to literary genres with relatively short histories and low status, especially the detective story and science fiction. This forms a striking parallel to the late seventeenth and early eighteenth centuries, when women first tried in any numbers to negotiate a place in the world of literary publication, and made greatest headway in non-canonical genres, and in particular the novel, which they could shape to their own concerns without the anxieties of influence that haunted more established forms. It is likely that the intervention of women in modern popular genres will prove as decisive. Certainly many critics have noted the increased participation of women writers in science fiction, and this is perhaps best understood in the light of Darko Suvin's assertion that science fiction is 'historically part of a submerged or plebeian "lower literature" expressing the yearnings of previously repressed or at any rate non-hegemonic social groups'.[1]

Women writers have found the tropes of science fiction particularly useful for dealing with the politics of gender. Rosemary Jackson suggests that fantasy 'traces the unsaid and unseen of culture: that which has been silenced, made invisible, covered over, and made "absent".'[2] as such, it is a highly appropriate form for women whose language expresses, according to feminist theories, 'the unsaid, the unmeaningful, the repressed holes in masculine discourse'.[3] Indeed, feminist theory, which speculates about the future and about different ways of living, has often been written in modes strongly influenced by fantasy and science fiction: Monique Wittig's work in particular forms an interface between fantasy and theoretic.[4] To take only one further example, when in an account of an eighteenth-century novelist, a feminist critic writes of 'women's parallel reality, the other-world state in which women live, relative to the...world of men',[5] her idiom is close to that of science fiction texts that depict the two sexes inhabiting literally different worlds. Conversely, fantasy and science fiction have proved useful tools for examining some of the recurrent themes of feminism – the battle of the sexes as 'two groups with opposite interests',[6] the inequities encoded in language – which have produced science fiction texts which function as heuristic for feminist theory.

'Fantasies', of course, 'are never ideologically "innocent" texts'. (Like Rosemary Jackson but unlike, for instance, Darko Suvin, I use 'fantasy' as a broad term for the continuum of counter-realist modes of which science fiction forms a part.)[7] Fantasy is 'important precisely because it is wholly dependent on reality for its existence',[8] so that it can depict a culture very minutely through its desires, its anxieties and its repressions. Thus Mary E. Bradley Lane's *Mizora*, an early separatist feminist utopia first published in 1880-1, makes opposite points from exercises in a similar mode in the 1970s. It reveals, for instance, nineteenth-century optimism about science, for the women have succeeded in cleansing food of natural impurities and eat only synthetics: it therefore suggests very different relations between women and the natural world from, say, Sally Miller Gearhart's mystically ecological *The wanderground* (1979).[9]

Images of women in science fiction

Utopian fiction has, since its origins, experimented with new roles for women. Plato's Republic, More's Utopia, or Swift's Lilliput, while wholly androcentric, recommend a greater participation of women in education, government, or public life. However, a tension between a culturally constructed androcentrism and a philosophical desire to question social assumptions can be found even in radical texts. James Lawrence's utopian accounts of the matriarchal society of the Nairs (c. 1798-1801),[10] for instance, argue vigorously for the individual's right to sexual freedom, and his titles make approving reference to the Wollstonecraftian 'Rights of Women'. European society, which represses 'both sexes' (Empire Vol. I, p. 16) is contrasted with the world of the Nairs, where rape, seduction, prostitution, jealousy, sexual frustration and chastity do not exist. However, Lawrence's plea for the equality of the sexes − 'why shoold the woman obey the man, more than the man shoold obey the woman?' (System, p. 7) − reveals awkward inconsistencies. He is undecided, for instance, about the extent to which the differences between the sexes are innate or socially constructed, at one moment arguing that the 'equality ov the sexes' (System, p. 5) is self-evident, the next offering a wholly conventional ideology of separate spheres in which 'Man is designed for activ, woman for domestic, life' (System, p. 28). Moreover, his view of liberated women sometimes seems merely to pander to male fantasies, and once it is no longer forbidden for women to be sexually active, it becomes compulsory. The Nair woman Camilla tells us that 'To make a worthy man happy no goodnatured woman would refuse; her compliance is a trifle ...' (Empire, Vol. III, p. 28-9). Here Lawrence's radical model of female sexual autonomy comes perilously close to conventional models of women as passive objects of male desire. Lawrence's view of the sexes as 'equal ... neither subservient to the other' (System, p. 28), like all ideologies of separate spheres, reveals hidden contradictions.

Later male writers also present strong female characters without actually questioning the sexual status quo.[11] Even the 'New Wave' of the sixties 'showed no specific awareness of feminism and did not do much to advance the improvement of the image of women in sf'.[12] The same can be said even of such a pioneering work as Philip José Farmer's The lovers.[13] Many readers in the fifties found this excitingly innovative in allowing SF to acknowledge sexual desires: and yet its treatment of power and gender is actually highly conventional. The male protagonist transgresses the codes of his repressive patriarchy by a sexual relationship with a 'woman' he meets on an alien planet. She, however, is really a lalitha, a member of an all-female, insectoid species only mimicking humanity. The lalitha provide an image for women and are used to articulate and endorse misogynist stereotypes. They have wonderful powers of mimicry but no originality, and they exert a strong force for conservatism − 'They tried to keep the status quo in every aspect of culture, and ... to eliminate all new and progressive ideas' (p. 188). The novel moves towards the sexual emancipation of the male, but its images of the female are wholly traditional.

Images of women in 'pre-feminist' women's science fiction

While male writers of science fiction often produce traditional views of gender even while apparently questioning '"natural" social arrangements',[14] female writers show their usual chameleon ability to accommodate themselves to traditional androcentric models, and yet simultaneously to subvert these modes from within: to reconcile 'an implicitly rebellious vision with an explicitly decorous form'.[15] The most interesting of early female chameleons is C. L. Moore, one of the few women writers for the thirties pulp market. Despite her use of a male-identified narrative voice, her stories reveal peculiarly female preoccupations as well as a sharp awareness of what was going on in the real world. In the background of her stories lurk disquietingly precise images of the Depression: in 'Scarlet dream' her regular hero Northwest Smith enters a dreamworld inhabited by down-and-outs who have become inert and apathetic like people without work, feed on blood at soup kitchens, and are prey to a shadowy 'Thing' that 'hungers and must be fed' (p. 115),[16] a kind of image of the devouring power of capital. Indeed, most of Moore's horrors are rewritings, often highly imaginative, of the vampire, and the Northwest Smith stories deal obsessively with images of food and eating. 'Hunger' and 'hungry' are key words (e.g. 'Black thirst' p. 62, 'The tree of life' p. 92, 'Lost paradise' p. 186, 'Julhi' p. 210, 'Yvala', p. 286, etc.): this, in a culture where women are still given major responsibility for shopping for and preparing food, dramatises specifically female anxieties. Despite this, Moore was, from commercial necessity, 'adept at writing from the male point of view'.[17] As a result her stories of Northwest Smith are usually seen as accommodating themselves entirely to traditional forms with a tough male hero fighting off sinister, often female, aliens – as depicting, from a male point of view, a 'battle between the sexes figured as two different species'.[18]

These stories typically begin with Northwest Smith meeting an alien female, usually casting her as victim and him as rescuer: this is the starting point of 'Shambleau', 'Black thirst', 'The tree of life', 'Julhi' and 'The cold gray god'. These encounters, however, are rarely what they seem, and Moore is ingenious in deconstructing the 'damsel in distress' trope. In 'Shambleau', Smith saves a 'berry-brown girl' (p. 2) from a mob. She seems 'like a woman ... sweet and submissive and demure' (p. 18): but in fact she is Medusa, and an allegedly 'natural' balance of power between male and female is abruptly reversed. She ceases to be 'submissive' while he descends 'into a blind abyss of submission' (p. 21). She usurps the active/phallic role with her 'snaky ... tresses' (p. 21), while he becomes wholly passive. This process of 'feminisation' of Northwest Smith, the deconstruction of the macho hero, is unusual among pulp writers of the thirties. In fact, Smith is an oddly ineffectual hero, rarely able to save himself from peril, but dependent for rescue upon male friends (in 'Shambleau', 'Dust of gods', 'Lost paradise', and 'The cold gray god'), or the self-sacrificing heroism of women (in 'Black thirst', 'Scarlet dream' and 'Julhi'). Reversals of libidinal economy are also frequent. The vampiric Shambleau forces Smith into a 'submission' previously defined as womanish, and in 'Julhi' this powerful vampiric female renders him 'impotent' (p. 225, twice), while her potency is demonstrated as 'her plume whipped erect... '(p. 228).

Moore, then, undermines stereotypes of the damsel in distress and of the macho hero. It might seem, however, that she is conventional in defining powerful females as evil. Critics have acknowledged the erotic power of her tales, but have seen it as a male-identified, misogynous eroticism: 'the Shambleau's unfettered sexuality ... suggests that such sensuality is evil, destructive',[19] the tale is read as a 'recapitulation of male anxieties' about the vagina, and Moore is said to share the 'socially induced dread of female sexuality and the intense misogyny that marked her historical moment'.[20] But if male texts image strong women as monsters, the female reader/spectator, and in this case the hidden female author, 'is always caught up in a double desire', identifying safely with the victorious male but also, subversively, with the defeated female.[21] Shambleau may thus not only recall Freud's Medusa, with her 'failed because multiplied phallicism', but also anticipate Cixous', 'beautiful and ... laughing' .[22] The tale ends with the destruction of the Shambleau, but the ultimate victory of the female may be only deferred, for Smith is unable to promise that he will successfully resist female sexuality in future. In this tale, and in others, there is a discernible tension between Moore's male-identified narrative voice and a delight in powerful women and sexual role-reversals.

The tale which reveals these contradictions most clearly is 'Yvala'. Smith is employed by slavers to investigate rumours of beautiful 'sirens' (p. 265) on one of Jupiter's moons. The jungle in which the slave-ship lands suggests some misogynous stereotypes of female sexuality – 'the worst type of semi-animate, ravenous super-tropical jungle, reeking with fertility and sudden death, hot...' (p. 266). Here dwells Yvala, a powerful female who has authored the illusory 'sirens' to attract men, on whose 'worship' she will feed (p. 291). The male hunters, bent on enslaving helpless women, become her victims. In its ironic reversals, 'Yvala' simultaneously offers two contradictory fables of sexual politics. On the surface, Yvala is Circe, vampirically feeding on men and wickedly turning them into beasts. In the subtext, however, she is the innocent victim of male aggression, which she exposes by revealing their natural animality, 'the very core of savagery that dwells in every man' (p. 287). Smith is turned into a wolf, with all that suggests about male sexuality. Moore as creator covertly identifies with Yvala as creator, and at the end of the tale Smith escapes but Yvala remains undefeated. Moore assumes the protective coloration of misogynist convention in order to enter a male-dominated literary market, but behind this she covertly offers subversive images of gender which mock the male hero and are potentially liberating for the female reader.

Between the 1950s and the 1980s women writers of science fiction, as in mainstream fiction, can be seen moving from a strategy of female chameleonism to more overt and radical feminist strategies. This development can be seen economically exemplified in the Darkover tales of Marion Zimmer Bradley, from The planet savers (1958) to City of sorcery (1984). Early novels are highly androcentric and ethnocentric, privileging white, Terran, males and allowing us to see female, Darkovan, characters only through their eyes. Many of these early novels are quite specifically male rites of passage, with few female characters, and none who are highly developed. An extreme case is Star of danger (1965), where the central character is the boy Larry Montray and there are no important female characters at all.

Bradley's rewriting of the life of Lew Alton best illustrates her changing views on gender and women's roles. The sword of Aldones (1962) produced the 'prequel' The heritage of Hastur (1975) and was rewritten as Sharra's exile (1981). Sword is told in the first person by Lew; in the rewritings this first-person voice is retained, but, on the model of Bleak House, alternates with an objective third-person narrative. This results in a less overpowering androcentricity, and a new respect for the female characters, especially Dio Ridenow, Lew's mistress. In Sword, Lew speaks in the hard-boiled, macho idiom of the sub-Chandlerian

detective novel, and in a particularly nasty scene strikes Dio - 'You
ought to be hurt!...You ought to be beaten!...I brought my hand back
and slapped her, hard. The blow sent her reeling...' (pp. 115-16). In
the revisions, Bradley substitutes for this male-identified sadism a new
literary model, Jane Eyre, so that Lew is identified with a more
ambiguous image of masculinity, Rochester. Like Rochester Lew is
mutilated — both lose a hand in a conflagration caused by an
uncontrolled female — and embittered by past sufferings. And, if Lew
becomes Rochester, Dio becomes Jane. In Sharra's exile the face-slapping
scene is excised, and their first meeting is modelled on that of Jane and
Rochester, where the man's horse throws him and he has to be rescued
by the woman (Exile, pp. 52-4), which allows for wholesale reversals
of conventional hero/heroine roles.

In mid-career Bradley clearly had problems with feminism. Although 'under various pseudonyms she wrote several lesbian paperback novels during the 1960s',[23] her Darkover novels of the sixties and
early seventies are conventional in gender relations (an apparent
exception, The world wreckers, will be discussed later). Some novels of the
seventies indeed, express overt hostility to the women's movement.
In Darkover landfall (1972) Ewen Ross attacks the career spacer Camilla
Del Rey for being unwilling to give birth to the child with which she
has been impregnated. He patronisingly explains that she is suffering
from 'a pathology ... sociologists called it "Women's Liberation" ... but
what it amounted to was a pathological reaction to overpopulation and
overcrowding' (p. 113): and the novel nowhere criticises this view.
In Bradley's novels such attitudes persist to some extent: but when in
Thendara house (1983) Ellemir puts forward a similar view this is only
one side of an argument which she does not necessarily win (pp. 409-
11). By the mid 1980s Bradley is making very different statements,
writing of her enthusiasm for 'Gay Rights and Women's Rights', and
of her belief that not planetary discovery but 'Women's Liberation is
the great event of the twentieth century'.[24]

Bradley's fame among feminists is mostly due to the matriarchal
culture in The ruins of Isis (1978) and the Darkovan trilogy focusing on
the Free Amazons or Guild of Renunciates, The shattered chain (1976),
Thendara house (1983) and City of sorcery (1984). Bradley's fictions tend
to operate through the creation of polarised opposites which are then
reconciled — Darkovan/Terran, magic/technology, even the two
warring identities of Jay/Jason Allison in The planet savers (1962), a novel
orchestrated by powerful images of integration, and whose last word

is 'together' (p. 101). *Star of danger* ends as 'The brother worlds were once again reconciled' (p. 160): and the specifically masculine language of the discourse here is appropriate to this highly androcentric book. But the result of this strong movement towards reintegration can be, as in *The ruins of Isis*, soggy compromise, the bizarre situation in which a feminist writer is seen arguing for equal rights for men. Bradley's later novels are less optimistic about integration, and especially about whether the female can simply be integrated into a male world. To provide an alternative for Darkovan women, Bradley invented the Free Amazons, women who live autonomously in a woman-centred society. The Free Amazons haunted Bradley's imagination from *The planet savers*, though this story is seen through male eyes, and the tomboyish Kyla Raineach, a 'girl' (pp. 31, 39, 40, 48, etc.) who is not very physically co-ordinated and shows conventionally 'feminine' emotion, is very different from the tough, capable women of the later stories.

The Free Amazons − somewhat, it appears, to Bradley's embarrassment − caught the imagination of women readers. In the Darkover fanzine *Starstone*, Amazon stories submitted outnumbered all other submissions put together.[25] They clearly offer something that women felt was missing in the real world, for Bradley notes that women have changed their names to the Amazon style and have set up Amazon Guild Houses in the USA, and that she has become Oath-Mother to a number of Renunciates.[26] At the same time, Bradley seems to feel increasingly that even the Amazon alternative is not enough to allow her female characters to develop as whole human beings: she has written, 'I resolutely refuse to countenance apartheid, even when it is camouflaged and rationalized as "women's space"'.[27] An apparent disillusion with feminism as a political movement makes her end the trilogy in *City of sorcery* with Magda Lorne leaving the Guild House behind as an outgrown stage of her life, seeking a mystic rather than a political 'Sisterhood'. Bradley's long career leads from androcentrism to feminism to 'post-feminism', and thus economically reflects trends in society and in mainstream women's writing.

Some themes in feminist science fiction

The themes of women's science fiction coincide with their 'mainstream' writing to a greater extent than is true in writing by men.

Women's novels, or feminist theoretic, provide metaphors of gender difference which can be given detailed materiality in science fiction. The literal war between the sexes in a novel like Joanna Russ's The female man is only a continuation in another form of the metaphorical war in women's novels from Aphra Behn's to Alison Lurie's The war between the Tates. The women-dominated communities so popular in feminist science fiction of the seventies and eighties are only a step from the community dominated by 'Amazons' in Gaskell's Cranford, or in other novels centring on 'Communities of Women'.[28]

The same continuity can be seen in themes of women's language. In their linguistic innovations modernist writers like Gertrude Stein and Virginia Woolf have been seen as producing 'a fantasy about a utopian linguistic structure'.[29] But only science fiction can imagine more fully new, non-oppressive, female languages which explicitly rectify some of the omissions of the linguistics of the dominant group. Some fictions, for instance, invent a singular common-gender pronoun, like 'kin' in Dorothy Bryant's The kin of Ata are waiting for you, 'na' in June Arnold's The cook and the carpenter, or 'per' in Marge Piercy's Woman on the edge of time: in a culture with such a language, discrimination on the grounds of sex becomes literally unspeakable. Other texts imagine what the language of a truly liberated female future will be like: in the 'Glorious Age' of Wittig and Zeig's Lesbian peoples there is 'an avoidance of fixed meanings', many words, like 'woman' and 'wife', have become obsolete, and some have changed their meaning, like 'have', which will no longer mean 'to possess' (pp. 166, 164-5, 71).

Women in feminist theory seem to have a paradoxical relationship with language, and this is reflected in feminist science fiction. On the one hand, they form a 'muted group', disadvantaged and made 'inarticulate' within their own language because that language is specifically 'man-made' to serve male needs.[30] On the other hand, there is also the suggestion that women's language is potentially, or even covertly, superior to that of the dominant group, since it is possessed of a rich 'plurality', where 'meanings' are 'redoubled and multiplied', and which images women's plural sexuality.[31] Feminist science fiction sometimes dramatises patriarchy's power to silence women: Elnoa in Suzy McKee Charnas's Motherlines (1978) has had her tongue cut out, in The wanderground we hear of many silenced women, including Gwen Aquarius, 'the libber' – 'they cut out her tongue' (p. 83). In Margaret Atwood's The handmaid's tale (1985) 'silent' (pp. 100, 231) and 'silence' (pp. 233, 266) are key words: women in this repressive theocratic patriarchy are rendered 'speechless' (p. 56). However, science fiction also speculates on the power of female languages. In *The wanderground* women develop telepathic powers which compensate for their cultural silencing, and in *The handmaid's tale* silenced women develop 'a secret language' (p. 287) composed of a knowledge of traditions of female opposition, and of the use of puns, 'Body language' (p. 190), illegal graffiti (pp. 156, 234), and a subversive language of whispers (p. 234). In Suzette Haden Elgin's *Native tongue* (1984) and *The Judas rose* (1986), a sort of feminist *Foundation and empire*, women devise a 'secret language' (*Tongue*, p. 266), which will have 'the right words in it' to express female insights and concerns (*Tongue*, p. 267), and will consequently 'change reality' (*Tongue*, p. 296).

Some of the themes of feminist science fiction have already been well discussed elsewhere, like women's rewriting of the nuclear family and their creation of female-dominated or separatist utopias, so at present it will only be necessary to note the popularity of these tropes. I want instead to examine two other themes: woman as alien, and images of transsexuality, as part of a continuing discussion of whether gender differences are innate or socially constructed.

Central to science fiction, which inhabits 'the semantic space created by the opposition of human versus nonhuman',[32] is the figure of the alien. Theorists like Suvin and Robert Scholes have read science fiction as a literature of 'cognitive estrangement', which works to make the familiar seem strange, operating on its audience through a Brechtian 'alienation effect'.[33] The alien is thus not only subject but also the very medium of the working of the text. In addition, the alien has a special meaning to women. SF by men tends to define women as alien, for 'to be human is to be male',[34] and the female is cast as 'other'. It may even hint that the damsel in distress is somehow 'secretly in league' with the alien monster against whom she seeks the hero's aid, her uncontrolled emotionalism rendering him vulnerable to the forces of irrationality which the alien represents even as it is apparently defeated.[35]

While male writers' use of aliens may encode anxieties about women, feminists tend to reclaim metaphors of otherness. It is a recurrent theme of feminist science fiction that men and women are 'not all of one race', or even 'of two different species', 'no longer of the same species'. 'Sexually', men and women 'meet ... as aliens':[36] and women often specifically identify with the alien. Spock in *Star Trek* appealed to women as an outsider within his society, who had to manage a hidden emotional life, was forbidden by his cultural context from being the sexual initiator, and was thus psychically 'feminised', while also possessing immense physical and psychic power.[37] Even in 'mainstream' fiction, 'alien' is a key word for women writers in their dramatisation of the dilemma of women within patriarchy: one example among many would be the fiction of Jean Rhys, full of women who are literally or figuratively displaced, expatriate, alienated, and who find themselves 'the stranger, the alien'[38] within their society.

Feminists may repeat the human/alien dyad, but privilege an alien (i.e. female) point of view, or may define the male rather than the female as alien. To take a single example, in James Tiptree Jr's 'The women men don't see', the female protagonist finds the aliens less alien than men of her own species, including the male narrator. Sarah Lefanu points out how in Tiptree's work, '[t]he alienation of one sex from another stands as the paradigm ... of other forms of difference',[39] and the same is true of much feminist science fiction. Alternatively, feminists can deconstruct the human/alien polarity altogether. Both of these strategies can be seen in the work of C. J. Cherryh, who is famous for the sympathy and conviction of her presentation of aliens. Many novels begin within an alien culture, usually egalitarian or female dominated, and introduce the human male through alien, often female, eyes. *Cuckoo's egg* (1985) begins with a double reversal as we see the human child Thorn through alien eyes, and the alien male warrior Duun becomes his 'mother'. *Pride of Chanur* (1982) begins with the female world of the spacegoing *hani*, and shows us the human male Tully − 'it' (p. 7) − through their compassionate but objective eyes, filthy, terrified, inarticulate, 'other'. *Serpent's reach* (1980) goes beyond the reversal of codes of privilege to the deconstruction of the human/ alien polarity. It begins with the alien Kontrin and especially with the heroine Raen, and only later shows us human, 'beta', culture through her eyes: though to describe it in this way distorts the novel, for both Kontrin and betas are in some respects human, in some alien. In fact the novel disintegrates the human/alien dyad by the range of its depiction of different cultures and their complexity, and by Raen's deep and sympathetic involvement both with the ant-like, female-dominated Hive culture of the *majat* and with the world of the artificially-created *azi*. The distinction between human and alien becomes, in other words, meaningless.

The fiction of Lisa Tuttle also uses the image of the alien for specifically feminist purposes, showing men and women approaching each other from wholly different levels of reality, meeting briefly before moving back into their own separate universes. In 'The hollow man' (orig. 1979) she is alive, he a revived corpse, a 'barely human being' (p.153):[40] in 'No regrets' (orig. 1985) the male and female understand the past in radically different ways and so inhabit wholly different presents. 'Wives' retells the story of The lovers from the viewpoint of the subjugated female/alien people whose culture has been destroyed by 'the men' (p. 25). As a desperate tactic for survival they have accepted the loss of their 'identities' (p. 30), and have camouflaged themselves as wives, even if they can be only 'imitations, creatures moulded by the men' (p. 31). This bleakly pessimistic tale exposes femininity as a social construct with no connection with biological realities. 'The family monkey' is a dazzling series of variations on themes of alienation. A southern family has adopted the shipwrecked ET they call Pete, but the story focuses less on the alienness of Pete than on that of Emily, the intellectual, and of Jody, the girl-child who has learned Pete's empathic powers and thereby become 'different' (p. 74). Both of these women find Pete less alien than the human males around them. The tale draws the alienness not only of the alien but of the spinster, the rebellious daughter, the liberated woman, the female artist, the female anti-racist, the female adolescent – in fact of the female altogether.

The metaphor of the alien deeply colours women's science fiction in its depiction of gender relations. It has been said that it is characteristic of women writers of fantasy to 'direct their narratives toward acceptance of the Other, not merely dealienating ... but actually integrating Self and Other',[41] and this is true of the more optimistic writers, like Cherryh: human and majat, human and hani, are siblings under the skin, and her fictions imagine gender and sex relations which will no longer be oppressive to women, like Raen's affair with the azi Jim. More pessimistic writers reproduce the trope of alienness, though replacing a male with a female viewpoint, and emphasise the alienness not only of human and extra-terrestrial, but of man and woman. We live, feminist theorists have told us, 'in a culture where sexual relations are impracticable, since the desire of man and the desire of woman are so foreign to each other',[42] and this insight is dramatised in the fictions of Tuttle and Tiptree.

Images of the alien are particularly dealienated in lesbian feminist science fiction. If men and women meet sexually as aliens, these writers hope that this will be less true in the case of two women. Thus

Jody Scott's I, vampire (1984) concludes not that 'alien is evil' (p. 199), but that '[t]here are no aliens' (p. 61). Both the heroines, a 600-year-old vampire and a Rysemian fishwoman currently disguised as Virginia Woolf (!), are 'unhuman' (p. 59), but their alienness from conventional standards of normality only makes them less alien to each other, and both vampirism and alienness are used to figure both lesbianism and, more broadly, femininity. Moreover, lesbian feminist science fiction assigns new meanings to the alienness of the alien planet. In traditional SF the 'conquest' of the alien planet figures victory over the 'other' and often specifically over the female: titles like Poul Anderson's Virgin planet make this explicit, as do the phallic spaceships mocked by James Tiptree Jr.[43] In lesbian and feminist fiction, planetary discovery is more likely to be a metaphor for self-discovery (as in much feminist crime fiction what is detected is less the criminal than the real self of the detective). Thus in Katherine V. Forrest's Daughters of a coral dawn (1984) the important discovery is not that of the alien planet, but the part-alien Megan's coming to terms with her own lesbian sexuality and her love for the human Laurel.

Like contemporary feminist theory, feminist science fiction is preoccupied with questions about the origins of gender difference: is it innate and biologically determined, or socially constructed? Writers of science fiction, like feminist theorists, are divided between essentialist and androgynous views. Simone de Beauvoir holds the androgynous position, arguing that 'the eternal feminine is a lie',[44] while feminists like Mary Daly argue that woman's nature is innately different from man's. In science fiction the same plot structures, for instance the separatist feminist utopia, can encode either view. Pamela Sargent's The shore of women (1986) takes an androgynous position, arguing that 'We are more malleable than we realize' (p. 340), and answering with a tentative affirmative the question of a woman from a female-dominated society, 'Would men, living here, become more like us?' (p. 90). Sally Miller Gearhart's The wanderground uses the same form to express instead a 'gynocentric essentialism'.[45] Here the Gentles, males who voluntarily forego sexual potency to live outside the cities and communicate with the women, remain inherently different from them. While female telepathy is imaged as non-violent, 'an enfoldment', men's is 'like a bridge ... like a sword' (p. 178).

Feminist writers of SF make powerful use of images of transsexualism in their examinations of sexual difference: gender is presented as unstable, and consequently any social organisation founded upon gender inequality is shown to be manifestly absurd. The seminal SF text here is Ursula K. Le Guin's The left hand of darkness: it is also the most problematic. The inhabitants of Gethen are normally neuter, though in their sexually receptive period they temporarily develop as either male or female. Any individual will in the course of her/his life develop both roles and will be able to father as well as give birth to children. Gender roles are therefore unknown, a state of affairs which the stuffily conventional male human narrator finds 'appalling' (p. 70). Le Guin's world is fascinating, but many feminist critics have found it ultimately unsatisfying, for the androgynous world of Gethen does not empower the female but effectively renders her invisible, since the androgynous ruler is a 'king' and the male pronoun is persistently used. In a 1989 edition of her collection of essays, The language of the night, though, Le Guin has annotated her 1976 defence of this novel, 'Is gender necessary?', showing her now occupying a much more radical feminist position than she did then, and assigning new importance to the politics of gender and of language.

Le Guin's successors vary from the most optimistic to the most pessimistic, and from the most androgynous to the most essentialist. Mary Gentle's Golden witchbreed (1983) and Ancient light (1987) offer a wholly androgynous vision. Her Orthians are sexually neuter until adolescence, when they develop unpredictably as either male or female. In their culture, therefore, there can be no difference between male and female education, and consequently no discernible differences in role. The same motif is used for a more conventional essentialism in Marion Zimmer Bradley's The world wreckers (1971), a watershed novel in the Darkover saga because of the centrality of themes of sex and gender. The telepath Keral is a member of the androgynous chieri race. However, rather than deconstructing gender difference, the androgyne is used to reinforce it: 'In its positiveness and strength ... it seemed like a man; yet the ... timidity...was altogether feminine' (p. 57). The Terran David Hamilton falls in love with Keral, and as a result the chieri moves into female phase. Despite the novel's sympathetic arguments for sexual liberation, it does not question gender stereotypes, seeing heterosexual intercourse as confirming that the male is naturally active, the female passive. As David and Keral make love, 'As the infinitely delicate polarity tipped, male to female, Keral would become more shy, more passive. It was David's turn to take the lead...' (p. 186).

Lisa Tuttle's 'The other kind' (orig. 1984) explores the process of gender construction more ironically. The misfit hero can make satisfying relationships only with the colonised Ederrans, 'teddies', so he chooses to be made an alien through surgery. The tale is an allegory of gender construction and particularly of transsexualism. In the entry on 'Transsexualism' in Tuttle's Encyclopedia of feminism (Arrow 1987, pp. 325–6), Gloria Steinem is quoted as saying that it is 'better to turn anger outward toward changing the world than inward toward transforming ... bodies': in 'The other kind' the Steinemian psychologist attacks the hero for believing 'Don't change the world, change your body' (p.181). Gender – and perhaps also race – is not innate but constructed: 'They made me: the psychologists, my parents, teachers, society' (p. 182). In 'The other kind', the final irony is that the real Ederrans are extinct: all the 'teddies' are now altered, mutilated human beings, who have chosen to sacrifice their vocal chords and wear fur, as male to female transsexuals choose to sacrifice their penises, to enter a 'muted' social group, and to wear women's clothes. Supposedly 'innate' Ederran qualities of gentleness and emotional intuitiveness are as phoney as supposedly 'innate' feminine qualities. The metaphor implies that the natural differences between male and female (humans and 'Ederrans') are negligible, and social construction all-important.

Tuttle uses similar metaphors of transsexuality in 'Mrs T' and in 'The wound',[46] an ironic dramatisation of Beauvoir's comment that 'one is not born, but rather becomes, a woman'.[47] It extrapolates from the generic use of the noun 'man' and the common-gender pronoun 'he' to imagine a world where the standard form of humankind is the male, but if one man falls in love with another, he undergoes a humiliating transformation to the female: 'it was terrible to be a woman ... To lose was to become a woman' (p. 233). The inauthenticity of socially constructed gender is starkly revealed.

Feminism, and especially the 'New French Feminisms' collected by Marks and de Courtivron, has problematised the whole notion of what it means to be a woman: 'The belief that "one is a woman" is almost as absurd and obscurantist as the belief that "one is a man".'[48] Feminists have emphasised the differences between biological sex and social gender – 'as soon as she desires ..., as soon as she speaks..., the woman is a man' – and this collection is full of images of the instability of gender and changes of sex.[49] This is another area where feminist theoretic and women's science fiction share a vocabulary of images.

Science fiction has changed spectacularly because of the intervention of women writers who have radically revised the tropes of a male-dominated literary form. Today science fiction is almost as likely to deal with separatist female utopias or with themes of androgyny as it is to deal with male astronauts subduing virgin planets or alien races. Fantasy and science fiction provide a rich series of metaphors for gender, which have influenced the feminist theories which in their turn have fed back into the fiction, making it the most vivid, vigorous and politically intelligent of modes in popular fiction today.

Notes

1 Darko Suvin, Metamorphoses of science fiction: on the poetics and history of a literary genre (Yale University Press: New Haven, 1979), p. 115.

2 Rosemary Jackson, Fantasy: the literature of subversion (Methuen: London, 1981), p. 3.

3 Xavière Gauthier, ' Pourquoi sorcières?' in Elaine Marks and Isabelle de Courtivron (eds.), New French feminisms (Harvester Press: Brighton, 1981), p. 200.

4 Monique Wittig, Les Guérillères (orig. 1971; Women's Press: London, 1979): Wittig and Sande Zeig, Lesbian peoples: materials for a dictionary (orig. 1979; Virago: London,1980).

5 Deborah Downs-Miers, 'Springing the trap: subtexts and subversions' in Mary Anne Schofield and Cecilia Macheski (eds.), Fetter'd or free? British women novelists 1670-1815 (Ohio University Press: Athens, Ohio, 1986), p. 308.

6 'Variations sur des thèmes communs', The editorial collective, Questions féministes 1, cited in Marks and de Courtivron, New French feminisms, p. 217.

7 Jackson, Literature of Subversion, p. 122; Suvin, Metamorphoses, pp. 8, 19, etc.

8 Eric S. Rabkin, The fantastic in literature (Princeton University Press: Princeton, NJ, 1976), p. 28.

9 Mary E. Bradley Lane, Mizora (Gregg Press: Boston, 1975; orig New York, 1890); Sally Miller Gearhart, The wanderground (Persephone Press: Watertown, Mass., 1979).

10 James Lawrence, An Essay on the Nair System of Gallantry and Inheritance: Shewing its Superiority over Marriage, as Insuring an Indubitable Genuineness ov Birth, and Being More Favorable tu Population, the Rights ov Women, and the Active Disposition ov Men (London, no date, but 1790s); The empire of the Nairs: or the rights of women. An utopian romance (London, 1811: but written by 1800). Lawrence was an exponent of phonetic spelling, and I retain his spelling.

11 See, e.g., Miriam Youngerman Miller, 'Women of Dune: Frank Herbert as social reactionary' in Jane B. Weedman (ed.), Women worldwalkers: new dimensions of fantasy and science fiction (Lubbock, Texas, 1985); Anne Hudson Jones, 'Alexei Panshin's almost non-sexist Rite of Passage' in Marleen S. Barr (ed.), Future females: a critical anthology (Bowling Green, Ohio, 1981).

12 Colin Greenland, The entropy exhibition: Michael Moorcock and the British 'New Wave' in science fiction (Routledge and Kegan Paul: London, 1983), p. 35 .

13 Originally a short story in Startling stories, 1952, rewritten as a novel in 1961: quotations from the Del Rey edition, New York, 1981.

14 Joanna Russ, 'Images of women in science fiction' in Susan Koppelman Cornillon (ed.), Images of women in fiction: feminist perspectives (Bowling Green, Ohio, 1973), p. 80.

15 Sandra M. Gilbert and Susan Gubar, The madwoman in the attic (Yale University Press: New Haven, CT,1979), p. 153.

16 C. L. Moore, Northwest Smith (Ace Science Fiction: New York, 1982): all references are

to this edition.

17 Pamela Sargent, 'Women in Science Fiction' in P. Sargent (ed.), *Women of wonder* (orig. 1974: Penguin: Harmondsworth, Middx.,1978), p. 15.

18 Gilbert and Gubar, *No man's land: the place of the woman writer in the twentieth century*, vol. 1, *The war of the words* (Yale University Press: New Haven, CT, 1988), p. 101.

19 Frank Cioffi, *Formula fiction? An anatomy of American science fiction 1930-1940* (Greenwood Press: Westport, CT, 1982), p. 59.

20 Gilbert and Gubar, *No man's land*.

21 Tania Modleski, *The women who knew too much: Hitchcock and feminist theory* (Methuen: New York, 1988), p. 2.

22 Gilbert and Gubar, *No man's land*;, Hélène Cixous, 'The laugh of the medusa' (orig. 1976; in Marks and de Courtivron (eds.), *op. cit.*, p. 255).

23 Eric Garber and Lyn Paleo, *Uranian worlds: a reader's guide to alternative sexuality in science fction and fantasy* (G. K. Hall & Co.: Boston, Mass., 1983), p. 51.

24 M. Z.. Bradley in Martin H. Greenberg (ed.), *The best of Marion Zimmer Bradley* (orig. 1985; DAW Books: New York, 1988), p. xiii.

25 M. Z. Bradley (ed.), *The keeper's price* (DAW Books: New York, 1980), p. 110.

26 M. Z. Bradley (ed.), *Free amazons of Darkover* (DAW Books: New York, 1985), pp. 7, 302.

27 Bradley, *The keeper's price*, p. 9.

28 Elizabeth Gaskell, *Cranford* (orig. 1853; Everyman: London, 1906), p. 1: Nina Auerbach, *Communities of women: an idea in fiction* (Harvard University Press: Cambridge, Mass., 1978).

29 Gilbert and Gubar, *No man's land*, p. 230.

30 Cheris Kramarae, *Women and men speaking* (Newbury, Mass., 1981), p. 1; Edwin Ardener, 'The "Problem" revisited', cited in Kramarae, *Women and men speaking*; Dale Spender, *Man-made language* (Routledge and Kegan Paul: London,1980).

31 Luce Irigaray, cited in Kramarae, *Women and men speaking*, p. 69; Wittig and Zeig, *Lesbian peoples*, p. 94.

32 Mark Rose, *Alien encounters: anatomy of science fiction* (Harvard University Press: Cambridge, Mass., 1981), pp. 31-2.

33 Darko Suvin, 'On the poetics of the science fiction genre', *College English*, December 1972, pp. 372-82; Robert Scholes, *Structural fabulation: an essay on the fiction of the future* (University of Notre Dame Press: Notre Dame, Indiana, 1975), p. 46; Suvin, *Metamorphoses*, pp. 4-7.

34 Judith Fetterley, *The resisting reader: a feminist approach to American fiction* (Bloomington, Indiana, 1978), p. ix.

35 Scott Sanders, 'Woman as nature in science fiction' in Barr, *Future females*, p. 49.

36 Lane, *Mizora*, p. 89; Ursula Le Guin, *The left hand of darkness* (orig. 1969; Panther: London, 1973), p. 199; Gearhart, *The wanderground*, p. 115; Le Guin, *Left Hand*, p. 168.

37 See Patricia Frazer Lamb and Diana L.Vieth, 'Romantic myth, transcendence, and Star Trek zines' in Donald Palumbo (ed.), *Erotic universe: sexuality and fantastic literature* (New York, 1986), pp. 235-55; Karin Blair, 'Sex and Star Trek', *Science fiction studies*, 10, 1983, pp. 292-7.

38 Jean Rhys, *Good morning, midnight* (orig. 1939; Penguin: Harmondsworth, Middx., 1969), p. 46.

39 Sarah Lefanu, *In the chinks of the world machine: feminism and science fiction* (Women' s Press: London, 1988), p. 108.

40 Unless otherwise stated, Tuttle stories are quoted from her collection, *A spaceship built of stone and other stories* (Women's Press: London 1987).

41 Charlotte Spivack, *Merlin's daughters: contemporary women writers of fantasy* (Greenwood Press: New York, 1987), p. 14.

42 Luce Irigaray, 'Ce sexe qui n' en est pas un', in Marks and de Courtivron, *New French feminisms*, p. 102.

43 E.g. in 'A momentary taste of being' in J. Tiptree, Jr, *Star songs of an old primate* (New

York, 1978).

44 Simone de Beauvoir in Marks and de Courtivron, *New French feminisms*, pp. 152-3.
45 Natalie M. Rosinsky, *Feminist futures: contemporary women's speculative fiction* (Ann Arbor, Mich., 1984), p. x.
46 *Other Edens*, ed. Christopher Evans and Robert Holdstock (London, 1987), pp. 217-34.
47 Simone de Beauvoir, *The second sex* (Penguin: Harmondsworth, Middx., 1972), p. 295.
48 Julia Kristeva, 'La femme, ce n'est jamais ça' in Marks and de Courtivron, *New French feminisms*, p. 137.
49 Luce Irigaray, 'Des marchandises entre elles' in Marks and de Courtivron, *New French feminisms*, p. 107. See also Antoinette Fouque in Marks and de Courtivron, *New French feminisms*, p. 117.

3

Yellow, black, metal and tentacled: the race question in American science fiction

Edward James

The 'race question', the problem of the relations between different 'racial' groups, has been in existence in North America since the earliest contacts between Europeans and Amerindians. With the arrival of other ethnic groups, above all African slaves, and with the rise of nineteenth-century science, which perceived those groups as biologically distinct races and ready to be ranked in terms of ability and potential, the 'race question' took a very different form. In some circumstances during the history of the United States it has been the occasion of considerable political and social turmoil; it has always been simmering beneath the surface, with great potential for tension and social conflict. The celebrated English medieval historian, E. A. Freeman, who narrated the course of the eleventh-century conquest of the Anglo-Saxon race by the Normans, caused a minor scandal on a lecture tour of the United States in 1881 by pronouncing that this race question would be solved if every Irishman in America could be hanged for the murder of a Negro.[1] It is a useful reminder that the problem does not just involve American blacks. Nor is the race question, of course, quite as simple as Freeman envisaged; it involved, and to some extent still does involve, native Americans, Hispanics, Jews, Poles, Italians, Chinese, Japanese and others, as well as blacks and the Irish. The 'science' of race has been written almost entirely by Anglo-Saxons, who used all kinds of measurements - particularly of skulls and of intelligence - to demonstrate the fact (which was obvious to them before they began) that Anglo-Saxons were superior in almost every way.[2] In the late twentieth century there are very few scientists who subscribe to nineteenth century racial science; but popular prejudices remain, and those scientific ideas to some extent survive to feed them.

As authors of a genre of popular literature, we might expect science fiction writers to reflect racial prejudice to some extent by science; we might also expect that as *science* fiction writers they may be using their fiction to educate their readers in the current state of scientific opinion – although that itself, of course, is often the product of current political and social realities. It is worth emphasising at this point that almost all the writers whom we are discussing are themselves white, and most of them WASP; the attitudes of the two best-known black American SF authors, Samuel R. Delany and Octavia Butler, have been discussed by Littlefield and by Bonner and Salvaggio.

Robert Scholes and Eric Rabkin, in their general book on science fiction, congratulate the science fiction author, collectively, on having moved well in advance of public opinion on race.[3] They see the xenophobia that created Bug-Eyed Monsters in the early days of SF (as characterised by the Martians of Wells's *The war of the worlds*) yield to more hospitable notions of the alien in the 1930s, under the influence of writers such as Stanley Weinbaum. They suggest that there has for some time been a general assumption among SF writers that in the future the question of black/white relations would wither away. This is often conveyed subtly, by the absence of reference to the problem, that is, by an unstated assumption that it has been solved; they cite the shock of pleasure felt by the young Samuel R. Delany when he was reading Robert Heinlein's *Starship troopers* (published 1959) and 'half-way through the book the hero looks into a mirror and a black face looks back at him. In the book, this is not remarkable in any way, and many readers are probably not even aware that the hero is black.'[4] Similarly, it would take a very careful reader of Ursula Le Guin's *The left hand of darkness* (1971) to notice that the only Earthman in the story is dark-skinned and flat-nosed. William Hjortsberg's *Grey matters* (1971) is even more direct; the hero chooses to move his consciousness into a black body because of its beauty; thereafter, in Hjortsberg's book as in Heinlein's and Le Guin's, the reader loses any sense of 'race' as being special. Scholes and Rabkin do bemoan the 'boys' of Asimov's *I, robot* stories, which we shall discuss below, and gently chide Bradbury for making his point in 'Way in the middle of the air' (a story in *The Martian chronicles*) by means of racial stereotypes (shambling blacks and southern rednecks), but nevertheless they celebrate the fact that SF has moved the racial boundaries: the human race is seen as one and united, and the problem is what attitude to take to the aliens beyond. 'Science fiction, in fact, has taken the question so spiritedly raised by the founding fathers of the United States – of whether the rights of man included black slaves as well as white slave-owners – and raised it to a higher power by asking whether the rights of being end at the boundaries of the human race.'

A cynic might wonder at this point whether the latent xenophobia of so many members of the human race – including SF writers – has not been transferred from the human to the alien. The black soldier of *Starship troopers* spent his time slaughtering the Bugs; Ender Wiggin, the hero of Orson Scott Card's enormously successful *Ender's game*, committed successful genocide on the Buggers (although he spent *Speaker for the dead* feeling guilty about it), while in the 1987 film *Aliens*, another reprise of *Starship troopers*, Ms Sigourney Weaver's liberated heroine Ripley again wipes out the insect-like aliens. Bug-Eyed Monsters have perhaps had a revival since Scholes and Rabkin put them to rest in 1977. And indeed the role of the race question in science fiction may be rather more complex than Scholes and Rabkin imply. Earthly races do appear in science fiction. But they may also appear in disguise, in what Gary K. Wolfe has seen as two of the most powerful icons in SF, both of which represent the Other in its relationship to humanity: the icon of the robot and the icon of the monster. The problem of the recognition of race in SF will be dealt with at the end, after discussion of the more obvious treatments of the theme

That science fiction does indeed share the general change in racial attitudes which we have witnessed this century is clear enough, however, and can be appreciated most obviously when looking at the treatment of the 'yellow races' in SF.[5] These are much more significant than the blacks in nineteenth-century SF, perhaps because blacks were so disregarded as not to appear a threat. Clareson finds only one story where there is a rebellion of American blacks against the whites: King Wallace's *The next war* (1897) – where the American blacks flee into the Southern swamps, there to disappear, after their plot to poison their employers fails (Clareson, pp. 54-5). But there are any number of late-nineteenth-century stories of the invasion of the US by the Chinese, even before the Englishman M. P. Shiel's *The yellow danger* (1899) unleashed the Chinese on Europe, and created the phrase 'the Yellow Peril'.[6] The theme dates back, as Clareson has noted, to the importation of Chinese coolie labour into California, denounced, for instance, in Pierton W. Dooner's *Last days of the republic* (1880) as 'a race of people whom Nature has marked as inferior, and who are incapable of progress or intellectual development beyond a certain point' (Clareson, p. 69). Robert Wolton in 1882 imagined the Chinese taking over California and Oregon in 1899; Arthur Dudley Vinton's Looking further backward (1890) had Professor Wun Lung Lai as the successor to Julian West – the main character, of course, of Edward Bellamy's Looking backward (1888) – as professor of modern history at Shawmut College, following the Chinese takeover of 2020. After 1905, and the Japanese victory over the Russian Empire, the racial epithets once used of the Chinese are transferred to the Japanese, as they attack the States in such books as Marsden Manson's The yellow peril in action (1907) or J. U. Giesy's All for his country (1915). Among a welter of racist futures, one eccentric stands out; Clareson reckons him 'unique among both American and Western European writers' (p. 76). This is Floyd Gibbons, who published The red Napoleon in 1929. This documents the conquests of Karakhan, the Mongol leader of the Soviet Union, during the 1930s; he takes Poland in 1933, and Boston in 1934. Like most Oriental invaders of the civilised West, Karakhan's hordes rape the white women they find; the idea of miscegenation can be relied upon to horrify (and secretly to fascinate?) readers of the time. Unlike most authors, however, Gibbons almost approves of Karakhan's order to, 'CONQUER AND BREED' (p. 2), because of his sympathy with Karakhan's aims, which were to end racial prejudice via miscegenation: 'The hatred between the colours and the species must be stamped out ... I recognise but one race – the HUMAN RACE' (p. 463).

Most writers are much less broad-minded than Gibbons, and race-hatred continues right through the fiction of the 1920s and 1930s. The editor Hugo Gernsback noted in 1930 that both writers and readers of Air wonder stories seemed to assume that all the magazine wanted to print were stories of air banditry, of men who wanted to control the world, and of aerial warfare between the yellow races and the white.[7] Stories of the Asian conquest of the United States in fact continued to be published for a long time, up to and beyond the greatest of them all, Philip K. Dick's The man in the high castle (1962), the alternate history novel in which the Japanese and Germans parcel out the world after their victory in the Second World War; a recent example is Frederik Pohl's Black star rising (1985). The modern manifestation of the fear of 'the Yellow Peril', I suppose, can be found in those numerous cyberpunk futures of the last decade in which the Japanese are the dominant world power; the classic manifestation is the short-story by the 'proto-cyberpunk' Norman Spinrad, 'A thing of beauty'. But Dick,

Pohl, Spinrad and the cyberpunks depict the resulting racism in a neutral way, and portray the conquerors or dominant people in sympathetic fashion. The last major SF writer to use the theme in an apparently racist way was Robert A. Heinlein, in his very early novel *The day after tomorrow*.[8]

In this novel the PanAsians have conquered the United States; the story tells of the founding of the resistance movement and its ultimate success. PanAsians are 'monkeys' and 'flat-faces', who speak in a 'meaningless sing-song'; the final battle was 'more in the nature of vermin extermination' (p. 157). But alongside the racial invective Heinlein does offer a more reflective view of the enemy. At the beginning, Ardmore, one of the leaders of the resistance, wonders about this 'crazy new world – a world in which the superiority of western culture was not a casually accepted "Of course "' (p. 15). Soon afterwards another member of the resistance, Thomas, meets Finny, an old anarchist, who makes him realise that he should not view the PanAsians as *bad*. 'Since the anarchist believed that all government was wrong and that all men were to him in *fact* brothers, the difference was to him one of degree only. Looking at the PanAsians through Finny's eyes there was nothing to hate; they were simply more misguided souls whose excesses were deplorable' (p. 27). Finny told Thomas,

Don't make the mistake of thinking of the PanAsians as *bad* – they're not – but they *are* different. Behind their arrogance is a racial inferiority complex, a mass paranoia, that makes it necessary for them to prove to themselves by proving to us that a yellow man is just as good as a white man, and a damned sight better.

The PanAsians, 'a mixed race, strong, proud, and prolific', are '"... simply human beings, who have been duped into the old fallacy of the State as a super-entity. '*Ich habe einen Kameraden.*' Once you understand the nature of – " He went off into a long dissertation, a mixture of Rousseau, Rocker, Thoreau and others. Thomas found it inspirational, but unconvincing' (p. 27). Thomas is not convinced – but Heinlein very soon puts him in a position which again teaches him that particular characteristics are a result of political conditioning, not racial inheritance. He goes to a hobo hideout and meets his old friend Frank Roosevelt Mitsui, a Californian farmer, 'as American as Will Rogers, and much more American than that English aristocrat, George Washington' (p. 29). Thomas has the common prejudices. He talks of 'the swarm of brown kids that were Frank's most important crop', and 'the sight of a flat, yellow face in a hobo jungle made Thomas' hackles rise ... Well as he knew Frank, Thomas was in no mood to trust an Oriental' (p. 30). But when he learns how much Frank Matsui had suffered (the PanAsians were slaughtering Americanised orientals), Thomas realises and conquers his own prejudice: it is a theme which, as we shall see, Heinlein developed in the course of the 1950s.

This novel by Heinlein, published almost on the eve of Pearl Harbor (and the consequent internment of thousands of Americanised orientals like Matsui), despite its use of racial terminology, seems to be an attempt to get people to think about common prejudices, as well as about the nature of religion (the PanAsians are in the end defeated thanks to the creation of a fake religion by the resistance). That no doubt explains how it can have continued to be reprinted in a very different climate. Another fate entirely was in store for a much better known veteran of war against the Yellow Peril: Buck Rogers.

The Buck Rogers opus has been very nicely used by Alan Kalish and others, in the course of an examination of textual variants, as an illustration of the changes in racial attitudes between the heyday of the 'Yellow Peril' and our own more circumspect times. The first versions are the two original stories of 1928 and 1929, by Philip Francis Nowlan; the fix-up novelisation called *Armageddon 2419* was produced in 1962; and the most recent revision, by the SF writer Spider Robinson, dates from 1978. The original Buck Rogers stories tell of the invasion of the Chinese, 'fierce Mongolians, who, as scientists now [AD 2419] contend, had in their blood a taint not of this earth'; they crush the United States, and kill over four-fifths of the 'American race'. The Mongolians are also referred to as the Hans (the text also, confusingly, refers to the 'non-Han Mongolians of Japan'); the possibility that they are in fact not human, but alien, presumably makes their annihilation somewhat more acceptable. The epic ends as the Han cities 'were destroyed and their populations hunted down', and the American example gives a lead to the other subject peoples of the Han, leading to the utter 'extermination' of 'that monstrosity among the races' (Kalish *et al.*, p. 305).

Kalish and his co-authors look at a number of different aspects of textual variants in the Buck Rogers opus, reflecting on changes over a fifty-year period in humour, in vocabulary and style, in scientific knowledge, in attitudes to gender and sex,[9] and to ethnicity and race. Even the picture of the United States of the future has been subtly altered. Nowlan gave all his future Americans pure Anglo-Saxon names; the later editions made America much more ethnically diverse, Boss Hart becoming Boss Ciardi, for instance, and Barker becoming Fabre. More importantly, the references to the enemies of America and of Buck Rogers have been softened. 'Yellow incubus' becomes 'Hans'; 'inhuman yellow blight' becomes 'inhuman blight'; the fight to the death between the 'Yellow and White Races in America' becomes the war between 'the Mongolians and our forces'. The 1962 edition also removes paneygyrics on 'the utmost of nobility in this modem, virile, rugged American race', and the 1978 version makes the 'simple and spiritual' blacks of Africa 'wise and spiritual'. The elimination of the racial slurs in the later editions, as Kalish et al. note, makes the final excuses that the Han may in fact be alien in origin rather less hypocritical. But:

> Whether they are 'yellow devils' or just 'Hans', it is clear that the story's intent is to stir up hatred and attempt to justify massacre. Extraterrestrial or not, the Hans look like humans, talk like humans, breed fertile offspring with humans, and create a recognisably human culture. Ethically considered, they are human beings, and killing one is a homicide. We are asked to rejoice at the end of all three versions at killing all of the Hans, at the utter extermination of a people.[10]

Another writer of the early decades of the twentieth century, and far more popular than Nowlan, was Edgar Rice Burroughs. The racism of the Tarzan books, directed against the blacks of Africa, is apparent and open, and has often been commented on. The racism of the Martian novels is more apposite here, and if it is equally apparent, it is veiled in what would become typically science fictional guises, as Benjamin S. Lawson has shown (esp. pp. 213-16). Burroughs' Mars is a multiracial and multicoloured society – with whites, blacks, reds, greens, blacks, and men 'with skins the colour of a ripe lemon', who each play the part of Orientals, Africans and American Indians rolled into one. This is sometimes revealed by Burroughs with charming simplicity, as when (with perhaps quite unconscious punning) he refers to the magnificent caravan of the green Martians as having 'a barbaric splendour ... which would have turned an East Indian potentate green with envy' (A princess of Mars, p. 83). But Lawson has convincingly argued that American Indians supply the major analogy;[11] the series starts with John Carter fleeing the Apache in Arizona, and is transported to 'Barsoom', Mars, with its deserts and exotic natives – one of whom, the red-skinned Dejah Thoris, becomes his own (egg-laying) Pocahontas: it is an Arizona transformed, and romanticised to excess. John Carter, with his Southern American prejudices, finds this multiracial society difficult, even though the natives act not unlike the lower races back home, with Martians such as the monstrous green Tal Hajus lusting after Carter's red princess. 'The thought that the divine Dejah Thoris might fall into the clutches of such an abysmal atavism started the cold sweat' on John Carter; he hoped that she would act like those 'brave frontier women of my lost land who took their own lives rather than fall into the hands of the Indian braves' (*A princess of Mars*, p. 66). Later Carter imagines her being torn apart by great apes 'her bleeding corpse ... dragged through the dirt and the dust, until at last a part of it would be rescued to be served as food upon the tables of the black nobles' (*The gods of Mars*, p. 162): a centuries-old fear of the European, which would have been relished by the celebrated inmate of Charenton. Yet, after slaughtering the coloured folks of Mars by the thousand, Carter, or Burroughs, comes in the end to imagine the possibility of reconciliation. He learns that the magnificent red men of Mars are in fact the result of the miscegenation between blacks and a yellow-reddish people who flourished in the past. 'Ages of close relationship and intermarriage had resulted in the race of red men, of which Dejah Thoris was a fair and beautiful daughter' (*A princess of Mars*, p. 63). Carter himself had lived, in disguise, as a red, a white and a yellow, and his best friend was the jolly green giant Tars Tarkas. *The warlord of Mars* ends (p. 124) with Carter musing on the possibilities of peace. 'The hand of every race and nation was raised in continual strife against the men of every other land and colour. Today, by the might of my sword and the loyalty of the friends my sword has made for me, black man and white, red man and green, rubbed shoulders in peace and good fellowship.' All he needed was to cement the 'fierce yellow race' to the others and he would rest happy.

An appreciation of the unAmericanness of racism became much more apparent to American writers after the rise of Hitler. As early as December 1933, *Astounding* published 'Ancestral voices' by Nat Schachner, which had Attila the Hun being killed in an encounter with a time machine, which caused, in the twentieth century, the immediate disappearance of two of his descendants – a Jew called Max Bernstein and a German called Hans Schilling – all while a dictator called Herr Hellwig is ranting about racial purity. As Carter notes (p. 117), readers seem to have readily understood the political point, but did not comment on this idea that, racially speaking, all Europeans were totally mongrelised. It was the same Nat Schachner who in The writer in August 1945 called on authors to avoid the standard ethnic stereotypes, telling them that if they portray members of ethnic minorities as individuals 'we will be doing more to eliminate the vicious Nazi myths ... than a thousand pulpit sermons and a thousand ponderous editorials' (Carter, p. 138).

After the Second World War it is clear that the 'race question' is above all the question of the place of blacks in American society. Many of the stories we shall be looking at come from the crucial period of the fifties. Let us briefly recall some dates, as a reminder of the political background. In 1950 the NAACP (the National Association for the Advancement of Colored Peoples) agreed to launch a legal assault on racial segregation in schools. In 1954 the Supreme Court created the 'Brown Decision', condemning such discrimination as contrary to the Fourteenth Amendment; almost exactly a year later it ruled that the Brown decision be implemented 'with all deliberate speed'. In December 1955 the young Martin Luther King led the bus boycott in Montgomery, Alabama. In 1957 nine black students were enrolled in the Central High School at Little Rock, Arkansas; thousands of soldiers and National Guard were called in to keep the peace. In February 1960 the restaurant sit-ins began, in Greensboro, North Carolina. In 1963, after a massive protest march on Washington, Kennedy launched a comprehensive Civil Rights bill; bloody riots swept northern cities as well as states like Mississippi. The bill became law in 1964; Martin Luther King was awarded the Nobel Peace prize.

Science fiction writers respond to this prolonged process with bitter stories of indignation, and with underplayed educational fervour. As an example, we can take four novels - three of them aimed at the young – which Robert Heinlein wrote during a short period in the mid-fifties; Fred Erisman has looked at these recently, and sees them, surely correctly, as being a deliberate attempt at education in racial tolerance. Heinlein's interest in the question emerges fairly soon after the war. There is a black among the scientists 'Who died for the truth that makes men free' in 'The black pits of Luna' (1948); the Interplanetary Patrol of Space cadet (1948) is multiracial, with race relations emerging as a specific issue when three Patrol cadets have to deal with a clash between a civilian pilot and the natives of Venus. But the four novels of the mid fifties The star beast (1954), Tunnel in the sky (1955), Time for the stars (1956) and Double star (1956), are all, Erisman argues, powered by this contemporary debate about civil rights.

The *star beast* has its inevitable all-knowing all-competent Heinlein father-figure; he is the Right Hon. Henry Gladstone Kiku, a Kenyan. His main problem, as a diplomat, is to deal with an alien race; yet he has an irrational hostility towards the alien ambassador:

He knew that he should not harbor race prejudice, not in this job. He was aware intellectually that he himself was relatively safe from persecution that could arise from differences of skin and hair and facial contour for the one reason that weird creatures such as Dr Ftaemi had made the differences between breeds of men seem less important (p. 83).

The alien, interestingly, understands the problem: all races everywhere have this in-built hostility: 'All languages carry within them a portrait of their users, and the idioms of every language say over and over again, "He is a stranger and therefore a barbarian"' (p. 113). Racial prejudices are natural, therefore, but have to be recognised as illogical and harmful.

The symbol of competence in *Tunnel in the sky* is not only black, but female: Caroline Mshiyeni. She becomes City Manager; her sister is an assault captain in the Amazons. Alfred McNeil ('Uncle' or 'Unc'), in *Time for the stars*, on the other hand, is, outwardly, Uncle Tom reborn. Yet he too is shown to be intelligent, a good manager of people, and a model of humanity. Heinlein used Kiku, Mshiyeni and Unc to demonstrate that 'if a society is to endure … it must look to what a person *is* and *can do* rather than to that person's color or sex' (Erisman, p. 219).

The final novel of the quartet was not intended, as the others were, as a juvenile; *Double star* was serialised in the leading SF magazine of the day, *Astounding* (serialised, as Erisman noted, during the turmoil following the admission of the first black into the University of Alabama), and won the year's leading award, the Hugo for best novel. And, from the point of view of Heinlein's message, it is much more subtle and much more effective. Its protagonist, Lawrence Smith, a down-at-heel actor known professionally as 'The Great Lorenzo', is egotistical, immoral, and a racial bigot. He cannot stand Martians; their smell, their sexual habits, their looks. 'Nobody could accuse me of race prejudice. I didn't care what a man's color, race, or religion was. But men were men, whereas Martians were *things*. They weren't even animals to my way of thinking … Permitting them in restaurants and bars used by men struck me as outrageous'(p. 7).

But Lorenzo is employed as the double of the kidnapped statesman

Joseph Bonforte, and as he lives himself into the role he gradually takes on the ideals and beliefs of his model. Bonforte aims to bring humans and Martians together; 'he kept harping on the notion that the human race must never again make the mistakes that the white subrace had made in Africa and Asia' (p. 84) (back in 'the late Dark Ages', p. 68). His enemy is the Humanity Party, who believe we

have a God-given mandate to spread enlightenment through the stars, dispensing our own brand of Civilisation to the savages. This is the Uncle Remus school of sociology - the good dahkies singin' spirituals and Ole Massa lubbin' every one of dem! It is a beautiful picture, but the frame is too small; it fails to show the whip, the slave block - and the counting-house! (p. 85).

At the end of the book Lorenzo actually meets Bonforte, and experiences 'that warm, almost holy, shock one feels when first coming into sight of that great statue of Abraham Lincoln' (p. 119). *Double star* has traced the personal and logical transformation of a bigot into a man who realised the importance of tolerance as a basic feature of the American way of life; it is a powerful message, yet conveyed quite subtly beneath the fast-moving action. (It is also the story of a professional actor who, thanks to excellent coaching by his aides, manages to become President; quite implausible, really.)

The message of the later novel *Farnham's freehold* (1964) is more complex, in that it depicts a future (into which Hugh Farnham and his household have been involuntarily thrown) ruled by vicious slave-owning African blacks. But Heinlein's point is that an evil system is not the result of race, but of circumstance: 'Color does not matter to me. I want to know other things about a man. Is his work good? Does he meet his obligations? Does he do honest work? Is he brave? Does he stand up and be counted?' (p. 95). The survival of the individual is, perhaps, even more important than his own sense of honour. Thus Joe, their black house-boy, joins the future black establishment, despite its evil nature. When his former employer objects that he had once been a decently treated employee, not a slave, Joe replies: 'Have you ever made a bus trip through Alabama. As a "nigger"?' (p. 206).

Hugh recalled an area of Pernambuco he had seen while in the Navy, a place where rich plantation owners, dignified, polished, educated in France, were black, while their servants and field-hands – giggling, shuffling, shiftless knuckleheads 'obviously' incapable of better things – were mostly white men. He had stopped telling this anecdote in the States; it was never really believed, and it was almost always resented – even by those whites who made a big thing of how anxious they were to 'help the American Negro improve himself'. Hugh had formed the opinion that almost all of those bleeding hearts wanted the Negro's lot improved until it was *almost* as high as their own - and no longer on their consciences – but the idea that the tables could ever be turned was one they rejected emotionally (p. 226).

As the Civil Rights struggle reached its climax came the only SF anthology, to my knowledge, actually devoted to the problems of racial intolerance: Allen DeGraeff's *Humans and other beings*. It is a powerful set of sixteen stories, many of them anthologised before or since, ranging in publication date from 1949 to 1961, but coming mostly from the mid fifties. The earliest is also the bitterest and most powerful: 'The NRACP', by George P. Elliott (an author who has done little or nothing else in the SF field). The 'National Relocation Authority: Colored Persons' is 'relocating' American blacks in reservations. The story comprises letters written from an NRACP bureaucrat to a friend outside, as he slowly learns the secret. 'Remember, back in the simple days of the Spanish Civil war, when Guernica was bombed, we speculated all one evening what the worst thing in the world could be? This is the worst thing in the world, Herb, I tell you, the worst. After this, nothing.' (DeGraeff, p.172). Elliott's story is, of course, a response to the experience of German concentration camps; but the NRACP (the fictional mirror-reversal of the NAACP) is sending trainloads of blacks not just to slaughter, but to meat canneries. The bleak message, I presume, is: it can happen here too.

The other stories in DeGraeff's collection are more traditional science fiction, and all by well-known authors. Several concern mixed marriages. Richard Wilson's 'Love' and its sequel 'Honor' are about a Martian and his human bride; she is an outcast from Earth society, because of her marriage – the couple live near the Earth colony on Mars, which humans called Spidertown, until his scientific discovery, which opens the way for his acceptance on Earth. J. T. McIntosh's 'Made in USA' is about the prejudice experienced by an android girl – indistinguishable from white Americans apart from the small mark 'Made in USA' stamped on her navel. Fredric Brown and Mack Reynolds's 'Dark interlude' tells how a traveller from the future comes to rural America, and marries a local girl. He gets on well with the locals, despite his dubious origins, until one day he gets discussing race with the girl's brother.

'He said that by his time – starting after the war of something-or-other, I forget its name – all the races had blended into one. That the whites and the yellows had mostly killed one another off, and then all the races had begun to blend into one by colonization and intermarriage and that by his time the process was complete. I just stared at him and asked him, "You mean you got nigger blood in you?" and he said, just like it didn't mean anything, "At least one-fourth." ... I just saw red. He'd married Sis; he was sleeping with her. I was so crazy-mad I don't even remember getting my gun.'

'Well, don't worry about it, boy [said the sheriff]. You did right.'[12]

Another story in the collection deals with the same cultural absurdity from another viewpoint: Robert Sheckley's 'Holdout', in which a space-travelling southerner from Georgia has conquered all racial prejudices except that cultural taboo which prevents him from working with another white Georgian. His determination not to work on the spaceship with another Georgian dissolves once he discovers that the newcomer is not all white.

'I'm one-eighth Cherokee on my mother's side ...

'They should a told me in the first place you was a Cherokee. Come on, I'll show you your bunk.'

When the incident was reported to Captain Sven, several hours after blast-off, he was completely perplexed. How, he asked himself, could one-eighth Cherokee blood make a man a Cherokee? Wasn't the other seven-eighths more indicative?

He decided he didn't understand American Southerners at all.

The story by Eric Frank Russell (an English author who published largely in American magazines, and who fairly effectively disguised his Englishness from American readers) was 'Test piece', which also imagines a future in which racial prejudice will have disappeared without trace. An Earthman comes to an alien planet and is treated virtually like a god. Before he dies he orders his followers to show any arriving Earthman his statue and portrait, and to kill them if they utter the two words which he makes the aliens memorise. The Earthmen look at this grey-haired black-skinned space scout's likenesses, and, nonplussed, ask the aliens what the two words were. 'Two simple words of two syllables each' – the reader is left to surmise that they are something like 'fucking nigger' – but the offending words are simply gabble to the Earthmen. They have passed the test.

A more serious point is made in Leigh Brackett's 'All the colors of the rainbow', about the fear which lies behind hatred and prejudice. A green alien comes with his wife to a rural backwater (the urban SF writer is often happy to find prejudice in the country) and lashes out at those who are persecuting him – 'a nigger, even if he is a green one': '"Yes, we have white folks out there, about one in every ten thousand,

and they don't think anything of it, and neither do we. You can't hide from the universe. You're going to be trampled under with color – all the colors of the rainbow!" And he understood then that that was exactly what they feared.' The result was corruption; the alien learned hatred: 'The physical outrage and the pain were soon over, but the other things were harder to eradicate – the sense of injustice, the rankling fury, the blind hatred of all men whose faces were white.' Hatred is also the theme of Frederik Pohl and Cyril Kornbluth's 'The world of Myrion Flowers', in which Flowers, a well-to-do and complacent Harlem black, tries on a device which he is told would render him telepathic.

'It didn't stop. It's not like a radio. You can't turn it off. Now I can hear – everybody! Every mind for miles around is pouring into my head WHAT IT THINKS ABOUT ME – ABOUT ME – ABOUT US!'
... The machine ... was maddening and dizzying, and the man who wore the helmet would be harmed in any world; but only in the world of Myrion Flowers would he be hated to death.

DeGraeff's collection shows that, for him, stories about blacks, aliens, robots and androids are equally valid ways of commenting upon racial prejudice in contemporary society. However, there is a real methodological problem faced by anyone who wants to investigate changing ideas about race and, specifically, race relations in the United States: to distinguish those stories which actually *are* about race from those which are not, and, secondarily perhaps, to separate those stories which are *consciously* about race from those which are not. The field is very wide, for one of the most ubiquitous themes in science fiction is Contact with the Other: there are potentially a huge number of stories which might 'really' be about race. The problem of deciding whether the Other - an alien, a robot, an android – is actually intended as a metaphor for the racial Other is a crucial problem if we want to understand the role played by race in SF.

We may start by looking at the approach taken to this question by one of the general introductions to SF which appeared in the 1970s, that written by the Swedish author and critic Sam Lundwall. He argues that 'the android functions as sf's contribution to the race debate ... It is guilt for the Negroes, the Indians, the Jews, the Vietnamese, the peoples of South America and mankind's rape of weaker individuals that comes back in the android' (p. 166). Androids, Lundwall argues, are quite different from other stock representatives of the Other in SF.

Androids are created by mankind, and so are technically secondary or inferior, but they have their own individuality, and constantly strive towards equality with man. 'The robots pose no problem, because they just obey, and the extraterrestrials are so different from us that some kind of understanding must be found in the end' (p. 167). Lundwall takes Algis Budrys's story 'Dream of victory' as a typical example of one common use of the android in American SF. A nuclear war has killed most humans; androids form the bulk of the post-holocaust population, and are largely responsible for the survival of civilisation. As the human birth rate grows, the androids are gradually eased out. The story is seen from the viewpoint of one android, who is replaced as office boss by a human being and turns to alcoholism and, eventually, murder. When he murders his (human) mistress, it unleashes a campaign of hatred aimed at the androids. The reference to the white male perception of the black as a threat to white jobs and to white women is clear.

However, we shall have to think whether Lundwall's neat distinction between androids on the one hand and robots, aliens and the like on the other stands up in practice. Alongside Budrys's androids, for instance, can be placed Asimov's robots, which, as several critics have pointed out, seem to function as the equivalent of blacks. The caves of steel (1954), for instance, 'begins with the bitter musings of the protagonist upon the dismissal of an office boy who has been replaced by a humanoid robot' – a robot who 'shuffles his feet', with a vacuous grin on his face, in clear parody of the stereotypical black (Portelli, p. 151). The protagonist Lije Baley is an anti-robot extremist; his partner R. Daneel Olivaw represents the constant fear of the racist – the light-skinned black who might 'pass' for white. Even so, the Three Laws restrain robots, just as the slave-owner expected (or hoped) that his black slaves would be restrained by custom, fear and conditioning to obey his every order. The dangers come when the conditioning is somehow overcome (a theme of a number of the classic early robot stories, collected as I, robot) or when a slave/robot is misused by another slave-owner (the explanation of the murder in both the Daneel Olivaw whodunits, The caves of steel and The naked sun (1957)).

Gary K. Wolfe points to Isaac Asimov's well-known story 'Little lost robot' as providing 'discomfiting support to the assertion made by some critics that robots provide science fiction with a means of dealing with racism' (p. 162). Susan Calvin repeatedly refers to her robots as 'boys' when she interrogates them to find out which robot's First Law was not working properly; the story is designed to find this 'boy' and to deal with him. 'To make the analogy stronger, the means Nestor uses to hide from the humans – mixing anonymously with a group of sixty-two identical slaves – calls to mind the legend of Spartacus and his rebellious slaves': not improbably a conscious analogy, given Asimov's wide reading in ancient history and mythology.

However, there are problems. Slaves, obviously, are not necessarily racially separate, particularly for someone who (as in Foundation) drew so widely on ancient history. And there may well be other messages in the author's mind. Asimov himself describes how he wrote his robot stories as a conscious reaction against what, in the stories themselves, he called 'the Frankenstein complex': the obsession with the idea that robots might destroy their creators. 'My robots were machines designed by engineers, not pseudo-men created by blasphemers' (Asimov,1964, p. 14). Portelli plausibly argues that this set Asimov up in a contradiction. His robots were machines, who inevitably tend to put people out of work, and hence create resentment in the work-force. This causes men to treat the robots as slaves, as 'boys'; this, however, creates sympathy in the reader, above all when we get humanoid robots, like Daneel Olivaw, who are seen to be the victims of blind prejudice. Asimov 'cannot support the comparatively respectable cause of racial integration without at the same time supporting the more controversial cause of automation and unemployment' (Portelli, p. 152). (But again we do not have to make that leap from 'slave' to 'black'.) At the same time, despite his profession of faith, Asimov is setting up the robots as Frankenstein monsters, with the help of his link character Susan Calvin. The efforts of the Society for Humanity to halt the robots will come to nothing. Robots, a superior breed, will triumph; humanity can only continue, and can only achieve happiness, through the Machine. When a character complains that mankind 'has lost its own say in its future' Calvin replied, 'it never had any, really' (I, robot, p. 192). The Machine will bring control to human society, and 'the Machine cannot, must not, make us unhappy.' '"How horrible!" "Perhaps how wonderful! Think, that for all time, all conflicts are finally evitable. Only the Machines, from now on, are inevitable!" And the fire behind the quartz went out and only a curl of smoke was left to indicate its place.'(I, robot, p. 192.) Those words, which conclude 'The evitable conflict' (1950), the last story of I, robot, are taken by Wolfe (p. 163) to represent the coming of a 'cheerfully totalitarian Utopia': 'the dying of the flame also carries a more ominous meaning that one assumes Asimov was aware of' (Wolfe, p. 163). I don't think Wolfe's cynicism about Asimov's choice of words is called for; it is surely not intended as a presaging of a 'cheerfully totalitarian Utopia', but an expression of uncertainty and unease about a Machine-led future. More important, however, it has little to do with the robot as American black, even if aspects of the black's position in American society might be mirrored in the position of the robot. Much more important in the early robot stories is the robot as representative of the ominous potentialities of man-made technology; the 'Frankenstein complex' lies in the background, even if it is frequently denied. As the last passage quoted suggests, we are not intended to be fooled into uncritical sympathy with Susan Calvin's fanaticism.

Much later in the robot series, by the time of the third anthology (The bicentennial man, 1976), the 'Frankenstein complex' had indeed vanished (as Asimov claimed he had intended all along), and robots appear much more obviously as beings searching for equality with humans. Here perhaps, as Portelli argues, we are getting closer to the parallel with the blacks. But Asimov's main concern is to ponder the problems of what distinguishes the machine from the human. In the title story of the collection, 'The bicentennial man', he related the story of Andrew, a perfectly loyal household robot. It is different from other robots in that it has an artistic gift, which it uses to make money for his owner and, at his owner's request (although no-one was sure it was legal) for its own private bank account. It, or perhaps he (Asimov uses 'he' throughout), uses the money to make technical improvements to his body; eventually he decides to use the money to buy his freedom. The judge and the World Court eventually decided that 'There is no right to deny freedom to any object with a mind advanced enough to grasp the concept and desire the state' (p. 136). An incident in which two robot-hating men order Andrew to dismember himself leads, eventually, to a law forbidding robot-harming orders; decades of more struggle lead him, finally, to be instrumental in procuring a law declaring humans and robots equal. In the meantime, technology has advanced to the point that he himself is humanoid – a proto-Daneel Olivaw; indeed, so desperate is his will to be human that he arranges for his own dying. The final decision for legal equality comes to a world in which medicine and technology are so far advanced that humans are themselves able to consist of a large number of artificial parts; androids, like Andrew. Portinelli, arguing that the story is a more deliberate discussion of racial themes than the earlier robot stories, sees this merging of human and machine as 'a skillful treatment of miscegenation' (p. 152). But as cultural historians we have to ask (and I say this in full realisation that most literary critics would deny the possibility of such a question) whether this was in Asimov's mind. Asimov may have written the scene where Andrew is baited by the robot-haters while thinking of similar scenes produced by racial tensions, but it is hardly a clear or profound comment on those racial tensions (particularly when we note that it is written in the 1970s rather than the 1950s). But for the rest he seems concerned only with a logical extrapolation about ideas of artificial intelligence, which was probably much in his mind in the mid-1970s, after he had become better acquainted with Marvin Minsky, the best known AI expert (and one of two people he acknowledges as brighter than he is: Asimov 1980, p. 302); the robopsychologist of 'The bicentennial man' is called Merton Mansky. That Asimov was rather more interested in the logical problems of robots and the Three Laws of Robotics than in anything that is happening in the wider contemporary world is suggested by his comments on 'That thou art mindful of him!' in Ferman and Malzberg's anthology Final stage (pp. 115-17). He points out that the deepest ambiguity inherent in the question of robot/ human relations is the definition of 'human'. Discussions with his former editor John W. Campbell, Jr, convinced him that if he dug too deeply into that question the Three Laws would be totally upset. But, with Campbell dead and the Three Laws thirty-four years old, Asimov decided to start digging. He has two robots work out for themselves that not only should they be regarded as human beings, but that logic demanded that they also be treated as superior human beings: 'those that followed in their shape and kind must dominate' (p. 115). Frankenstein's monsters rebel ... And in the process Asimov suggests that race was not something that preoccupied him at all.

The case of Asimov is a useful illustration of the problems there are in defining whether a particular SF story or novel is 'about' race. Where there are clear statements placed in the mouth of narrator or character – as in the Heinlein novels quoted above – there is little problem. But when it is the case that the message has to be inferred by the reader from the treatment of the plot, then it is much more difficult. It seems to me – an impression based on over thirty years' reading, rather than the proper exhaustive survey and analysis of hundreds or thousands of stories – that there is an historical progression in the treatment of the Other. In the 1950s and early sixties there is a constant treatment of the theme of a unified humanity; in the later sixties and early seventies the alien, in particular, became the oppressed colonial (and Vietnam Wars devastated planet after planet); and in the eighties the concerns have been primarily environmental. But also, by the 1980s, SF had very largely lost the sense of being the educational tool that SF writers had, in the 1950s, espoused with sometimes almost missionary zeal.

Such an impression clearly ought to be backed up by statistics. But here I do no more than offer a relatively random sample of science fiction stories, published respectively in 1990 and 1960. My present-day sample comes from the two monthly magazines published by Davis Inc., the two most popular SF magazines, *Analog* and *Isaac Asimov's science fiction magazine* for the first four months of 1990.[13] *Asimov's*, in those four issues (an average of 6·5 stories per issue) had precisely one story about aliens, and none about androids or robots. This can be partly explained by the nature of *Asimov's*: not given to traditional themes, and inclined to publish stories which are pure fantasy (ghosts, werewolves) as well as science fiction. The lone alien appears in Deborah Wessell's 'Joyride' (February 1990); he offers sexual satisfaction to the two women in the story — he is accepted as an exotic and interesting novelty, and if the story is making any serious point (which I doubt) it is that racial difference adds spice to life.

Analog, the sole 'hard-science' SF magazine around now, has a very different tally: both February and April 1990 have two stories each featuring aliens, March 1990 has three, and January 1990 has one story about aliens, and one about androids. (No robots in either magazine; computers have to a large extent replaced robots in SF iconography, and computers never seem to lend themselves to racial metaphor.) The January aliens (Michael F. Flynn's 'The feeders') are merely a conceit, concerning (among other things) the possible explanation for the Angels of Mons. One of the February aliens is concerned entirely with the problems of communication, and of learning whether or not a species is intelligent (Ray Brown's 'Tongues in trees'). In the other, 'Curlew's choice', by British academic Ian Stewart, the intelligent aliens are very much off-stage, having been totally wiped out before the action starts in an ecologically disastrous attempt to exploit the economic resources of a planet; the message is green rather than anti-racist. Of the March stories, Joe Haldeman's 'Passages' is merely a hunting story on an alien planet; Deborah D. Ross's 'Expression of the past' is another warning about messing with the ecology. The third

March story, on the other hand, W. R. Thompson's 'Backlash', is very reminiscent of some of the tales collected in Allen DeGraeff's anthology. There is a member of an alien embassy in New York, attacked in Central Park by muggers who, it is discovered, have been hired by the Human Brotherhood – an organisation we have met before in various guises: a racist group determined to keep the human race pure and on top. In addition, we have a human society in which some people are, before birth, 'gengineered' – genetically improved, as kind of super-beings. The Human Brotherhood are against them too, and we witness a good deal of popular prejudice against them. The primary message, however, is that politics is complex and dirty. It emerges that the Human Brotherhood and some aliens are being manipulated by people, in alliance with another group of aliens who are wanting power for themselves. If it is a comment on racism, as it must be, it is a much more cynical comment than we found in the 1950s: racists are fools, whose unthinking prejudices are manipulated by power-seeking politicians. Neither of the April alien stories carry such a message. Michael F. Flynn's 'The common goal of nature' speculates on alien psychology, while Lou Grinzo's 'Childhood's confession' reworks an ancient SF theme (which, in its origins, goes back to the Book of Genesis): that aliens will come to observe humanity and judge it lacking. Finally, there is that one story about androids: D. M. Vidrine's 'Lifer', in the January 1990 *Analog*. We have, very briefly, the obligatory sign of human prejudice against androids, in this case against the beautiful female android in charge of the rehabilitation of a retired spaceman. But her function seems to be a means of comparing machine obsolescence with human aging and retirement, rather than any sustained comment on prejudice against the Other.

Let us compare these eight issues with eight comparable issues, chosen equally randomly, from thirty years ago. *Asimov's* was not in existence then, but *Galaxy* makes a reasonably substitute; *Analog* was there, under its original name of *Astounding*. I have taken the first four issues of *Astounding* for 1960 (January to April) and the last four issues of the bi-monthly *Galaxy* to appear in the British edition (end of 1959 to April 1960).[14] Only one of these issues features robots. Charles Satterfield's 'Way up yonder' (*Galaxy* 76) is fairly undistinguished, even if it does have the memorable image of dancing robots. Humans run plantations; the robot workers have tribal dances, and voodoo beliefs, and all largely unknown to their owners. The historical parallel is fairly basic and obvious, but the story does not seem to be making any clear point about it. Aliens, however, figure quite largely in these issues: nine stories in *Galaxy*, and six in *Astounding* – although four of those are in the one issue, January 1960. Two of the *Galaxy* stories about aliens are by Clifford D. Simak, probably the greatest purveyor in the 1950s of the message that human beings will have to learn to live with the Other.[15] But only one of the stories in *Galaxy* seems to me to use aliens in any way as a comment on contemporary racial problems: Christopher Grimm's 'Someone to watch over me' (*Galaxy* 76), in which the hero learns to realise that appearance means nothing – the horrific aliens are at root 'human' – even if his alliance with them is viewed with great suspicion by more prejudiced humans.

The January issue of *Astounding*, however, has a number of interesting messages for its readers. The cover story, 'The aliens', by Murray Leinster, repeats the theme of his famous story 'First contact'; that the Other should be met with caution but with friendliness: xenophobia is unnecessary, and inefficient. In Randall Garrett's 'Dead giveaway' space explorers find a huge alien city, empty of inhabitants, which they recognise to be a screening device for humanity: to see whether humans can learn from a superior people and survive (like, a character says, the Mexicans and Peruvians) or whether it will refuse to learn, and perish (as he says, like the Amerindians). The next story, whether by design or poor editing, is on a similar theme: Bertram Chandler's 'The outsiders' also offers an alien test of mankind, a test, perhaps, to see whether humanity can bear to face some unutterably alien Otherness:

It's an ingenious test, and amazingly simple. It's ... a mirror that's held up to you, in which you see ... everything. Yes, *everything*. Things that you've forgotten and things that you've wished for years that you could forget. After all, a man can meet any alien monster without fear, without hate, without panic-motivated aggression, after he has met and faced that most horrible monster of all ...
Himself.

The final story in the issue was George Whitley's 'Familiar pattern', effectively illustrated by just three pictures, scattered through the text: a Polynesian war-canoe in action; the same Polynesian war-canoe, rotting on a beach; the same canoe in a museum, in the room next to the dinosaurs. The story runs through that pattern, with commentary supplied by a Polynesian, Tom. An alien ship comes to Earth; quarrels result in a race riot; Melbourne is destroyed in retaliation. '"The familiar pattern ... The chance contact – The Trader – The Missionary – The incident – And the gunboat – ""And after the gunboat?"asked Lessing. "We learned the answer to that many years ago," said Tom."Now it's your turn."'

The stories, as we see, reflect a number of ideas about meetings with other peoples, including a clear concept of the mistakes that have been made, or crimes committed, in the past when 'superior' races came across 'inferior' ones. And inherent in most of the stories from 1960 is the message that humanity is one race, which has emerged from an unhappy past of racial misunderstandings and conflicts. That message came across clear in the American science fiction of the 1950s; it seems much less regarded in 1990. We may trust that that is a hopeful sign.

Notes

1 See Gossett 1963, pp. 109-10. He later publicly claimed it was a joke, and said that the only people who really complained were those who would not be able to get domestic servants without the negroes and Irish. But privately he confessed: 'I feel a creep when I think that one of those great black apes may (in theory) be President.'

2 The whole sorry story is well described in Gould, 1981.

3 Scholes and Rabkin, pp. 187-9.

4 I have been unable to find this passage in my copy (Four Square: London, 1961); the hero is Johnny Rico, apparently Puerto Rican in origin but clearly from a rich and privileged family.

5 To a large extent I am here following Clareson, Some kind of paradise, pp. 69-78. I have unfortunately not been able to consult William F. Wu's The yellow peril.

6 These tales mirror the contemporary spate of English tales of German invasion (Clarke,1966), or Ulster tales of Irish wars (James,1986).

7 Letter of Hugo Gernsback to Henrik Dahl Juve, 23 January 1930, cited by Sam Moskowitz in Extrapolation, 30, 1989, p. 25.

8 McDermott (1982) discusses all the political assumptions in Heinlein's The day after tomorrow; she deals with racism on pp. 264-6. The novel was originally serialised as Sixth column in Astounding, January-March 1941 (as by Anson McDonald), and expanded into book form in 1949; my citations are from the first British paperback edition (Mayflower, 1962).

9 The chief weapons of the American resistance were air balls, referred to by Nowlan as 'our balls': such delights have been surgically removed from later texts. See Kalish et al., p. 312.

10 Kalish et al., p. 315. The point is also made by P. Stephensen-Payne in a review of Armageddon 2419 AD in Vector, 73/74, March 1976, pp. 16-17.

11 Christine Morris and Mary S. Weinkauf have both, separately, looked at the often patronising way in which American Indians are treated in American SF.

12 The editor of Galaxy, H. L. Gold, noted in an editorial in May 1951 that some readers had thought that this story was in favour of racial prejudice: Carter, p. 139.

13 Leaving out the extra stories printed in the sixtieth anniversary issue of Analog, January 1990, which were reprints of some classic stories from the previous sixty years.

14 The four issues of Astounding are the British reprints (which continued to August 1963):

January-April 1960 (British ed.) are reprints of August 1959, November 1959, December 1959 and January 1960 (September and October were never reprinted in the UK). The four issues of *Galaxy* are 76-9, British edition, released one month later than in the US. No. 80 was the first US edition to be distributed in the UK, in June 1960.

15   On Simak's treatment of aliens, see Pringle, 1977.

References

Asimov, Isaac, 'Little lost robot', first published in *Astounding*, 1947, and republished in Asimov's I, *robot* (New York, 1950), pp. 100-26.

Asimov, Isaac, I, *robot* (1950), consulted here in the Fawcett edition (Greenwich, CT, 1970).

Asimov, Isaac, *The rest of the robots* (1964), consulted here in the Panther edition (London, 1968).

Asimov, Isaac, 'That thou art mindful of him!', first published in *Magazine of fantasy and science fiction*, May 1974; anthologised in Asimov, *The bicentennial man* (1976) and quoted here from Edward L. Ferman and Barry N. Malzberg (eds.), *Final stage* (Penguin: New York, 1975), pp. 91-117.

Asimov, Isaac, 'The bicentennial man', published in *The bicentennial man and other stories* (1976); consulted here in *Wollheim's world's best SF, series 6* (DAW Books: New York, 1977), ed. D. A.Wollheim, pp. 127-65.

Asimov, Isaac, In joy still felt: the autobiography of Isaac Asimov, 1954-1978 (Avon: New York, 1981).

Bonner, Frances, 'Difference and desire, slavery and seduction: Octavia Butler's *Xenogenesis*', *Foundation*, 48, 1989, pp. 50-61.

Brackett, Leigh, 'All the colors of the rainbow', in Degraeff (ed.), pp. 219-40; originally published in *Venture science fiction*, November 1957.

Brown, Frederic and Mack Reynolds, 'Dark interlude' in DeGraeff (ed.), pp. 15-22; originally published in *Galaxy*, 1951.

Budrys, Algis, 'Dream of victory', published in *Amazing*, 1953; first published in the UK in A. Budrys, *The furious future* (Gollancz: London, 1964) and consulted here in the Panther paperback (London, 1966), pp. 128-54.

Burroughs, Edgar Rice, *A princess of Mars*, published in *All-story*, 1912, and in book form 1917; quoted here from Four Square edition (London, 1961).

Burroughs, Edgar Rice, *The gods of Mars*, published in *All-story*, 1913, and in book form 1918; quoted here from Four Square edition (London, 1961).

Burroughs, Edgar Rice, *The warlord of Mars*, published in *All-story*, 1913-14, and in book form 1919; quoted here from Four Square edition (London, 1961).

Carter, Paul A., *The creation of tomorrow: fifty years of magazine science fiction* (Colombia UP: New York, 1977).

Clareson, Thomas D., *Some kind of paradise: the emergence of American science fiction* (Greenwood: Westport, Conn., 1985).

Clarke, I. F., *Voices prophesying war, 1763-1984* (Oxford University Press: Oxford, 1966).

DeGraeff, Allen (ed.), *Humans and other beings* (Collier: New York, 1963).

Elliott, George P., 'The NRACP' in DeGraeff, 1963, pp. 141-72; originally published in *The Hudson Review*, 1949, and republished in the *Magazine of fantasy and science fiction*, September 1960.

Erisman, Fred, 'Robert Heinlein's case for racial tolerance, 1954-1956', *Extrapolation*, 29, 1988, pp. 216-26.

Gossett, Thomas F., *Race: the history of an idea in America* (Southern Methodist UP: Dallas, 1963).

Gould, Stephen Jay, *The mismeasure of man* (Norton: New York, 1981; Penguin: Harmondsworth, 1984).

Heinlein, Robert A., *The star beast* (1954), quoted in the Ace edition (New York, n.d.).

Heinlein, Robert A., *Double star* (1956), quoted in the Panther edition (London, 1960).

Heinlein, Robert A., *Farnham's freehold* (1964), quoted in the Corgi edition (London, 1967).

James, Edward, '1886; past views of Ireland's future', *Foundation*, 36, Summer 1986, pp. 21-30.

Kalish, Alan, Michael Fath, Chris Ehrman, John Gant and Richard D. Erlich, '"For our balls were sheathed in inertron": textural variants in "The seminal novel of *Buck Rogers*"', *Extrapolation*, 29, 1988, pp. 303-18.

Lawson, Benjamin S., 'The time and place of Edgar Rice Burroughs's early Martian trilogy', *Extrapolation*, 27, 1986, pp. 208-20.

Littlefield, Emerson, 'The mythologies of race and science in Samuel Delany's *The Einstein intersection* and *Nova*', *Extrapolation*, 23, 1982, pp. 235-42.

Lundwall, Sam, H., *Science fiction: what it's all about* (Ace: New York, 1971).

McDermott, K. A., 'Ideology and narrative: the cold war and Robert Heinlein', *Extrapolation*, 23, 1982, pp. 254-69.

McIntosh, J. T., 'Made in U.S.A.' in DeGraeff (ed.), pp. 107-38; originally published in *Galaxy*, April 1953.

Morris, Christine, 'Indians and other aliens: a Native American view of science fiction', *Extrapolation*, 20, 1979, pp. 301-7.

Pohl, Frederik and Cyril Kornbluth, 'The world of Myrion Flowers' in DeGraeff (ed.), pp. 243-8; originally published in *Magazine of fantasy and science fiction*, October 1961.

Portelli, Alessandro, 'The three laws of robotics: laws of the text, laws of production, laws of society', *Science-fiction studies*, 21, 1980, pp. 150-6.

Pringle, David, 'Aliens for neighbours: a reassessment of Clifford D. Simak', *Foundation*, 11, 1977, pp. 15-29.

Russell, Eric Frank, 'Test piece' in DeGraeff (ed.), pp. 303-19; originally published in *Other worlds science stories*, March 1951.

Scholes, Robert and Eric S. Rabkin, *Science fiction. History-science-vision* (Oxford UP: New York, 1977), pp. 187-9.

Salvaggio, Ruth, 'Octavia Butler and the black science fiction heroine', *Black American literature forum*, 18, 2, Summer 1984, pp. 78-81.

Sheckley, Robert, 'Holdout' in DeGraeff (ed.), 289-99; originally published in *Magazine of fantasy and science fiction*, December 1957.

Spinrad, Norman, 'A thing of beauty', first published in *Analog*, January 1973, and reprinted, e.g. in Spinrad, *No direction home* (1975) (Fontana: London, 1977).

Weinkauf, Mary, S., 'The indian in science fiction', *Extrapolation*, 20, 1979, pp. 308-20.

Wilson, Richard, 'Love' and 'Honor', in DeGraeff (ed.), pp. 25-31 and 35-44, originally published in 1952 and 1953.

Wolfe, Gary K., *The known and the unknown: the iconography of science fiction* (Kent State UP: Kent, Ohio, 1979).

Wu, William F., *The yellow peril: Chinese Americans in American fiction, 1850-1940* (Shoe String: Hamden, Conn., 1982).

4

The personal and the political in utopian science fiction

Antony Easthope

Utopia's deepest subject, and the source of all that is most vibrantly political about it, is precisely our inability to conceive it.

Fredric Jameson

'Mesmer awoke, his dream falling away from him with the dawn mist shrouding the Mersey this first of May, New Year's Day, 2411. Dreaming, he'd been, of times long gone, before the Californian Redoubt, last stand of garagism, had surrendered without a bolt being fired and the Revo made worldwide.' So, in the unmistakable tone and style of science fiction, begins Michael Westlake's novel, The utopian (1989). Here is the young man Mesmer – Mesmer Partridge actually – waking up in the year 2411, in a matriarchal utopia, and setting out on his Journey towards sexual maturity by riding his horse, Golden, down the now grassed over motorway of the M6 – 'man and horse bounded forth into the great wide Communist world'.

Such a striking and original novel as The utopian forces us to re-examine and rethink our own habitual understanding of the politics of both science fiction and utopian writing. From the time of Bacon's New Atlantis (1627) the two modes have been inextricable, since to imagine a better future has been to imagine a better use of science and technology. But someone will only invent a science fiction utopia if they are dissatisfied with the real world they live in. So Fredric Jameson has argued that trying 'to imagine Utopia' (in Nelson, p. 355) constitutes an important political act because it challenges and criticises the alienation of late capitalist society (Mesmer's 'garagism'). Such politics, however, cannot be separated from textual questions: if the genre ensues from the unhappiness of someone in the present – a utopian driven to invent a utopia – what form should this writing take? I shall discuss this question of rhetorical strategy by comparing Marge Piercy's feminist science fiction utopia, Woman on the edge of time (1976), with Westlake's The utopian.

Strictly, neither of these texts is science fiction and only science fiction – rather, they are both 'serious' high cultural novels which, as suggested, for their political purpose and utopian aims are necessarily deeply indebted to more conventional popular cultural writing in the science fiction genre. I shall not have space to discuss a full range of science fiction writing so will draw on a particularly brilliant example, Philip K. Dick's *The man in the high castle* and treat this in detail as a representative of the genre (and of course in some respects it is not wholly typical). However, before coming to any of these textual questions we need to think about present society, why the utopian might wish to imagine a future alternative to it, and how this essentially political contrast between now and a future then is to be understood.

Utopia and the politics of alienation

Shakespeare's *Hamlet*, a play which stands at the very beginning of the modern period, dramatises a profound and unbridgeable opposition between the individual and society. Hamlet thinks that the Danish court is corrupt – the court thinks that Hamlet is mad. As it transpires, the action does bring these two points of view into some alignment, for the denouement reveals that Hamlet was not mad, but right in thinking King Claudius was a villain and that his Denmark was corrupt. The play continues to mean a lot to us because it signals a conflict or contradiction now deeply instituted in post-Renaissance culture: that the social is to be conceived as 'objective', while the individual must be defined in radical opposition to it as 'subjective'.

Or must it? For on this issue itself there are opposed arguments. One, which has to be named as liberal humanist, would accept Hamlet's dilemma as an ultimate reality: no matter how defined and however much he or she is influenced, even determined, in their choices by their social environment, the individual finally maintains his/her freedom in a domain beyond the social and cannot be practically or theoretically reduced to it. In this sense the individual as subject is always alienated from the objective social world he/she inhabits, and rightly so: subject and object are necessarily opposed. To envisage a better world may indeed involve many kinds of social amelioration, but in the end utopia can only lie in a form of subjective transcendence.

The other view, given essentially by the Marxist account of alienation, would claim the liberal vision sees the world upside-down. Thus, Marxist political economy is founded on the assumption that the human species in creating its world through labour creates itself, that production 'not only creates an object for the subject, but also a subject for the object' (Marx, p. 92) so that the objective mode of production reciprocally conditions subjective experience. Even when alienated from each other as they are within capitalism (commodity production), subject and object still actively define each other. Because the means of production (factories, universities) belong not to them but to private capital (and the state), people as active and productive subjects become separated from the objective fruits of their labour. Work is experienced as dead time (Monday to Friday) and through a process of compensation 'real life' is felt as something personal that takes place on Saturday night and Sunday morning.

A Marxist account would therefore criticise the presumed liberal opposition between subject and object, individual and social, as *itself* a symptom of alienation in bourgeois society. It might further point to a whole series of oppositions as corresponding to this original split: sociologically determined oppositions (production/consumption, work/leisure, factory/home); ideological terms (the political/the personal, the idea of 'the city'/the idea of 'the country'); philosophic oppositions (fact/value); internal psychic contrasts (reason/emotion, duty/desire). According to this critique of late capitalist society, pre-history and class conflict (Mesmer's memory of 'times long gone') will end and the communist utopia begin only when the originating subject/object opposition has been reworked and superseded with 'the Revo made worldwide'.

But we do not have to wait till then to see ways in which the equation social = objective/personal = subjective is under attack. Especially in the past twenty years the women's movement has advanced with the assertion that 'the personal is political'. It has applied this principle by urging, for example, that sexual relationships are not simply personal but always have political meanings, or that the question of who cleans the lavatory in a home is not just domestic and trivial but has important implications for the roles of women and men in a society. Feminist writers have combined to make a comprehensive challenge to all the ways masculine and feminine have been categorised as objective and subjective so that 'masculine' = work/the factory/the political/the city/fact/reason/duty and 'feminine' = leisure/home/

the personal/the country/value/emotion/desire.

A second and more abstruse field in which the subject/object dichotomy has been interrogated occurs in the theoretical intervention of Louis Althusser. Developing the Marxist premiss that who you are depends on where you are, he has argued that our individuality is constituted in the different ways we each live out the objective rules assigned to us in the social formation. And Althusser has followed this critique of the supposedly autonomous individual by rejecting traditional theories of knowledge. Conventional epistemology, in presuming that the knowing subject extracts from the object to be known truth as an essence already contained in it, conforms to the well-known 'ideological scenario' in which the transcendental or absolute Subject confronts 'the transcendental or absolute Object' (Althusser, pp. 55-5). In contrast, he argues that knowledge is actively produced through a process of construction for which there can be no final guarantees because both subject and object are always *situated* so that the object of knowledge is always defined in relation to the knowing subject.

Both the view that 'the personal is political' and this critique of the 'ideological scenario' of traditional epistemology indicate, in very different ways, the need to transcend inherited oppositions between the subject and the object. Both imply the need to confront the interconnection between utopia and utopian, the subject in the present (whether as writer or reader) who knows about this better world and who wishes for it. There is a question, then, not only of cognition but also of fantasy.

Future object and present subject in science fiction

Philip K. Dick's *The man in the high castle* (1962) is imagined as written from within a North America which, in the early sixties, has lost the Second World War so that the western half of the United States is occupied by Japan while the East is part of the Third Reich. At one point Mr Baynes, who claims to be Swedish, tells a young German that he doesn't like modern art: 'I like the old prewar cubists and abstractionists. I like a picture to mean something, not merely represent the ideal' (p. 43). This is a good joke, but in a kind particular to the science fiction genre. The conventional popular attitude is that modern art (cubism and abstract expressionism) doesn't mean anything; but art, in this now dominant National Socialist culture, consists only of fascist idealisations; therefore Baynes says he prefers the actualities of modernism.

The Baynes joke is consistent with the science fiction effect well analysed by Darko Suvin as 'cognitive estrangement' (see 1979). Here there is estrangement because the reader is forced to acknowledge a sense in which modernist art acts out of a kind of realism but it is cognitive (as distinct from a consequence of fantasy) in that it is entirely consistent with an empirical possibility: if the Axis had won the Second World War, then the relation between cubism and the fascist idealisation in art would be exactly what Baynes presumes in making his comment.

Crucially, it is a joke for us, not for Baynes, for he speaks quite literally of what for him is a real situation. The determining rhetorical feature of the genre consists of what might be called 'the science fiction synecdoche' (or part for whole) in which a single feature or group of features empirically plausible in our present becomes extrapolated to occupy the whole space of an imagined future. On the one hand, this future world is or should be realised from its broadest outlines into its most minute details. In *An artificial intelligence approach to understanding natural language* (a book dedicated, incidentally, 'to the first computer program to understand it') Jacques Pitrat takes science fiction to exemplify the degree to which all language use rests on a corpus of socially-constituted and pre-conscious assumptions:

Science fiction is a domain where questions of pragmatic knowledge raise delicate problems. A science fiction novel is difficult to write: the action takes place in a world of strange objects whose properties we do not know beforehand. Social behaviour may also be quite different from what we are familiar with. Sometimes we encounter non-human intelligences. Most of what we rely on to understand a 'normal' novel is no longer valid (p. 8).

Thus, on the premiss of a future now, a self-consistent and objective world is projected whose effectivity depends upon how specifically and concretely the pragmatic knowledge of that world is worked out and naturalised. But on the other hand, this world takes on a completely different meaning when experienced by a reader in the present who thus brings to it his/her own pragmatic knowledge. At another point in Philip Dick's novel, an American, Robert Childan, recalls the war: 'Think how it would have been had we won! Would have crushed them out of existence. No Japan today, and the USA gleaming great sole power in entire wide world' (p. 113). This reminds us (not Childan) of what we know – that the West did win, Japan was crushed, but now is a great power in the world. The science fiction effect of defamiliarising pragmatic knowledge arises from the juxtaposition of an objectively conceived future world with a subject – the writer or reader – bearing their own knowledge in the present.

In this respect the science fiction text is both like and unlike more conventional novels. There is now a fairly well established body of criticism which affirms that the realist text – most typically the nineteenth-century realist novel – sets up a would-be autonomous and objective world, that plausible characterisation, a consistent and contemporary everyday setting, concatenated linear narrative, a seemingly transparent 'documentary' style and careful control of the narrative point of view all work together to consolidate what the text represents as a real object distanced from and external to its reader (see particularly Barthes 1970 and MacCabe 1985). The realist text, then, like the commodity in the Marxist account of capitalism, is an object produced so as to deny or disavow the fact of its own production.

Much mainstream science fiction writing is very close in form to the procedures of traditional realism except for the temporal location – once the premiss about a setting in the future is granted, much of the rest follows as it would in George Eliot. As Jameson says in a most perceptive essay on the genre, science fiction is 'the very prototype of the narrative without a narrative subject' (p. 78). But the effect of cognitive estrangement depends on the way everyday practical knowledge is exercised in a world which at every point reminds us that it is not ours. To a much greater degree than conventional realist writing, science fiction presses on the reader the question of the narrative subject.

Even so, it is unusual for this to become an issue in the science fiction text itself, though Philip Dick's novel provides an instructive exception. It contains a character, Hawthorne Abendsen, the man in the high castle, who has written a novel, The grasshopper lies heavy, which imagines that the Allies and not the Axis won the Second World War. Factual historical narrative (though one subtlety is that Abendsen's book is not completely accurate) is presented therefore as a fiction within Dick's fictional text. In what we have now learned to describe as a postmodernist technique, this is a defamiliarising effect which threatens to enforce for the reader the knowledge that all writing, whether 'novelistic' or 'historical', constructs its represented meaning.

Cognitive estrangement in science fiction directs itself at, but does not overtly address, the reader; utopian writing, in addition to this, calls on the reader as a subject of desire. While undeniably all fictional texts engage the reader's fantasy at both conscious and unconscious levels, utopian writing in a specific way operates through a politics of desire. As Tom Moylan notes, utopian fiction registers an opposition 'between what is and what is not, between the "evil" of the given world and the "good" of the alternative' (p. 197). In so far as the utopian future is imagined from a position in what relatively is cast as an imperfect present, it performs not merely cognitively as a mode of empirical prediction and rational critique but as an active and largely unconscious wish or complex of wishes for a better world: who in the present *needs* to imagine this better future and why? For in this respect, as Raymond Williams says in his essay on utopia and science fiction, utopian writing, arising in a less than utopian present, always supposes 'a desire displaced by alienation' (p. 63), a desire symptomatic of all that is wrong now. What is this subjective desire and what status does it assign to the objectively imagined futureworld?

To the extent that a utopia, as an objectively conceived future, is seen to rely upon present desire, its validity is both weakened and strengthened. It is weakened in that the force of a cognitively real and attainable social possibility as a critique of existing social conditions ('Denmark is corrupt') is diminished if the utopian dream seems no more than a distorted wish-fulfilment consequent upon present frustrations and repressions, merely a sickness and form of neurosis ('Hamlet is mad'). Yet at the same time, and by the same token, the claims of the future are strengthened if these subjective frustrations and the ensuing need to satisfy desire in fantasy can be re-evaluated as *themselves* objective evidence that the present order is unsatisfactory and wrong (this move of course presupposes the personal as index not opposite of the social). However this understanding is pursued, the question of the utopianising subject for the utopian object becomes inescapable: by what discursive means may this dialectic best be articulated and explored?

In both Marge Piercy's *Woman on the edge of time* and Michael Westlake's *The utopian* the interest and investment of a present subject in the fantasy object of a future good society becomes an explicit concern of the text. To encompass this dialectic the rhetorical strategy in both texts is to break with most conventional science fiction writing by working with a dialogic or double discourse, one originating in the present, one in the future. Over this significant differences emerge.

Woman on the edge of time

She saw ... a river, little no account buildings, strange structures like long-legged birds with sails that turned in the wind, a few large terracotta and yellow buildings and one blue dome, irregular buildings, none bigger than a supermarket of her day, an ordinary supermarket in any shopping plaza. The bird objects were the tallest things around and they were scarcely higher than some of the pine trees she could see. A few lumpy free-form structures overrun with green vines' (p. 68).

This is Mattapoisett in 2137. After 'the Age of Greed and Waste' its utopian science concentrates on genetics and an ecologically sound relationship with nature. There are 'floaters', a kind of balloon for fast air travel and a 'bus-train object' which moves just above the earth for local transport; and everyone wears a portable 'kenner' providing all forms of information. But science has harnessed intuition and sympathetic magic in the form of 'inknowing resources' for the purposes of farming and healing and communicating with the higher mammals. Since 'most everything is automated' and there is no market economy, production is firmly local and agrarian: 'we care for our brooder, cook in our fooder, care for animals, do basic routines like cleaning, politic and meet. That leaves hours to talk, to study, to play, to love, to enjoy the river' (p. 128). Town meetings, its leaders chosen by lot, take political decisions or refer them up to the 'grandcil' or grand council. Justice, mainly over personal hassles, is achieved through 'worming', a process of argument, though criminals who do not reform after one chance are executed (p. 209).

As Jackrabbit explains, 'the crux' in 2137 lies 'in the biological sciences' (p. 233). Embryos are conceived and nurtured outside the uterus in brooders so there are no natural parents. Instead of the biologically determined family there is a 'core' of individuals who have chosen a binding relationship with each other; everybody has three 'comothers'. A spell of enforced separation, when at puberty an individual is left to fend for him/herself in the wilderness, is enough to 'break dependencies' in a rite of passage called 'the end of mothering'. Sexual intercourse ('coupling') is for pleasure, not reproduction, and proceeds without regard to biological gender. Since there are no natural parents, there are no patronymics and no fathers. There are songs, including a hymn to 'how it flows', funerals and other rituals, but there is no god − 'god is a patriarchal concept' (p. 104).

Recounted in bald summary like this, the utopia of 2137 cannot but sound ironically inadequate. Such, however, is by no means its effect in the text of the novel. For in *Woman on the edge of time* there is a subject for the object of 2137, a dreamer for 'the dreams' (p. 33). The world of Mattapoisett appears within another discourse, an encompassing narrative rooted in a contemporary and everyday present.

Consuelo (Connie) Ramos is a Hispanic American woman living on welfare in the slums of New York in 1976. She had a lover, Claud, a pickpocket, who died, but married Eddie Ramos, from whom she is now separated. Her only child, Angelina was adopted when Connie was accused of abusing her. Hospitalised, Connie is first given heavy tranquillisers (Thorazine and Prolixin), and then put in a psychiatric ward where she is submitted to a brain operation to give her a tranquilliser implant, Dialytrode. At one point she escapes from the hospital but after her recapture the novel ends when she poisons four of the doctors. This makes up the main discourse (though a further discourse is added when Chapter 20 gives excerpts from Consuelo's case notes) and the utopian future is explicitly presented on this basis as the imaginings or hallucinations of Consuelo.

Doubling the discourse, introducing the utopian for the utopia, has a number of different consequences. Piercy's text breaks with traditional realism to the extent that Connie can be felt as the on-stage author of the work – the novel conforms to the modernist tradition in which, for example, in Beckett's *Malone dies* (1951) all the writing is ascribed to Malone who sits in bed with paper and blue pencil telling his own story (or trying to). So an active relation between product and producer, object and subject, is openly admitted, in a way that it is not in *Man in the high castle*. The world of 2137 nevertheless remains as an empirical possibility, a science fiction utopia able to defamiliarise and provide a point of critique for our knowledge of our own present, as when Luciente is horrified to come into Connie's kitchen because, as he says, it is 'full of poisonous chemicals, nitrites, hormone residues, DDT, hydrocarbons, sodium benzoate' (p. 54).

But the doubling of the discourse tends to be easily recuperated in *Woman on the edge of time*. A not wholly unsympathetic nurse says that Connie is 'a sick woman' (p. 30) and though we are meant to reject this view, to the extent that the imagined objective future is revealed as a symptom of a merely subjective malaise – unhappiness seeking solace in wish-fulfilment – its claims to be a critique and desirable alternative to the present are diminished. Although the reader seems to be faced with two contrasting discourses – the present, the future – the text is narrativised so that Connie's present becomes a real centre in comparison with which the discourse of 2137 is rendered a subordinate, marginal appearance, an expression mainly of her own needs.

The effect is intensified thematically. No one in 2137 has an unconscious – this non-patriarchal world foresees the break with mothering as achievable simply through bodily separation since there is no unconscious bond with the idea of the mother to be broken. Connie, however, does have unconscious feelings manifest in her dreams about Claud and drive towards self-destruction, as when she has 'torn at herself with her nails' (p. 61). In her unhappiness she is more psychologically vivid and persuasive than any of the inhabitants of 2137 who, like Swift's Houyhnhnms, are simply rational consciousness incorporated in bodies. Since the realism of the contemporary narrative individualises her so distinctly, Connie's unsatisfied desire is rendered merely personal, merely her problem rather than an expression of the boundaries within which a society constructs its members. Arguably, then, the novel, despite its ambition and frequent power, offers a liberal vision of personal transcendence rather than any more comprehensively radical politics.

The utopian

The future perfect of 2411 is a sexual – mainly heterosexual – utopia whose feel and flavour may be conveyed by the incident in which Beth, a 'seabitch', described as 'six foot four and two hundred and fifty pounds, blue-black in colour, and at seventy or so in the prime of life' (she also has a wooden leg) meets a reincarnation of Vladimir Lenin, now called Very Light, who is rising 120 and rides a donkey called Bert. She asks him directly, 'How are you in the hammock?', and on obtaining a satisfactory reply, they retire. Throughout the evening Mesmer and his companion are entertained

by a whole symphony of sounds from beyond Beth's cabin door, including nautical expressions, circus cries, odd sentences in Russian, grunts of satisfaction, gasps, farts, the creaking of the hammock, the sound of wood on flesh, and of wood on wood, and on several climactic occasions, drowning out all else, a bout of braying from Bert, evidently responsive in the hold to the cavortings of his master's body-actual' (p. 117).

This post-Communist matriarchal utopia is presided over by the slogan, 'To each according to his need! From each according to her desire!' (pp. 40-1),

The *utopian* is written primarily in two radically opposed discourses, each the other of the other and so occurring in effectively alternating sections separated only by asterisks. Neither discourse is central, a metalanguage for the object language of its subordinate, so — which to mention first? In one, Mesmer Partridge is a young man who sets out from Stock Port on the Journey towards mature sexual identity in 2411, leaving his breast-mother and his two sisters (in this matriarchy the family persists in the form of 'multiple mothering and occluded fathering', p. 9), meets Very Light, travels with him to New Stoke, borrows a dragon's tooth from VL, makes love (in fantasy?) with April and May and their mothers, June and Julie, and finds the task set to him by VL is to try to bring back to life Candle, VL's mother, destroyed by him during a circus act which meant leaping into a tank of gasoline while carrying a lighted candle. After voyaging south with Very and Julie, first to Bright On and then to Medi Terra, Mesmer goes to Wick, scene of Candle's extinction, where his trick is to rekindle by walking a high wire. Mesmer falls but is saved in mid-air by the dragon 'come back for *her* tooth' (my italics). VL flies off on the dragon which leaves only the marks made by her tail in the dust.

Simultaneously, in the discourse of the present (1980) Mesmer Partridge is a young man from Stockport who has had a breakdown. After an incident in which he carefully swallows the aerial of a television and reconnects it so that, threaded 'like a bead on a wire', all the meanings of 1980 pass through him, he comes to think he lives in 2411 (and can't tell dreaming 'apart from the real thing', p. 135). For a cure he has been sent by his father to a Harley Street psychoanalyst, Dr Reed. This other discourse is spoken by Reed in the first person, though it includes also ten sections from Reed's case study, which include Mesmer's three sets of Blue Prints (of which more later) as well as 'White Heap', a list of the twenty-three coupled rhyming terms around which 2411 is constructed. Reed's cure fails, he decides to marry (for a third time), takes Mesmer with him on the honeymoon and, partly because he imagines Mesmer is making love with his new wife, Sonia, decides he must kill him but, failing, kills himself.

We are at some distance here from such traditional socialist utopias as Morris and *News from Nowhere*. My cumbersome but necessary retelling of the two narratives reduces their rich complexity but immediately indicates that *The utopian* founds itself in the subject/object dialectic by taking as its theme the relation between evil present and good future, utopian and utopia. And it does so in textual terms which completely resist recuperation to a main and a subordinate discourse, such as that between real present and imagined future which limits the project of *Woman on the edge of time*. At a stroke, therefore, it resolves a textual difficulty which has always inhibited utopian writing, as Jameson notes, that the narrative 'tends to be effaced by and assimilated to sheer description' (p. 95). Present and future worlds remain merely synchronic and static, without diachronic possibilities. *The utopian* is able to recapture for the utopian fiction a virtue from science fiction, that in committing itself entirely to projecting an imagined world and excluding the point of view of the narrating subject it assumes a world to be interestingly traversed by the characters of its narrative. There is a story both in 1980 and in 2411, and the suggestiveness of this relatively short text, 158 pages, derives from the constant interaction between the two.

Though mixing other genres besides utopian writing (there is more than a touch of Tolkien), *The utopian* continues the science fiction tradition in which the unfamiliar outlines of another world are experienced as practical, everyday knowledge. In 2411 it is always a perfect day, since meteorology is at last fully a science and seasonal weather is controlled 'in accordance with the theory of Regional Difference' (p. 12). Mesmer, like Luciente in 2137, carries all the information he needs with him in the form of an 'allcock' projected from which he and Very Light, resting in the woods, watch one of the Soviet classics, Vertov's *Man with a movie camera* as they finish a nicely chilled bottle of 'Meursault '97'. Meanwhile the expository business of the science fiction utopia is summarised neatly on pp. 149-52 in the rhyming terms of 'White Heap' including the NOBLE-GLOBAL (international world government), the SIFTING-SHIFTING (a fully socialised or strictly communist economy in which all production is reorganised on the basis of need and ability), the CARING-SHARING of the social group or elected family or even couple, and the CET-SET, which specifies a sympathetic rather than exploitative relationship with the natural world.

These four suffice to indicate the rest for the problem lies not in inventing the conditions for utopia today – in many ways as a fuller comparison with Piercy's 2137 would show, this now comes with standard features – but in making it possible, and, as a condition for this, socially desirable, by bringing into significant reciprocity subjective wish and political reality. The utopian gives weight to and justifies its deployment of what in itself would be no more than a technical trope – the on-stage dreamer for the utopia – because at a deeper level it reworks the social/personal relation. It does so on the seemingly unpromising terrain of psychoanalysis and its account of the unconscious.

For psychoanalysis all dreams of paradise are forms of infantile regression, images of a pre-Oedipal existence. And this explains adult resistance to utopian writing for subjectively it is the product of a wish to return from the problems of maturity to memories of a childish state, a flight from the reality to the pleasure principal (sexuality in Piercy's Mattapoisett, indifferently hetero- and homosexual, is what Freud termed 'polymorphously perverse', an expression of the pre-Oedipal subject). But psychoanalysis is often misunderstood if it is thought to be just another universalising abstraction of the personal. For the subject of psychoanalysis is always also a social being. The male Oedipal transition, for example, a process of the unconscious in which the little boy becomes a man by surrendering his drive towards the symbolic mother because of a threat from the symbolic father, can only take place in historically specific terms, terms in which the father's symbolic role is played by a given representative of social order and law.

It is precisely this imbrication of ideology and the unconscious, the political and the personal (signalled in the work of Jacques Lacan, a character who appears as a colleague of Dr Reed on pp. 124-5) which The utopian exploits in its dialectic. From the point of view of present social reality Mesmer is sick and it is only right and proper that he should be made well, if possible, and turned into an ordinary, functioning member of his society; from the point of view of 2411, where desire is to be gratified, his unsatisfied desires are themselves evidence that the present of late capitalism is corrupt and a restriction on human fulfilment. Reed seeks to impose the law of the symbolic father on the infantile and incestuous wishes of Mesmer, Mesmer resists that imposition because that law as embodied in Reed, haut bourgeois to his fingertips, is socially repressive.

Thematically the subject/object dialectic, the interdependence of the personal and the political, is focused in the idea of Mesmer's illness. Prefixed with fifteen synonyms for 'sick of' ('MADDENED BY',

'ESTRANGED BY', 'STUPIFIED BY' etc.) the second Blue Print lists six pages of things Mesmer finds wrong with present society, a list carried over from the five pages of the first Blue Print which include:

NEO-NAZISM
THE PENTAGON
DESTRUCTION OF HABITAT
PROHIBITION OF BIRTH CONTROL
RADIATION HAZARDS
ESTATE AGENTS
THE CHICAGO SCHOOL
COMPULSORY SPORT
ALL MALE POLITBUREAUX ... (p. 55)

The ambivalent significance of 'sick of' (and its synonyms) opens in one direction onto a subjective state (Mesmer's utopianism is a symptom of his personal problem) and onto an objective condition (the social realities of late capitalism). To the extent Mesmer is shown to be sick because his world makes him sick, and as his personal symptoms become objectified, the *necessity* for a better futureworld is validated – Mesmer's alienation cannot be dismissed as 'merely personal' because the personal documents an alienated society.

Textually, the dialectic between the utopian and 2411 is narrativised as an interaction between the discourses of Mesmer and Reed. Psychoanalytic therapy relies upon transference, that is, that the analysand will come to live out his/her neuroses by projecting them onto the supposedly impartial figure of the analyst. So Reed's attempt to curtail Mesmer's incestuous fixation on the mother appears in Mesmer's discourse in the character of the matricide, Very Light, correctly interpreted by the good doctor as phallic because of his 'piercing gaze, bald head and aerial brilliance' (p. 14), just as June stands for Sonia and the dragon presumably for Mesmer's symbolic mother. But as Freud's case history of Dora notoriously instances, the analyst always risks counter-transference, projecting his or her own problems onto the patient. Far from immune to this, Reed first decides to marry yet again in response to the sexual challenge to him posed by Mesmer, and then to kill him because his utopia so completely subverts everything Reed stands for, his expensive Harley Street practice, his Rolls Royce Silver Cloud, his instrumental and fetishistic relation to women as fantasy objects of an endlessly metonymic desire but not of satisfaction and pleasure. Mesmer's utopian vision counts not merely as an individual's disorder but accrues social and objective force because Reed in his 1980 so actively – and unconsciously – needs to defend himself against 2411 and all it stands for.

In the doubled narrative, events in Mesmer's and Reed's discourses repeat, rhyme and counter each other, making it impossible to catch all the questions the text poses. Can there be a world without law and fathers and the repression, both social and psychic, they mutually enforce? Why does the phallus, the dragon's tooth Mesmer acquires from Very Light, belong in 2411 not to a male but emphatically to a female and maternal figure (her tooth)? In what kind of discourse can the future be written? In its textual complexity, doubled discourse, Blue Prints, the 'White Heap' of coupled terms, The utopian goes further in articulating such questions than any other comparable work, though ends with the full conditions of possibility for 2411 unavailable, for the last sentence, referring to marks made by the diamond tip of the dragon's tail, says 'There, in the dust, was written the word' (p. 158, and there is no full stop). Mesmerising in its brilliance and suggestion, The utopian is a text we do not yet really know how to read.

Total utopia

Renewing older debates about utopianism (to be found in Ernst Bloch and Louis Marin), Fredric Jameson has consistently taken the position that to imagine utopia is a necessary political intervention. Following through Pierre Macherey's account of literature, Jameson in The political unconscious (1981) argues that all literary texts are in some degree utopian in enacting an imaginary resolution to ideological contradictions and affirming a collective class consciousness, a view he has extended with reference to science fiction in an essay of 1977.

In his advocacy of utopianism Jameson's point of departure is Marx's famous discussion of commodity fetishism and its development by Georg Lukács in History and class consciousness (1923). Like the human imagination in Blake, bourgeois culture is trapped within the categories of Experience; subject and object are felt as necessarily split and opposed; the objective world of commodity production itself seems to determine human action; people treat themselves as isolated individuals whose only choice is what to consume; the subject, unable even to imagine being objectively active in its own constitution, is diverted into fetishism, aestheticism and fantasy; partiality, specialisation and fragmentation replace awareness of interconnection; there ensues 'destruction of every image of the whole' (Lukács, p. 103).

Although Jameson has been criticised (notably by Terry Eagleton, pp. 65–78) for reinstating the somewhat Hegelian politics of Lukács in place of more traditional critiques in terms of class and social contradiction, his analysis has gained considerable purchase through its convincing application to postmodernism (Jameson, 1984). In contemporary conditions it is a central concern of ideological critique and intervention to recreate an image of the whole, a sense of connection, of totality.

In this present chapter I have worked within that theoretical framework. For the Lukácsian (and Jamesonian) concept of totality presumes that a radical dichotomy in the subject/object relation necessarily arises in correspondence with the capitalist mode of production and reproduces itself across different levels of the social formation as the sociological, ideological, psychological and gender oppositions discussed at the beginning, as well as promoting within traditional epistemology the alienation and hypostatisation of Subject and Object criticised by Althusser. But these levels, though interdependent, remain also autonomous in that each operates through its own specific effectivity. A novel then, to be a novel, must succeed in the first place as writing of a particular kind in a particular genre or mixture of genres (such as utopian SF). If, as Jameson proposes, a progressive politics must affirm totality by reworking the subject/object dichotomy – the political versus the personal – a literary text can only do so effectively on its own specific terrain as a particular textuality.

Which is where utopianism comes in. Utopian writing (despite its own mode of existence within the alienated structures of late capitalism in which the literary aesthetic is maintained as a separated and (supposedly) absolutely autonomous domain), in imagining a future totality, should speak from present experience and subjectivity – 'the ultimate subject matter of Utopian discourse would then turn out to be its own conditions of possibility as a discourse' (Jameson, p. 101). Conventional science fiction, in setting up another world as the sphere for its narrative, puts a distance between its represented object and the reading subject (even if its effect may be cognitively estranging); utopian writing, as in Piercy's novel, poses the utopian subject in an active relation to the utopian object, but at the price of stasis – description replaces the narrative proper to the novel genre. A text such as Westlake's The utopian, by taking as its subject matter a dialectic between utopian and utopia, answers more completely than any other work I know to Jameson's prescription. It may be that literature here once again anticipates resolutions to what are otherwise seen as inevitable contradictions.

For, despite Jameson's American pessimism, we do not in fact live only under conditions set by commodity production. Communism, defined as providing for each according to their need, like capitalism in the late feudal period, is already growing within contemporary western society. The family is a communist institution – no-one sells food to their own children. International corporations do not treat their subordinate divisions as rival companies but distribute capital to them according to their needs within the overall corporate strategy. In Britain, despite its present difficulties, the National Health Service has since 1948 treated patients according to need, not by how much they can pay. Since 1945 the western world generally has seen the end of the material deprivation of the masses, at least as it was up to 1939, and this has provided a space for people to give unprecedented attention to questions of gender, sexuality and personal happiness. Of course in one respect this once again enforces the liberal humanist vision of subjective transcendence but, in that it discovers that the personal is political, it points beyond present conditions to a world governed by freedom rather than necessity. It is not necessarily utopian to think we live in an age more profoundly transitional than we frequently imagine.

References

Althusser, Louis, and Balibar, Etienne, *Reading Capital* (London, 1975).

Barthes, Roland, *S/Z* (London, 1975).

Dick, Philip K., *The man in the high castle* (Harmondsworth, Middx., 1965).

Eagleton, Terry, *Against the grain* (London, 1986).

Jameson, Fredric, 'Of islands and trenches: neutralisation and the production of utopian discourse' (1977) in *The ideologies of theory* (London, 1988), 2 vols., vol. 2, pp. 75-101.

Jameson, Fredric, 'Cognitive mapping' (1983) in Cary Nelson and Lawrence Grossberg (eds.), *Marxism and the interpretation of culture* (London, 1988, pp. 347-57).

Lukács, George, *History and class consciousness* (London, 1971).

MacCabe, Colin, *Theoretical essays* (Manchester, 1985).

Marx, Karl, *Grundrisse* (Harmondsworth, Middx., 1973).

Moylan, Tom, 'Demand the impossible: science fiction and the utopian imagination' in Bob Ashley (ed.), *The study of popular fiction, a source book* (London, 1989), pp. 195-9.

Piercy, Marge, *Woman on the edge of time* (London, 1979).

Pitrat, Jacques, *An artificial intelligence approach to understanding natural languages* (London, 1988).

Suvin, Darko, *Metamorphoses of science fiction* (New Haven, CT, 1979).

Westlake, Michael, The utopian (Manchester, 1989).
Williams, Raymond, 'Utopia and science fiction' in Patrick Parrinder (ed.), Science fiction, a critical guide (London, 1979), pp. 52-66.

5

Kozmik kommie konflikts: Stanisław Lem's *Solaris* – an Eastern Bloc parable

Carl Tighe

The existing criteria of value have been falsified and distorted. The force brought to bear against consciousness must, sooner or later, develop into physical force. To take note of this and to give warning is the role of literature.

S. Baranczak, *Więz*

This chapter will look at SF – and in particular Stanisław Lem's novel *Solaris* – as a form of dissidence in the Eastern Bloc, as an oblique way of considering important social and political themes, of side-stepping the censor in the never-ending battle to get unpoliced ideas out of the writer's head and into the heads of a reading public. The subject is directly related to the way the Communist Parties of the Eastern Bloc run their societies and their cultural and political media via the office of the censor.

Post-war East European writers have become increasingly fascinated by the way their societies have created and maintained themselves as closed information systems which control ideas. However, in so far as this idea and theme reveals the ways in which Eastern Bloc societies work, writers have rarely been allowed to discuss it openly. Stanisław Lem has come to see human society as a complex mechanism for transmitting information and for furthering a common sense of identity through particular kinds of state-approved language, ideas, plots and characters. Lem has been able to produce 'serious' works of SF on these themes precisely because he works in a medium that is considered to be an intellectual backwater of little or no serious thought, a trash medium where nothing lasts and where readers who have a taste for SF are unlikely to be those who will fathom social message, political commentary, or moral significance.

The jump from SF to the problems of social structure and censorship may seem a huge one, but virtually all of Lem's novels may be read as parables about what happens to society and to people when channels of communication are blocked, the difficulty of making a revolutionary society or fundamentally changing human nature by social and political engineering on the slender basis of the knowledge of humanity that we have at our disposal. As such his novels may he seen as profoundly humanistic, a critique of the kind of societies that developed under Stalin and a plea for a socialism of gradual change and with a human face

The Czech novelist Milan Kundera described Eastern Europe as 'a laboratory where history made a strange experiment with humanity'. The defeat of Germany in 1918 brought forth a magnificent flowering of art and thought from among the 'smaller nations'. It was here that some of the most adventurous and far-reaching developments in modern fiction took place. Writers revealed what had been unleashed on the world in both personal and national terms by probing the collapse of the old empires and the rise of the new. They also anticipated many of the developments of the post-war world too. East European literature has a rich tradition of utopian and absurdist writing developed in reaction to the bureaucratic procedures and administration of the Austro-Hungarian, Prussian and Russian empires. Much East European literature is marked by strong anti-authoritarian elements, grotesque appreciation of human contradictions, very perceptive reactions to power structures and a keen appreciation of the social, personal and familial structures that underlie government.

Eastern Europe up to the start of World War Two was the haunt of artists and writers who recorded the process of transition from agricultural folk cultures into modern industrial nation-states, and they recorded it in all its ambiguities. This was where Freud explored dreams and the unconscious: and writers such as Franz Kafka, Bruno Schultz, Stanisław Witkiewicz, the brothers Karol and Josef Čapek, Frigyes Karinthy, Josef Mesvadba and Jaroslav Hašek explored not only the 'outer limits' but the inner limits of humanity. They all wrote of the effects of modern social structures and political systems on the inner life of the individual – the borderlands of perception, of consciousness and its links with citizenship. They pursued relentlessly those elements that go to make up personal, public and political decisions.

Eastern Europe experienced the whole range of twentieth-century possibility within a very short time-span. The nations of Eastern Europe saw the growth and break-up of the old European empires, the development and impact of large-scale industry and the effects of increasingly centralised and often military government upon their daily life. They experienced these developments first as distant provinces of the old empires, and then through the experience of building small, would-be democratic nations from the ruins of those empires. All experienced the totalitarian regimes first of Hitler and then of Stalin.

Without doubt Stanisław Lem is a product of this intense history and literary tradition. Lem was born in the Polish-Ukrainian town of Lwów on 12 September 1921. Both his parents were doctors of very distant Jewish ancestry. Between 1939 and 1941 he was prevented from pursuing his studies by the Russian invasion of Poland and then by the German invasion of Russia. Since under the Nazis Poles were forbidden any kind of further education, Lem worked as a garage mechanic; he scavenged ammunition from the local German arms dump, and on one occasion transported a gun for the resistance under the noses of the Occupation forces. In 1945 Lwów passed under Russian control and Lem, along with millions of other Poles, moved westwards to the new Polish People's Republic. In 1947 he resumed his studies, this time at Kraków University. He became a junior research assistant at the Kraków Conservatorium where he made abstracts of scientific literature for learned journals. Eventually he graduated as an MD, practised as an intern and began to study philosophy. Lem began writing in the late 1940s and his early work was part of the very rigid Stalinist literary bureaucratic world – he has since dubbed this period as 'devoid of any value'.

With *Solaris* (Warsaw, 1961) he achieved considerable success. The book was translated into a number of languages but is probably best known as the basis for Andrei Tarkovski's (1972) film of the same name. His books are translated into more than thirty languages, with over six million copies currently in circulation – two and a half million of these in the Soviet Union. On average over thirty new translations of his work are made every year. With his books recently reissued in a uniform Polish edition, published in expensive hardback editions in Britain and the USA, and in a two-volume selection by Penguin, it is probably fair to say that Lem is one of the world's most successful SF writers.

It is often assumed that because Lem is so well known in the Eastern Bloc his work has somehow been encouraged by state patronage and official favour. Lem, however, feels that his work was tolerated by the authorities rather than encouraged. Almost all of his books appeared first in editions of less than 20,000. *Summa technologiae*, for example, was published in 1963 in an edition of 3,000 copies; even the highly successful *Robotic fables* first appeared in an edition of 7,000 – small even by Polish standards. Almost all of Lem's books appeared in initial print runs of 20,000 or less. Only after 1978 did Lem achieve an edition of 100,000 on any of his books. The third edition of *Solaris* published (Kraków, 1976) consisted of only 30,000 copies, but by the third joint edition of *Solaris* and *Invincible* (1986) the print run rose grudgingly to 100,000. Lem believes that state 'patronage' held him back. In its absence he feels he might have achieved greater recognition without having to wait more than twenty years for his international reputation to establish him in Poland.[1]

Lem's situation is the same as that of any other Eastern Bloc SF writer. Because SF is seen to be a minority interest it has a very low priority within Eastern Bloc publishing programmes; whenever the inevitable print and paper shortages show themselves, SF publication is one of the first casualties. This inevitably means that serious Polish writers tend to favour work in other more stable and rewarding areas. At first the authorities say they can publish only a limited edition because the writer is an unknown and because he is working in SF. Then, when his books have sold out, received good reviews and come to the notice of foreign readers, the authorities worry that perhaps the public has read something into the work that they or the censor has missed. No reprint is forthcoming until public interest has died down, or until the censor has checked that the work is perfectly safe, that there is, after all, nothing dangerous lurking between the lines.

Western readers encountering Lem for the first time often sense the power of his writing, his massive literary and linguistic inventiveness, but find his playfulness, false naïvety, grotesquery, his huge engagement with SF as a serious art form both daunting and unsettling – though in the terms of East European fiction these traits and manoeuvres are perfectly acceptable. Lem's writings may be seen as an escape out into orbit, but also and more productively, as deeply subversive, telling critiques of the prevailing political system and the mentalities it has created. *Solaris* is a powerful parable about the difficulty of breaking into or out of closed information systems – whether that system be a language, a country or a political set-up. Lem anticipated the almost obsessive development of this theme in dissident writings of the 1970s and 1980s. Dissidents like Leszek Kołakowski, Adam Michnik, Władysław Bieńkowski, Jacek Kuroń, and novelist like Kazimierz Brandys have all raised similar topics – and have provoked the censor to take immediate action against them.

In this novel Lem pursues the idea of society as a 'closed information system' through the image of Solaris, a huge implacable yet apparently intelligent planet. The planet is covered by a mysterious sea which from time to time produces semi-solid 'mimoids' – forms of wondrous shape and size. Some of the mimoids imitate vast human forms. There has been a long history of research into the planet, yet after years of investigation Solaris remains an enigma: 'For a great many, particularly the young, the "affair" gradually became a kind of touchstone for certain values: "Basically", they said, "there is greater matter at stake than the probing of Solaris civilisation. This is a game that turns on us alone, about the very borders of human cognition." '[2]

Kelvin, a psychologist, is sent to investigate events on a space station orbiting the planet. There he finds that in response to human attempts to 'jolt' the planet into acknowledging humanity by bombarding it with massive doses of lethal X-rays, the planet has retaliated by digging into the subconscious of its human explorers to reproduce their most shameful fantasies and memories. For as long as they hover over Solaris they are doomed to relive their most severe failures of sympathy and humanity, doomed to live with their presumption and inability to recognise those aspects of their own life and mentality that are deeply and limitingly human. They are haunted by apparitions manufactured out of their unconscious by the planet. Thus a giant negress, naked except for a grass skirt, follows the scientist Gibarian; something huge and childish lives in Dr Sartorius's room. At one and the same time these things are newly identified and as old as humanity. The scientist Snow explains to Kelvin:

We moved out into the cosmos ready for anything. That means for loneliness, struggle, martyrdom and death. Modesty does not allow us to say so, but over a period of time, we think we're rather excellent. Meanwhile this isn't it at all, and our readiness becomes a pose. We don't want to capture the cosmos, we want only to extend Earth to cosmic frontiers. One planet might be desert like the Sahara, another frozen like the poles, or tropical like the jungles of Brazil. We are humanitarian and noble, we don't want to enslave other races; we want only to pass on our values and in exchange to penetrate their heritage. We have become followers of the Knights of the Holy Contact. This is an expensive falsehood. We are searching for nothing other than people. It is not necessary to have other worlds. It is necessary only to own a mirror. We do not know what to do with other worlds. One world is enough, but still we are stifling. It has to be the 'right thing', an idealised picture; it must be a globe, a civilisation higher than ours, but at the same time we hope again for a likeness that had developed like our own primitive past. At the same time on the other hand there is something unpleasant against which we defend ourselves, and we don't take with us from earth only the distilled virtue of humanity! We arrive here just like this, as we are in reality, and when we are shown that truth, that other part of us about which we would rather remain silent — we don't like it.[3]

Lem is mainly interested in the dilemma of investigator Kelvin. The planet very quickly digs into Kelvin's subconscious to find that he once had a girlfriend called Harey and that she, as a result of Kelvin's inattention and refusal to take her seriously, killed herself. Now the planet provides Kelvin with a new Harey, a woman who with her innocence and trust forces Kelvin to acknowledge the limits of his sympathy and his inabilities as a human being. Kelvin locks the new Harey in a space capsule and ejects her into space, but that night he wakes up to find her - or a new facsimile of her — beside him in bed again.

Solaris forces the humans to face up to certain basic facts about themselves. What the planet has found in each of them is the core experience, the mainspring of their personality and presumption, their most shameful area of moral turpitude, the driving force that has led them to Solaris. The planet shows them that it is this which has driven them to conquer the stars. Not a desire to meet or understand aliens. The planet, as far as we can know, has mastered its inner life, the humans have not. By its action it asks them to consider why it should respond and break its communication with itself when humanity is so lacking in self-knowledge and driven by piffling motives. The planet calls into question the human notion of 'I'. It asks them to consider that perhaps humans only mirror each other's preconceptions, run along in the tram tracks of human cognition, have not yet achieved the level of introspection and self-knowledge required to understand either the universe, the planet, or even themselves. Humanity is pouring its own inner chaos out into the universe.

Lem does not tell us if the planet is self-aware, or hint what communication with the planet might be like. He is much more interested in looking at the basis of the human characters and their drive into space. In many of Lem's novels the human protagonists begin to understand their new and alien environment only after all attempts at communication in human terms have failed: at this point they often experience a difficult aesthetic encounter. Kelvin feels that the planet has played despicable tricks with his unconscious, but while he will never understand or be able to communicate with it, he still has to come to terms with that entity, and experience it on its own terms rather than his. The only terms on which he can establish any contact with it are aesthetic. The beauty of the planet is a kind of truth, and truth resides in simply accepting that incomprehensible beauty. In the end the planet puts the humans in touch with a new perspective on their cosmic and personal failure, on their actual place in the universe.

At the close of the novel Harey realises that she is not human, that her presence is some kind of deception and that if she is not fully human she has no place in Kelvin's life. In a way, the more human she becomes the less she accepts the mystery of her own existence. In secret Harey offers herself as a target for a new 'Matter Disintegrator' that Snow has developed. Kelvin wakes up one morning to find that Harey is not beside him in bed. This time she does not come back. Kelvin recognises that Harey's appearance on the space station had been a 'cruel miracle', but it was one that gave him a second chance and her presence was something that he had come to accept and appreciate. Now that she is taken away from him for a second time he alternates between a desire to renew attempts at communication with the planet and a desire to annihilate it.

In despair Kelvin takes a flight out over the sea and experiences for the first time the power and mystery of the huge, intelligent entity, its massive boredom with him, the banality of his own personality and desires:

Are we then to be a watch that measures the flow of time, now smashed, then repaired anew, whose mechanism the watchmaker sets in motion and which from its very first movement generates despair and love, knowing that it is the recapitulation of suffering, apparently profound, yet in sum, amounting only to a multiplicity of comic repetition? To repeat human existence, fine, but to repeat it like a drunk thrashing the same record, again and again throwing his newly minted coin into the depths of a capacious juke-box.[4]

All of Lem's protagonists are intellectually active, they want to solve the problems that beset them. Yet without exception they pay for their 'cognitive impulse', for their effort to recognise another way of processing, thinking, developing, being. They pay for the extension of their humanity with the painful recognition of their human limitations. In Kelvin's case, by repeating his earlier mistake of taking Harey's presence for granted, he pays with the loss of the thing he has come to love.

Jerzy Jarzębski, perhaps Lem's most perceptive critic, points to a passage in *Memoirs found in a bathtub*:

What does it mean? Meaning. And so we enter the realm of semantics. One must tread carefully here! Consider: from earliest times man did little else but assign meanings – to the stones, the skulls, the sun, other people, and the meanings required that he create theories – life after death, totems, cults, all sorts of myths and legends, black bile and yellow bile, love of God and country, being and nothingness – and so it went, the meanings shaped and regulated human life, became its substance, its frame and foundation – but also a fatal limitation and a trap.[5]

Nature creates things; only humanity searches for and assigns meanings. To step outside that and accept the 'otherness' of another intelligence is perhaps to cease being entirely human.

Andrei Tarkovski's film version of the book displeased Lem. After seeing the shooting script he announced himself unpleasantly surprised at the long prologue set on earth and at the undue importance given to Kelvin's mother – a figure who came to symbolise Motherland, ideas of home and Mother Earth and which he felt had more to do with Russian folklore and Tarkovski's own preoccupations than with his novel. Lem managed to persuade Tarkovski to drop most of the alterations, but eventually he realised that the novel was a stalking horse for Tarkovski's own ideas and he withdrew from the project. Although accounted one of the finest of all SF films, Lem has only seen fragments of it on Polish TV.

I was expecting a visualisation of the 'Drama of Cognizance', seen as a contrast between the images of 'home, sweet Earth' and the 'Cold Cosmos', a drama in which the characters affecting the men in the station originate from the ocean and symbolise the antagonism between the vast open spaces of the planet and the small enclosed Station. Unfortunately Tarkovski took sides and favoured 'home sweet Earth' against the 'Cold Cosmos'. For a drama of cognizance in which the people, the envoys from Earth, keep on struggling with the enigma that cannot be solved by the human mind, Tarkovski substituted a moral drama *par excellence*, which in no way relates to the problem of cognizance and its extremes. For Tarkovski, the most important facet was Kelvin's problem of 'guilt and punishment', just as in a Dostoyevsky book...[6]

Lem has said that the writer whose characters visit an alien intelligence is in a better position than a writer who has an alien intelligence visit Earth because the motives for an alien visit must be simple: to fight, steal, conquer, learn, play. If these motives are not sufficient, the only other strategy is to keep their motivation a secret.

If humans stumble upon an alien intelligence, however, it is altogether a different matter: the alien is going nowhere, is living its life according to its own rules, and may therefore be utterly impenetrable. Thus in the encounter humanity may find only itself and its limitations.

Lem was quite clear about the theory and direction that lay behind *Solaris*. When he began work on the novel he had a developing design in mind: 'I knew there was to be an ocean on the planet and that it would interfere with the lives of the people in the station, although I was not aware, at that point, what the ocean was truly "up to", or what the interference would in fact be.'[7] The process of construction gave him a great deal of trouble and the final chapter of *Solaris* was particularly difficult precisely because Lem was wrestling with his own self-knowledge and the limits of is own cognition:

This process of writing, which is characterised by the signs of creation by trial and error, has always been arrested by blocks and blind alleys that forced me to retreat; sometimes there has even been a 'burning out' of the raw materials – the manifold resources necessary for further growth – stored somewhere in my skull. I was not able to finish *Solaris* for a full year, and could do it then only because I learned suddenly – from myself – how the last chapter had to be. (And then I could only wonder why I hadn't recognised it from the beginning.)[8]

Lem has little time for structuralist or post-structuralist attempts to divorce his work from its cultural and political context, and insists on a very close relation and obligation to the social norms that helped create his work. He has complained frequently about SF's lack of awareness of the problems of narrative and the relationship of the genre to the cultural and political problems of the real world. In his many essays Lem has identified stories that have only a passing fashion, which interest us because they are parts of a world which is marvellous, but is self-contained and has no bearing on the real world. He contrasts most SF, which he includes in this category, with other works like Kafka's 'Metamorphosis' which is not a fantastic marvel of the imagination, but a deep-seated recognition of the deformations of the human 'socio-psychological situation':

If the new phenomenon is of a qualitatively different scale – contact with 'aliens' in outer space, for example – it is all but certain that the repertoire of received, ready concepts will not be able to accommodate it without considerable friction. In all likelihood, a cultural, perceptual, and perhaps even a social-ethical revolution will be necessary. Thus instead of the assimilation of the new, we must imagine the re-ordering and even the destruction of fundamental concepts, the revaluation of truths that were previously indisputable, and so on.[9]

For Lem it is important that SF should be seen to depict a world that is not only morally neutral, but is a recognisable world described with a contemporary shape but situated at some point further along the space-time continuum:

Only the outer shell of this world is formed by the strange phenomena; the inner core has a solid non-fantastic meaning. Thus a story can depict the world as it is, or interpret the world ... or, in most cases, do both things at the same time.

As in life we can solve real problems with the help of images of non-existent beings, so in literature can we signal the existence of real problems with the help of prima facie impossible occurrences or objects. Even when the happenings it describes are totally impossible, SF work may still point out meaningful, indeed rational problems.[10]

It is usual for writers to leave messages 'between the lines'. Indeed, Polish literature sometimes resembles a gigantic cryptic crossword — to be read only by the initiate few. On a very crude level, the story could be said to portray a massively indifferent Party, smug in its own existence and in its failure to respond to any outside overtures. Lem, however, was not writing an allegory — he was to wary of the censor for that — and it would be mistaken to look for a series of point-for-point correspondences with Polish political life. Certainly the novel is informed by this experience, but, in the manner of all parables, it has much wider implications: it is very clearly about human ability to think within and outside a given set-up, about the limitations of human comprehension of things which are not human, about humanity's refusal to believe that it may be of no interest to an alien intelligence. It is also about the obsessive 'I' of human culture, and since the role of the individual is one which Communism has sought to redefine, the subject has further repercussions in that it seeks to reveal some of the mechanisms by which our perceptions are shaped and informed, how we see and how we are allowed to see the world and the universe around us.

Censorship is the main and all-pervasive feature of the business of perception in the Eastern Bloc. It may be a characteristic of Stalinism, but it was certainly not something of which Marx approved — in 1843 he said: 'Censorship, like slavery can never become lawful, even if it exists a thousand times over. A censored press corrupts social life and means that government hears nothing but its own voice.' In the post-war years censorship, rather than helping to smooth the path of progress towards socialism, actually suppressed legitimate grievances and set up a propaganda of success contradicted by everyday experience. This in turn bred cynicism and antagonism towards the state and the authorities which the society had no way of satisfying, diverting or even easing.

One of the effects of censorship, and one which literature continually struggles against, is that it makes the feelings and thought processes of human discovery and cognition increasingly difficult and irrational. Censorship blocks channels of information and feeling within society and individuals. It guards the difference between truth and propaganda, but because it erodes the language and the processes of cognition it also effectively destroys the perception that there is a difference. Not only does a society not know what it thinks, but it does not know what it feels; and before long society does not know what it knows.

Not all Polish readers are prepared to seek comfort in SF parables, however, and it is important to know something of the social and political context in which *Solaris* was written and in which its concerns have become increasingly relevant.

Through the 1960s and 1970s Poles turned increasingly to sources of information and feeling that were not in any way 'approved' and which were uncontaminated by the hand of the censor. They listened regularly (and illegally) to Polish-language broadcasts from the West – Radio Free Europe, heard by 17 million Poles per week; the Voice of America heard by 9 million Poles per week; and the BBC World Service and Polish service broadcasts heard by nearly 7 million Poles each week. They also came to depend increasingly on gossip. This meant that Poles became easy victims to malicious rumour-mongering and often tended to believe the most blatant nonsense simply because it came from some source other than their own official media.

Writers complained of the 'shell of falsification' that became increasingly effective in the 1970s. They regarded literature as an unofficial opposition that faced up to the moral bankruptcy of the regime and which acted as an alternative ideal within society. The readership of semi-legal magazines was enormous – particularly after the demonstrations and unrest of 1976. It has been estimated that for each copy of an underground journal there were at least thirty readers and countless others who heard the contents over the 'bush telegraph'.

While the underground press had virtually no contact with the authorities, their publications were read by those in power with a view to finding and suppressing publication. This was virtually the only transmission of ideas from the bottom to the top of Polish society. It was certainly not possible to voice criticism within the official trade unions, through elections to the *Sejm* (the Polish Parliament), or in newspapers: these 'organs of state' formed a one-way transmission belt for the orders and policies of the Party. Censorship shaped public consciousness and self-awareness as an incomplete and irrational, empty entity; it created a hunger for information, but did not foster introspection nor provide any framework in which information could be assessed.[11]

It was to counter some of the effects of misinformation and censorship, to combat ignorance and apathy and to curb the growing right-wing reaction to Party propaganda, that TKN (Flying University) was founded in January 1978. With the assistance of the Catholic Church TKN fostered some thirty uncensored journals dealing with cultural, historical and political matters in a manner that was open, reliable and accurate. TKN conducted unofficial lectures and seminars on the 'grey' areas of intellectual life – particularly events lost in 'official' Polish history such as the Katyn Massacre and the Molotov-Ribbentrop pact. The Polish authorities predictably resorted to breaking up meetings, beatings, harassment, the destruction of equipment and arrests on trumped-up charges.

The inevitable consequence of these actions were pointed out to the regime by the semi-official 'Experience and Future Group' in 1978-9:

The effects of politics and economic policies we experience literally every day, but we feel ourselves left out of the decision-making processes, not only as active subjects but even as mere observers. We are left out and hence cut off from responsibility. A Polish citizen experiences the meanderings of politics and planning more or less as he experiences changes in the weather: as important changes he must adapt to but whose causes – wholly external – are not worth exploring more deeply, since he has no way of influencing them …

What is more, this system has created something that is more dangerous than indifference and cynicism, something that surely was not intended: it has created a state of collective *informational* psychosis.[12]

Poles began to feel that in their own private lives they were no longer in control and that therefore they were no longer responsible for their actions, that somehow 'They' (the government and the Party) were to blame for everything. The result was mounting frustration, mutual hostility, a complete failure of social responsiveness and responsibility - undirected, unspecific antagonism towards the state and society.

In autumn 1979 – just before the strikes that gave birth to Solidarność Michnik, Lipski and Kuroń agreed that there was every possibility of a sudden explosion of public anger at government economic policies. Knowing the strength of anti-government feeling they worried about how 'Democratic Oppositionists' like themselves would function in such an event. Michnik saw the growth of Polish right-wing opinion as a mark of confusion resulting directly from the work of the censor and from the government's failure to establish or foster self-knowledge and responsibility within society:

I think that in Poland the conflict between the right and the left belongs to the past. It used to divide a society that was torn by struggles for bourgeois freedoms, universal voting rights, land reform, secularisation, the eight hour workday, welfare, universal schooling, or the democratisation of culture. A different distinction comes to the fore in the era of totalitarian dictatorships: one between the proponents of an open society and the proponents of a closed society. In the former, social order is based on self-government and collective agreements; in the latter, order is achieved through repression and discipline. In the vision of an open society, the state acts as the guardian of safety for citizens; in the vision of a closed society the state is a master and overseer who determines all modes of society's existence.[13]

At his grimmest Michnik claimed that every human move, feeling and reaction under censorship, even violent efforts to overthrow the regime, were nothing more than manifestations of 'slave mentality'.

As in Lem's novel, indifference provoked violence, but not necessarily further understanding on either side. Lem called into question the underlying human feelings that informed the processes of civil society. How can politicians remake society (or humanity dare contact aliens) when they know so little of how society works, and so little about the influence their own individual fears and ambitions have on the processes of power, when there are no mechanisms of feedback on the effects of their restructuring? They know themselves so little, yet are powerful enough to subvert and pervert political thinking and theory. Lem is interested in the mainsprings of human ambition and activity. He is concerned about the values and the true extent of the human knowledge and understanding that humanity is planning to export into space, and in the sense that the space race is also a revolution he worries about the presumption that humanity knows enough (morally and personally) to undertake any such engineering project when it has failed so spectacularly at home.

Bieńkowski (an ex-Minister of Education) has pointed out that censorship has made the business of integrating new knowledge about systems, social structures, the inner workings of human thought and its social and political manifestations almost impossible by creating barriers to resist all notions alien to a very narrow and highly selective interpretation of Marx. Bieńkowski believes that twentieth-century society has slowly abandoned force as a way of controlling its citizens and has concentrated on reordering social structures so that freedoms of all kinds are increasingly seen as some kind of commercial commodity – rights must be bought or earned by conforming to social norms. In Eastern Europe this has meant that the relationship between behaviour and consciousness, the very idea of internalisation, of individual moral responsibility, have lost all meaning and instead have been replaced by learned behaviour patterns which have no personal rationale behind them. The Polish sociologist Julia Sowa has dubbed this phenomenon the 'dead field of public normative indifference'. It is a state of 'intellectual innocence' in which the citizen falls prey to chance impulse. While believing they are 'free' to decide for themselves on any issue, in fact they lack all self-knowledge and therefore lack all social and political judgement. The result – as in Kelvin's case – is an increasingly chaotic social and inner life for the bulk of the population.[14]

In the same way that the failure of the planet Solaris to respond to the scientists provokes them to bombard it with massive doses of harmful X-rays, the monolithic indifference of the Polish Communist Party to public opinion and common sense provoked increasing hostility. Many writers and observers had warned that Polish society was heading for an explosion of discontent. Although the Party blamed Solidarność, the economic collapse of 1980 had been inevitable since the early 1970s. Had the government chosen to monitor the success of its own performance instead of using the office of the censor to suppress discontent, they would have picked up the first rumblings from deep within Polish society long before the earthquake of 1980 and the declaration of Martial Law in 1981.[15]

Attempts to control the formation of opinion inevitably destroy the possibility of ever finding out what people think or might think. It is inconsistent to believe that free expression of thought – especially critical thought – should survive alongside a bid for total control. Ultimately the bid for control destroys knowledge. In this way political power and social- or self-knowledge are linked in opposition to each other. The office of the censor erected an insurmountable barrier between what Marxism might have offered the Poles and what the Party did in the name of Marxism. The great outburst of clandestine publication in Poland in the 1960s and 1970s was a direct effort on the part of Polish intellectuals not to succumb to the Party's bid for total control, to maintain some level of self-knowledge and social understanding. Lem's particular choice of themes was to a very great extent a direct response to that bid to control minds and remake society.

The Polish novelist Kazimierz Brandys has described the twentieth century as an era of 'self diagnostic and self critical culture', of 'thinking about thinking', a period of taking many senses and meanings, each of which reveals some part of an overall truth. For him everything fills a cognitive function, and he characterises the era as 'analysing itself while in the process of becoming', a process modified by introspection and self-analysis. For Brandys, as for Lem, it became essential to question the language in which the 'reality' of the closed, censored, 'socialist' world was presented. It became necessary to ponder anew the questions that tortured him as a schoolboy in order to restore some part of the faculty of cognition and introspection denied by censorship:

What is man? Does God Exist? Does death mean the end, and how ought one to live? These are actually adolescent's questions; if you ask them, the fear of being laughed at is well justified. Dare we ask them in a civilisation where research by specialists has replaced philosophy? Our world, which is interested in technology, in genetics, and in the structure of language, has grown humble in the face of the universal problems; it has set itself narrower, better defined goals. In such a world, to go deep within oneself and ponder the secrets of Being, without electronic microscopes, without laboratories or accelerators – that can only be the quirk of a thinker from the provinces seeking a proof of the existence of God. Yet sometimes there is nothing else to do. When choosing a way of life, only naïve questions remain, because in such a world all questions with an ethical content appear to be naïve.[16]

In the face of the cosmos Lem proposes a return to these considerations. In *Solaris* he questions the fundamentals of his own existence and the social order that both nurtures and stifles him. He writes out of a specific social and political context. What is it like to try to talk to an intelligent monolithic entity that consistently fails to respond? What are the effects of living under a regime/intelligence such as this? How can we know what we have created in a social revolution when we do not know ourselves sufficiently to understand what we are creating? Naïve questions these may be. However, they undercut the 'ethics' of the one-party state, restore the status of self-knowledge and self-examination, then raise again the issue of humanity's right to make a social revolution and to explore the cosmos.

Solaris was published at a time when the East–West space race was just getting under way and when the burden of military spending was clearly more than the inefficient Eastern bloc economies could support. The novel appeared after the first of the post-war Polish upheavals, but before the increasingly serious demonstrations of discontent in 1968, 1970, 1976 and 1980-1. Lem could not be expected to predict exactly how the influence of the censor would operate on the formation of moral and political attitudes, but working in a genre of limited appeal and small circulation and therefore largely ignored by the censor, he was able to pinpoint one long-term effect of blocks and barriers to the free flow of information and feeling within that particular society. Lem was able to foresee and indicate a very precise formation of discontent, of political and moral failure within Polish society, and to predict an area of increasing concern taken up by dissidents and by the leaders and thinkers of Solidarność some twenty years later.

Notes

1 In 1978, for example, Poland published a total of 54,000,000 volumes but this included 12,000,000 'modern classics' in translation; 11,849 new titles by contemporary Polish writers appeared in editions of about 10,000 copies. PF. VI 1-1 and 7-1 Literature, Facts about Poland (Polska Agencja Interpress: Warsaw, 1980).

2 Stanisław Lem, Solaris (Wydawnictwo Literackie: Kraków, 1976, p. 26). My translation. The English translation of the French translation from Polish has: '...it was essentially a test of ourselves, of the limitations of human knowledge'. Solaris, trans. J. Kilmartin and S. Cox (Arrow Press: London, 1973), p. 23.

3 Solaris, Kraków, 1976, pp. 76-7.

4 Ibid., pp. 208-9.

5 Jerzy Jarzębski, 'Stanisław Lem: rationalist and visionary', Science Fiction Studies, vol. 4, Part 2, July 1977, p. 119; Stanisław Lem, Memoirs found in a bathtub (Kraków, 1961) (Seabury Press: New York, 1973), p. 148.

6 'Stanisław Lem answers questions', Foundation, No. 15, January 1979, p. 46.

7 Ibid., p. 42.

8 'Reflections on my life' (1984) in Stanisław Lem, Microworlds: writings on fiction and fantasy (Secker & Warburg: London, 1985), ed. F. Rottensteiner, p. 22.

9 'Metafantasia: the possibilities of SF' (1981) in Lem, Microworlds, p. 196.

10 'On the structural analysis of SF' (1973) in Lem, Microworlds, pp. 35, 36-7.

11 On censorship in Poland see: Jane Leftwich Curry, The black book of Polish censorship (Vintage

Press: New York, 1984). Also: M. Korbel Albright, *Poland: the role of the press in political change* (Praeger Press: Washington, D.C., 1983).

12 *Poland: the state of the republic: two reports by the Experience and Future Group* (Pluto Press: London, 1981), p. 25. The reports never appeared in Poland, but were originally published by Instytut Literacki (Paris, 1980).

13 Adam Michnik, 'Letter from the Gdańsk Prison, 1985', *Letters from prison* (University of California Press: Berkeley, 1985), p. 91.

14 Władysław Bieńskowski, *Motory i Hamulce Socjalizmu* (Instytut Literacki: Paris, 1969), p. 82. Władysław Bieńkowski, *Theory and reality: the development of social systems* (Allison & Busby: London, 1981), pp. 72-3. Julia Sowa, 'Teoria grup odniesnia', *Studia socjologiczne*, no. 4, 1966.

15 On the economic collapse of 1980-1 see: D. M. Nutti: 'The Polish crisis: economic factors and constraints', *The socialist register 1981*, ed. R. Miliband and J. Saville (Merlin Press: London, 1981), pp. 104-43.

16 Kazimierz Brandys, *A question of reality: answers from Poland* (Blond & Briggs: London, 1981), p. 158. Unpublished in Poland.

6

Change and the individual in the work of the Strugatskys

Christopher Pike

Three issues have dominated Russian literature in the modern period: war, social and political conflict, and scientific progress. As is well known, war, both external and internal to Russian/Soviet territory, has had paradoxical effects: on the one hand, alliances with western powers have internationalised Russia within Europe and beyond; on the other, the destruction of invasion, civil war and terror has alienated it from the outside world and immured it in a self-obsessed martyrdom. It is also obvious that the nature and consequences of social and political conflict have been no less extreme. The country which has lacked, in both the nineteenth and the twentieth centuries, any stable mechanism for securing progress or reform, has instead suffered from sudden and often disastrous crises of change, but change which in this century has generated a socio-political culture of stasis and torpor. The third issue – that of scientific progress – is, like the other two, related almost inextricably to the unsolved question of Russia's relationship with the West, in particular with Europe. The desire of Russia, or the European USSR, to be regarded as European (displayed most recently in Mikhail Gorbachev's concept of the 'common European home') has been held in check, not just by political constraints, but also by the USSR's profound failure successfully to implement scientific progress on a large scale.

These three issues continue to be central to 'the Russian question' in the extraordinary period of glasnost and perestroika which has developed since the mid-1980s. In particular, glasnost has called attention not just to the need for freedom of information and expression for the collectives of society, but also to the absolute necessity of the individual's contribution to this process. At the same time, the pressure for economic perestroika relies not just on the individual's sense of responsibility, but also on the successful application of scientific progress to production and services; but glasnost has revealed the atrocious levels of ecological damage done by industrial development and has alerted the population to a strong 'green' concern. At every·point, therefore, Gorbachev's economic perestroika is faced by the cultural paradoxes which his 'second Russian revolution' has brought about: the primacy of the individual in relation to the need for massive social change (and the inevitably accompanying conflicts); the demand for scientific and technological modernisation against a society newly aware of and disturbed by its environment.

At a time of such monumental change, it seems equally important to emphasise the continuity of these cultural issues, if only as a means of further illuminating what is happening now. Consequently, this essay discusses the way in which change is treated in modern Russian literature, with reference to the relationship between scientific ideas, society and the individual. The intention is to place four of the Strugatskys' novels, The snail on the slope (1966-8), The ugly swans (1972), Roadside picnic (1974) and Definitely maybe (1976-7), in the context of Russian literature's treatment of science since the nineteenth century and to show that in the1960s and 1970s the Strugatskys combined questioning of the benefits of science with a defence of the integrity of the individual.[1] As Geoffrey Hosking has shown, these themes permeate much Soviet literature, especially the so-called 'village prose'. Hosking gives little credit to Soviet fantastic literature in this respect. 'Recent Soviet fiction of the "fantastic" type,' he says, 'intriguing though some of it is, has proved less penetrating and revealing than the best works of the relatively familiar realist type.'(Hosking, p. 198.) Nevertheless, it is arguable that the Strugatskys' work does articulate these issues effectively and that it treats problems not otherwise accessible to the Soviet readership of its time.

In his discussion of Russian literary attitudes, Richard Freeborn comments: 'All of Russian literature, from Pushkin to Gorky, tends to subsume that at some future point a change will occur, be it simply of heart or a trip to Moscow or a revolution.' (Freeborn, Literary attitudes, p.12.) The nineteenth century in an unbalanced Russia was indeed an age of change, actual and potential. Nor could change be envisaged simply as the alternative to an unchanging continuity. Change itself became the distinctive feature of existence and concepts of gradual change opposed notions of absolute change, the radical perelom ('break') of Chekhovian device, a discontinuity which could create a genuinely new future.

This opposition is also broadly canvassed by the work of Tolstoy and Dostoyevsky. Tolstoy's impulse is always towards continuity: the emphasis on search; the concept of gradual improvement through education; the quest for a comprehensive vision in history and religion; the notions of blending, rhythm and harmony which come to guide the lives of Pierre Bezukhov in *War and peace* and Levin in *Anna Karenina*. By contrast, Dostoyevsky is a creature of discontinuity and sudden, overwhelming change. Alex de Jonge sees Dostoyevsky as operating with 'an aesthetic code built upon the need to provoke a reaction at all costs. Its aim is neither beauty nor harmony of form, but sensation and intensity.' (de Jonge, p. 201.) The utopia with which Dostoyevsky repeatedly experiments is not one of the gradual reform and reorganisation of society, but a state which depends on a longed-for and dreamt-of *moment* when the millions of humanity will suddenly be transformed and happiness realised. Such is the cry of the eponymous hero of Dostoyevsky's *The dream of a ridiculous man* as he goes out to preach his vision of a perfected humanity.

Mention of utopianism brings us to the problem of science, of which Tolstoy and Dostoyevsky were well aware and profoundly mistrustful. Interestingly, Tolstoy himself has been described as 'a queer combination of the brain of an English chemist with the soul of an Indian Buddhist' (de Vogue, quoted in Berlin, p. 22), while Jacques Catteau reminds us that Dostoyevsky 'often finds a means to illustrate the complex thought of his heroes by borrowing an image from the theories of Cuvier, the non-Euclidean geometry of Lobachevsky or astro-physics' (Catteau, p. 33). But both writers resisted the rationalising, Europeanising force of scientific activity and, in *The idiot* and *Anna Karenina*, attacked technology, in the form of the train, as an instrument of menacing social instability.

Russian writers were no strangers to the impact of scientific developments in the first two decades of the twentieth century. Ian Bell observes that at that time 'the scientist recognized, primarily as a result of advances in wave theory, field theory and the postulates of relativity and of quantum mechanics, that nature could no longer be seen as constituted by the enduring objects of traditional physics' (Bell, p. 24). In Russia, always sensitive to theory, the intersection of this scientific crescendo with Futurism, Formalism and Bolshevism excited many. Roman Jakobson describes the poet Vladimir Mayakovsky's reaction to news about relativity theory:

The idea of the liberation of energy, the problem of the fourth dimension, and the idea that movement at the speed of light may actually be a reverse movement in time – all of these things fascinated Mayakovsky. I'd seldom seen him so interested and attentive. 'Don't you think,' he suddenly asked, 'that we'll at last achieve immortality?' I was astonished, and I mumbled a skeptical comment ... 'I'm absolutely convinced,' he said, 'that one day there will be no more death. And the dead will be raised from the dead. I've got to find some scientist who'll give me a precise account of what's in Einstein's books. It's out of the question that I shouldn't understand it. I'll see to it that that scientist receives an academician's ration. (Quoted in Pomorska, p. 371.)

There are echoes here of Dostoyevsky's initial enthusiasm for Fyodorov's so-called 'scientific' scheme to resurrect the dead, perhaps a search for the ultimate social harmony. For the moment, however, Futurism's interest in science was largely concentrated on its ambivalent concern with technology, with the 'machine' or 'engine' that both moved the future and might become it. Just as the development of vehicles such as the tank, the submarine and the aircraft were stimulating not only Futurism, but also science fiction, so more startling considerations such as those entailed in relativity theory had their effect on Mikhail Bakhtin who, in his treatment of time and space in literature, indicated intriguingly that he was 'borrowing' the concept of space-time from the theory of relativity 'almost as a metaphor (almost, but not entirely)' (Bakhtin, p. 84).

Russian revolutionary literature has been shown to celebrate 'the phoenix spirit', 'the idea of simultaneous death-birth' (Freeborn, *Revolutionary novel*, p. 70). Consideration of such revolutionary change, in the context of unprecedented scientific and technological advance, could not but herald the writing of utopias, to which Russian science fiction proceeded between this time and its suppression in the 1930s. But it was continuity with the nineteenth-century utopian heritage, with its emphasis on the transformation of the individual, which problematised the writing of utopias in the post-revolutionary world. Jurij Striedter discusses the tension between 'utopia' and 'science' in Soviet thought as follows:

This equation – utopianism = antiscientific: scientific = Marxist – had a crucial impact on Soviet criticism of utopian literature, including science fiction. Such a criticism, however, did not exclude the development of a productive Soviet Russian science fiction, as long as this 'scientific fantasy' (*nauchnaya fantastika*) did not contradict the only genuinely scientific approach, that is, the dialectical and historical materialism of Marxism-Leninism. (Striedter, p. 179.)

The principal early result of the attempt to create a Marxist scientific utopia was the *Red star* trilogy of Alexander Bogdanov, a story of class struggle, revolution and a perfect communist society on Mars. Richard Stites comments on Bogdanov's profound belief in the theory of systems:

Bogdanov's systems thinking, still developing when he wrote *Red Star* eventually blossomed into a full-scale theory which he called 'tectology'. The term, borrowed from Ernst Haeckel, denoted a study of the regulatory process and the organization of all systems, a 'general natural science' ... His main goal was to suggest a super-science of organization that would permit regulative mechanisms to preserve stability and prevent cataclysmic change in any of life's major processes – including the production and distribution of goods. As a Marxist he believed this to be possible only under a system of collective labor and collectivized means of production; but he also believed that Marx had to be updated by means of contemporary scientific and organizational discoveries. (Stites, p. 5.)

Bogdanov's utopia depended on a determinism which had already been subverted not only by the new physics, but by Dostoyevsky's Underground Man, with his defiant claim that '... wanting (desire) is the expression of all aspects of life, that is, of all life, including reason and all the itches' (Dostoyevsky, p. 27). It was the subversion of rational activity by desire, the a-rational, primarily erotic impulse which Zamyatin celebrated in *We*, that unsurpassed argument against a final revolution, which can survive only by endlessly recalling its own history or, eventually, obliterating the memory of its citizens.

The Stalinist era not only suppressed speculative literature, but stultified the Soviet attitude towards science itself. Modern genetics and biology were declared 'idealistic' and 'reactionary', discussion of relativity and quantum theory was banned. Many areas of scientific activity were distorted into pseudo-scientific approaches. Zhores Medvedev provides remarkable detail of this tendency:

The veterinarian G. Boshian 'discovered' that viruses could be 'transformed' into bacteria, and vice versa. His 'discovery' also received publicity as a success in Soviet science. Another 'innovator', A. J. Titov, declared that he had discovered plants on the planet Mars and established a so-called 'cosmo-botany'. As the only prominent representative of this new science, he was made a corresponding member of the Academy of Sciences of the USSR and obtained a special laboratory to study life outside earth. (Medvedev, pp. 54-5.)

So when 'normal' scientific activity and the writing of science fiction resumed in the late 1950s, it was the end of a prolonged hiatus in both professions. Certain distinctive features of the Strugatskys' work emerge most clearly when seen in this perspective. Issues such as technology, transforming change, and the effect on the individual of scientific developments within society are prominent in their writings. Moreover, some of their work reflects a 'reception' of issues such as nuclear power, relativity and quantum theory which is broader than that found in orthodox Soviet perception of the time.

The Strugatskys' novels are dominated by a questioning of the relationship between scientific progress and the welfare of the individual. Indeed, the Strugatskys' exploration of social and individual morality on this basis is one of the most impressive elements in their work by comparison with their western counterparts. This is particularly the case with technology, which has always been the principal, if distrusted feature of western science fiction. For historical and cultural reasons, technology is virtually absent from or irrelevant to much modern Soviet science fiction, but acted as its initial spur in the coincidence (not an accidental one) between the scientific-technological revolution (in Russian abbreviation, the NTR) of the 1960s and the development of the new Soviet fantasy. Here too, however, literature deflected external domination. As Halina Stephan has argued, Soviet science fiction 'soon ceased to be an unquestioning handmaiden of the NTR':

Obviously, science and technology could not replace the esthetic and ethical function of literature. In fact, they created new problems with moral dimensions to which literature could specifically address itself. Despite the development in recent years of the so-called NTR style of literature, fictional writing increasingly began to act as a counteragent to the technologization of life. It consciously stressed individual emotions, nature, and ethical authenticity. (Stephan, p. 362.)

This emphasis on individuality and authenticity becomes, in the Strugatskys, a search for the identity of the individual, of environment and society, of man. The identity of environment is particularly important in this respect. The Strugatskys work, and protect themselves, by creating in the major novels (with the exception of Definitely maybe) generalised or alienated non-Russian environments, be it the Forest and Directorate of Snail, the awful provincial town of Swans (like Skotoprigonevsk in Dostoyevsky's The brothers Karamazov) or the 'Canadian' zone of Picnic. The search for universal moral and social statements has led the Strugatskys in these novels to avoid extraterrestrial settings, but at the same time these locations all constitute environments which counteract notions of determinism or even rationalism. The title, epigraphs and events of Snail are parodies of 'progress'. The future, like a pine forest which 'keeps extending wider each day', is as unconquerable by the individual ('You won't draw it into arguments / Nor pet it away') as the slope of Mount Fuji by the snail. Kandid's 'progress' serves only to bury himself (and others) further in the forest:

He vaguely recalled that he had wanted to wait for somebody, wanted to find something out, there was something he was intending to do. Now all that was unimportant. What was important was to get away as far as possible, though he realized that he would never get away. He wouldn't, and neither would many, many, many another. (Strugatsky, Snail, p. 187.)

Although this perception is lightened at the end of the novel, it remains as telling within the thematics of Snail as the final grotesque lessons which Pepper learns about the Directorate and 'administrative activity' from Alevtina:

Just as the highway can't turn as it pleases to left or right, but has to follow the optical axis of your theodolite, just so every directive must be a continuation of all those preceding it ... Ducky, sweety, don't probe into it ... because probing stirs up doubts, doubts make people mark time, and marking time is the death of administrative activity ... (pp. 230-1.)

It is this parodied deterministic 'administrative activity', which achieves nothing but the absurd in Snail, which is further helpless to prevent the physical transformation of characters and environment in Swans. Such activity can do little more than stand guard over the zone in Picnic, its efforts subverted by the anomalous, a-rational Schuhart, and it is powerless before the Homeostatic Universe of Definitely maybe.

These environments of cognitive estrangement (Suvin, p. 12) confront their characters with sudden, total crisis – radical change or transformation. The crisis brings to the surface the latent structures of their personality, humanity and identity. Only the hero who bears a 'natural' identity has the will to go on. Change manifests itself in the distortion of both natural and rational processes in Snail, in the physical transformation of environment in Swans, in the imposition of alien structures on terrestrial reality in Picnic and in the inversion of causality in Definitely maybe. The Strugatskys thus preserve their continuity with the Russian tradition indicated earlier, by questioning the integrity of structures, systems, organisations and institutions and asserting the validity of random, individual response, interaction and adaptation.

The Strugatskys are deeply engaged with the issue of the identity

D

of the individual. Stephan comments: 'The initial [i.e. in earlier Soviet science fiction] positive figure of the hero-explorer is often replaced by an alienated individual whose inflexible emotional framework becomes a dissonant factor in the technologized and bureaucratized world.' (Stephan, p. 362-3.) After reviewing the development of the Strugatskys' work, she concludes: 'The confrontation with the unknown, with the charmed zone or the threat of Martian invasion, evoke traditional patterns of negative response because the protagonists are unable to transcend their psychological limitations.' (Stephan, p. 375.)

Stephan rightly perceives science fiction's place in the tradition which treats the endangerment of the individual in modern society. In Russian literature it is a tradition which goes back to Alexander Pushkin's The bronze horseman of 1833. Nevertheless, it is difficult to agree with Stephan's pessimism about the individual. Most of the central characters in the novels at issue do progress by overcoming their 'psychological limitations' and responding positively to their situations of crisis. It is this location of salvation or hope in the individual that is the principal thrust of the Strugatskys' outlook. The transformation of the individual will be accomplished as a reaction to, rather than the result of, 'science'. The change will not be evolutionary, but momentary, discontinuous, 'catastrophic', an ending which creates a beginning.

The Strugatskys' retreat from science as system and solution does not indicate any disregard for scientific developments. It is within the framework of scientific issues, often not otherwise accessible to the Soviet reader, that they realise these endings/beginnings, these deaths/births. The process begins with the Strugatskys' novel Monday begins on Saturday of 1965. The hero finds himself in the secret research institute of Solovetz, only to discover that it is staffed by the creatures of Russian folklore. The setting and events of Monday satirise the bureaucratism and failure of communication within Soviet science, as described by Medvedev in terms which could yet reflect the future of a fragmenting Soviet Union:

It was not unusual for a research institute in Estonia to receive an official letter written in the Uzbek language from the Uzbekistan Soviet Republic, and it could take months before anyone could be found who was able to read it. In retaliation, the reply would be written in Estonian, and this would create the same situation in Uzbekistan. (Medvedev, p. 128.)

More significantly, the multiple, apparently 'illogical' worlds of Snail reflect a physics which corresponds closely to the premises of quantum mechanics. The theory of a non-determined reality in a continuous state of flux suggested by quantum mechanics led to its suppression under Stalinist science. It may well be that the scarcity of notions of multiple reality in Soviet science fiction results from this suppression. This makes certain features of Snail all the more striking: the plurality and fluidity of life forms in the Forest, the questioning of the observation and reality of events, the emphasis on the emergence and transformation of beings (the deadlings, the Maidens). Meanwhile, the bureaucratic binarism of the Directorate, in its preservation and destruction of the Forest, is quantised through the polyphonic telephone system which simultaneously delivers a different message to each individual. Here, Pepper searches feverishly for 'his' telephone, which alone will convey words intelligible to him:

... every one of [the staff] had the telephone clamped close to his ear, as if afraid to miss even a word. There were no spare telephones. Pepper attempted to take a receiver away from one of the entranced ones ...
   'Where's my telephone?' Pepper was shouting. 'I'm a man like you and 1 have a right to know! Let me listen! Give me my telephone!' (Strugatsky, Snail, p. 83.)

The Director's message or messages travel through the telephone system as a wave of variants, collapsing into an individual intelligible monologue at each receiving point. Thus, in quantum terms, the hearer (observer) creates his own message (reality) by listening (observing).

   By contrast, Swans may well relate history rather than theory. One of the most sensational elements in Medvedev's study of Soviet science was the revelation of a Soviet nuclear catastrophe in Cheliabinsk in 1957, almost twenty years before Chernobyl. An explosion of nuclear waste is said to have irradiated more than 1,000 square miles and to have affected thousands of people. It is difficult not to see Swans as a covert treatment of this horror, which may well have reached the Strugatskys by word of mouth in the scientific community at the time. In Swans, however, the deadly rain actually transforms the bandaged 'slimies' and the children of the town, to usher in a new age. In an ending/beginning which will remind the Western reader of Walter M. Miller Jr's A canticle for Leibowitz (1960), the heroes walk down the main street towards these new people, as the town itself suffers symbolic nuclear annihilation:

Street lights twisted and melted, kiosks and billboards dissolved into thin air, and everything around was cracking and hissing, turning porous and transparent, changing into piles of dirt and disappearing. In the distance, the town hall tower lost its shape and merged into the blue of the sky. For some time, the old-fashioned tower clock hung in the sky, separate from everything, and then it too disappeared. 'My manuscripts are gone,' thought Victor, amused. (Strugatsky, Swans, p. 233.)

Roadside picnic is the Strugatskys' furthest exploration of the utopian theme and, in common with Arthur C. Clarke's Rendezvous with Rama (1973), is based on alien disregard for man and his world. Most importantly, however, Picnic is an essay against scientific determinism, concentrating on the moment of transformation or catastrophe:

A million years from now our instinct will have matured and we will stop making the mistakes that are probably integral to reason. And then, if something should change in the universe, we will all become extinct – precisely because we will have forgotten how to make mistakes, that is, to try various approaches not stipulated by an inflexible program of permitted alternatives (Strugatsky, Picnic, pp. 113-14.)

The positive reaction of humanity to the phenomenon of the alien zone lies not in human science's hopeless attempt to unravel the mysterious objects and effects of the zone itself, nor in the attempts of the authorities to control the administration of the zone and deter the stalkers, but in the transformation of Redrick Schuhart. His searching of the zone for the golden sphere capable of granting all wishes is a sifting of images of himself as outcast, law-breaker, father of a mutant child, a lone, beleaguered individual.

The system which confronts the scientist heroes of Definitely maybe is that of the homeostatic universe which itself determines the balance and, if necessary, the suppression of advances in human knowledge. Nature itself is on the attack against humanity, perceiving it as a developing intelligence which can have only one goal: to change nature (Strugatsky, Definitely, p. 103). Seeking to continue an infinity of progress in knowledge, the scientists encounter the determinedly finite limits permitted to them by an intelligent universe. Again, we find ourselves dealing with the recurrent Strugatskian theme of 'how much (or how little) the individual is permitted to see or know'. The reader recalls Kandid's attempts in Snail, limited even in linguistic expression, to uncover the meaning of Forest life, Pepper's lesson in the same novel in issuing directives 'without probing', the efforts of the authorities in Swans and Picnic to control situations of crisis and restrict the understanding and access of ordinary citizens. The scientists in Definitely maybe are subjected to quantum-jumping changes in their lives and surroundings. The marriage of one is disrupted, the sanity of another threatened, the stamina of a third, Gubar, sapped by the simultaneous manifestation in his apartment of all the women he has ever loved:

They came in droves – all the women he had ever been involved with. They hung around his apartment in twos and threes; there was one horrible day when there were five women in his apartment at the same time. And he simply did not understand what they wanted from him. And worse than that, he had the sneaking suspicion that the women didn't know either. They abused him; they grovelled at his feet; they begged for something or other; they fought among themselves like cats; they broke all his dishes, shattered the blue Japanese water bowl, and ruined his furniture. They had hysterical fits; they tried poisoning themselves, some threatened to poison him, and they were inexhaustible and extremely demanding in lovemaking. (Strugatsky, Definitely p. 66.)

The only resource of the surviving characters is their individual will and courage, an irrational human determination. There is a recurrent thought in Picnic that 'the really miraculous thing about man is that he has survived'. On the same basis, the characters of Definitely maybe experience their own kind of ending/beginning, a transformation from members of a community in a tolerant universe to lone individuals in an intolerant one. One character, the heroic Vecherovsky, pictures it thus:

I felt a strange, serious satisfaction, I was proud of myself and respected myself. I thought that a soldier who remained at the machine gun to cover his retreating comrades must feel like that. He knows he will be here forever, that he will never see anything other than the muddy field, the running figures in the enemy uniform and the low, grim sky. And he also knows that it's right, that it can be no other way, and is proud of it. (Strugatsky, Definitely, p. 125.)

Thus inspired, Vecherovsky resolves to continue his research alone, in an effort not to submit to the laws of nature, but to understand and utilise them. Change is in the air, even if there is still 'a billion years till the end of the world'.

There is a remarkable correspondence between these four Strugatsky novels and the thematics of glasnost. In their oblique, often cryptic way these works constitute a prehistory of the debate about values which glasnost has engendered. Just as the threat of war has been significantly lessened by the demands and initiatives of perestroika, so in their best work the Strugatskys had already turned away from the subject of military conflict (never such a strong theme in Soviet science fiction as in western), to present instead the individual's struggle with society, with environment and ultimately with self. Writing in periods of strict orthodoxy, the Strugatskys nevertheless were able to introduce the reader to a significantly 'dissident' view of science, society and the individual, which went much further than the traditional (and by no means subversive) satirisation of bureaucracy and entered areas such as the philosophical questioning of the collective organisation of society, the insistence on the primacy of individual morality, and the limitations and dangers of deterministic scientific progress. There is a debate which must take place elsewhere about the role of fantastic literature in facilitating glasnost. It is by no means easy to clarify the relationship between a long-tolerated strain of the fantastic and the brutally real and realistic confrontation of historical and contemporary truths which is taking place under glasnost. But it does seem plausible that the Strugatskys' writings on change and the individual helped to create the ethical agenda for a new era in Russian literature.

Note

1   Parts of this essay derive from a paper given by the author at the conference 'Discontinuous discourses in modern Russian literature' held at Mansfield College, Oxford in June 1984. A selection of the papers was subsequently published, see Kelly, Makin and Shepherd (eds.,) Discontinuous discourses in modern Russian literature (London, 1989).

References

Bakhtin, M. M., 'Forms of time and of the chronotope in the novel' in The dialogic imagination: four essays by M. M. Bakhtin (Austin, Texas, 1981), ed. Michael Holquist.
Bell, Ian F. A., Critic as scientist: the modernist poetics of Ezra Pound (London, 1981).
Berlin, Isaiah, Russian thinkers (London, 1978), eds. Henry Hardy and Aileen Kelly.
Catteau, Jacques, La création littéraire chez Dostoievski (Paris, 1978). Translated as Dostoyevsky and the process of literary creation (Cambridge, 1989), tr. A. Littlewood.
Dostoyevsky, Fyodor, Notes from underground (Washington, D.C., 1982), ed. Robert G. Durgy.
Freeborn, Richard (ed.), Russian literary attitudes from Pushkin to Solzhenitsyn (London, 1976).
Freeborn, Richard, The Russian revolutionary novel (Cambridge, 1982).
Hosking, Geoffrey A., Beyond socialist realism: Soviet fiction since Ivan Denisovich (London, 1980).
de Jonge, Alex, Dostoevsky and the age of intensity (London, 1975).
Kelly, Catriona, Michael Makin and David Shepherd (eds.), Discontinuous discourses in modern

Russian literature (London, 1989).

Medvedev, Zhores A., Soviet science (Oxford, 1979).

Pomorska, Krystyna, 'The Utopian future of the Russian avant-garde' in Debreczeny, Paul (ed.), American contributions to the ninth international congress of Slavists, vol. II (Columbus, Ohio, 1983).

Stephan, Halina, 'The changing protagonist in Soviet science fiction' in Birnbaum, Henrik and Thomas Eekman (eds.), Fiction and drama in Eastern and Southeastern Europe (Los Angeles, Cal., 1980).

Stites, Richard, 'Fantasy and revolution: Alexander Bogdanov and the origins of Bolshevik science fiction' in Bogdanov, Alexander, Red star (Bloomington, Indiana, 1984), eds. Loren R. Graham and Richard Stites.

Striedter, Jurij, 'Three postrevolutionary Russian Utopian novels' in Garrard, John (ed.), The Russian novel from Pushkin to Pasternak (New Haven, 1983).

Strugatsky, Arkady and Boris, The snail on the slope (London, 1980). First published as Ulitka na sklone in two parts as follows: in Ellinskii sekret (Leningrad, 1966) and in Baikal, nos. 1 and 2 (1968).

Strugatsky, Arkady and Boris, The ugly swans (London and New York, 1980). First published as Gadkie lebedi (Frankfurt/Main, 1972).

Strugatsky, Arkady and Boris, Roadside picnic (London, 1979). First published as Piknik na obochine in Avrora, nos. 7-10 (1972).

Strugatsky, Arkady and Boris, Definitely maybe (London and New York, 1978). First published as Za milliard let do kontsa sveta (A billion years before the end of the world) in Znanie-sila, nos. 9-12 (1976) and 1 (1977).

Suvin, Darko, Metamorphoses of science fiction (New Haven, 1979).

7

Violent revolution in modern American science fiction

Edward James

Chapter 13 of William Morris's *News from Nowhere*, entitled 'Concerning politics', consists of only a few sentences. When William Guest asks Old Hammond about politics in twenty-first century Utopia, he is told, 'We have none. If you ever make a book out of this conversation, put this in a chapter by itself, after the model of old Horrebow's Snakes in Iceland' (p. 267). It is tempting to suggest that a chapter on 'Revolution in American SF' should model itself on Horrebow and Morris; it is a theme remarkable above all for its absence. But an examination of its very rare appearances, and its transformations, and its very frequent absences, does tell us something about the political culture of American SF, and suggests something too about the nature of American culture itself.

The circumlocution in the title of this piece is an unsatisfactory attempt to resolve the confused and ambiguous usage of the word 'revolution' by historians and others. 'Revolution' can be applied to almost any process of change whereby one state of being is transformed into another: the Industrial Revolution was the semantic trailblazer, preparing the way for the Agrarian Revolution, the Scientific Revolution, the Darwinian Revolution, and countless others. 'Political revolution' is no more precise, since it has been applied to lengthy political processes by which change has been achieved, as, for instance, the winning of votes for women. But all these are secondary meanings of revolution from our immediate point of view: I wish to talk about the type of revolution for which the French and Russian revolutions form the historical paradigms – violent revolutions in which one political order is replaced by another, very different, system. But when it comes to precise definition of revolution, there are still problems, as Eric Hobsbawm has recently pointed out:

Arbitrary selections from the total complex of phenomena most of us think of as 'revolution' are of little use to historians ... Selection may define it simultaneously as 'change which is characterised by violence as a means and a specifiable range of goals as ends' (Zagorin) and as 'a fundamental change in social structure which is accomplished in a short period of time' (Galtung), two formulae which have nothing in common except the word 'change'. Without entering into their merits, their omissions are obvious. Zagorin does not enable us to distinguish the Mexican Revolution from the Chilean coup of 1973, while Galtung does not enable us to distinguish between the Russian Revolution and the social changes which occurred in Jamaica as a result of the abolition of slavery. (Hobsbawm, p. 8.)

In general, historians would regard a 'proper' political revolution as consisting of the overturning of existing institutions, the involvement of some kind of ideology, and the active engagement of, if not the masses, then certainly a wider political involvement than just that of a political élite: it usually also entails the use of violence. This still leaves problems at the boundaries. Presumably the Glorious Revolution of 1688, always termed a 'revolution', is thus not a 'real' revolution. Perhaps the Dutch Revolt of the sixteenth century, always termed a 'revolt' or 'rebellion', is indeed a revolution. Sometimes the terminology is an expression of the speaker's own politics: the distinction between, for instance, the Great Rebellion in England in the 1640s and the English Revolution of the 1640s is an obvious one. And, to a large extent, the semantics of 'revolution' has been dominated by Marx, whose followers are uneasy talking about Mussolini's Fascist revolution or the Hitlerian Revolution; but, as David Close has remarked (p. 13), Khomeini's Iranian Revolution 'ought to end the old-fashioned tendency to identify revolution with left-wing ideals'.

The American Revolution – the paradigm of revolution as far as American science fiction writers are concerned – is another problem. In many ways it is much closer to the Glorious Revolution in England than to the French Revolution which followed so soon after: the replacement of one government by another, but without any threat or change to the social order. Indeed, Edmund Burke himself made that comparison, and argued that it was James II and George III who had been the revolutionaries, trampling on time-honoured traditions and practices, which the 'revolutionaries' were only trying to restore and maintain. The French revolutionaries, on the other hand, were 'pulling down an edifice which [had] answered in any tolerable degree for ages the common purpose of society' (quoted by Bridge, p. 82). Historians today would certainly argue for the truly revolutionary nature of the

American Revolution, pointing above all to the innovatory nature of the American Constitution. 'It was a revolution against the characteristic institutions of Europe: monarchy, aristocratic privilege and patronage, imperialistic wars, colonialism, vestiges of feudalism ... mercantilism, and established churches' (Howell, p. 67). Yet 'the primary goal of the American Revolution, which transformed American life and introduced a new era in human history, was not the overthrow or even the alteration of the existing social order but the preservation of political liberty threatened by the apparent corruption of the constitution, and the establishment in principle of the existing conditions of liberty' (Bailyn, p. 19). The distinction between different types of revolution made by Edmund Burke – the conservative revolution designed to restore an (imagined) status quo and to overthrow the (alien) despot, as in America, and the destructive revolution designed to set up some kind of utopia, which unleashes chaos and a despotism of its own, as in France – has had a powerful impact upon subsequent political and popular thought, above all in America itself.

Positive images of violent revolution, à la Marx, are rare indeed in modern American science fiction. Hardly any Americans followed the lead set by novelists such as William Morris, who argues in *News from Nowhere* (1890) that Utopia could only have come into existence after a popular uprising against the propertied classes. There were some Americans in Morris's own day who espoused socialism. The most influential of all American utopians, Edward Bellamy, in his *Looking backward* (1889), had the socialist utopia emerge in the twentieth century as a result of economic evolution and rational consensus, not revolution. But Ignatius Donnelly's *Caesar's column* (1890), written, like Morris, in reaction to Bellamy, has his upper-class utopia of 1988 destroyed by a revolution on behalf of the oppressed millions; one of the anarchist leaders, Caesar Lomellini, plans to erect a massive column made up of the quarter-million corpses of soldiers and citizens. But the result of that revolution was not a workers' utopia, but chaos and anarchy; the utopia was, perhaps, to be set up by refugees from that chaos in Utopia, who emigrated to Uganda – but we are left in doubt about their ultimate success. Jack London's revolution in *The iron heel* (1907) was much more successful, but also very much off-stage: the socialist revolutionaries of the early twentieth century fail to dislodge the powerful despotism of the Oligarchy – the iron heel – but the footnotes of the text's editor, seven hundred years in the future, make it clear that a socialist utopia had been set up, after a successful revolution three hundred years and more in our own future. This is not unlike the device used much more recently in Margaret Atwood's *The handmaid's tale* (1985), whose Historical Notes − a marvellous parody of an academic conference talk − reassure us that the oppression described in the text is a thing of the past (and indeed, has become something one can, tastelessly, joke about), but whose text tells us only of the impossibility of change.

Since the Second World War very few American science fiction writers have conceived of radically different socio-economic systems; almost none have imagined those different socio-economic systems coming into existence as a result of violent revolution. Mack Reynolds, himself one of the most radical of American SF writers, used to complain about the conservatism of his fellow writers:

A story-teller of the ability of Isaac Asimov will spin his yarns of the Foundation, set a few thousand years hence. And what socio-economic system has evolved by then? Something new? Certainly not! They haven't even got capitalism. They've gone back to feudalism ... We in the West ... are free to picture a world which has risen above our dog eat dog society. A tomorrow that no longer knows war, exploitation of man by man ... and the multitude of other evils that are our present socio-economic system ... Why do we hesitate to deal with extrapolation in socio-economics, or, when we do, cry disaster?[1]

Reynolds very consciously presented himself as the science-fictional successor to the socialist Edward Bellamy − most obviously in his two novels *Looking backward from the year* 2000 (1973) and *Equality in the year* 2000 (1977) (the latter taking its title from *Equality* (1897), Bellamy's lack-lustre 'sequel' to *Looking backward*) But, like Bellamy, Reynolds was not convinced of the prime importance of class conflict in the socialist future, or of the perfectibility of human nature − and without these premises of Marx, revolution seems not only an unnecessary route to progress, but potentially a disastrous one. Moreover, the twentieth (and subsequent) centuries have not borne out the historical predictions of Marx in Reynold's view. With starvation a thing of the past (in the developed world, at least), revolution is unthinkable. As one of his characters says: 'One of the things most social-commentary writers, from Karl Marx to the latest current sob-sister, overlook is that *slobs like living like slobs and will defend their way of life.*'[2] Those who have what they believe they need will not rebel − not unless they are manipulated by the ruling classes to do so.

There were a number of stories in the early 1960s in which Reynolds looked at revolution and its results, one of the first of which was 'Revolution',[3] published in 1960. This is a speculation about what might replace the Soviet system after its collapse and fragmentation. An American agent is sent to help the Russian underground foment their counter-revolution. But he discovers that the counter-revolution was not going to establish Czarism, or capitalism, but intended to go back to the pure stream of Marx and Engels; the agent begins to wonder whether he should sell them out to the KGB. In 'Freedom' (*Analog*, February 1961) a KGB agent is sent into an East European country to investigate a subversive movement, and finds instead a spontaneous mass movement which is demanding the right of free speech: the agent himself rejects the KGB and opts for 'subversion'. (Stableford commented in 1979 (p. 36) that post-Dubcek the story looks 'a little on the optimistic side'; in 1990 it appears remarkably prescient.) In *Analog* for August 1960, Reynolds published 'Adaptation', which again featured criticism of the post-revolutionary Russian system. Here rival Stalinist and capitalist elements in a spaceship crew try to sell their respective systems to societies on an alien plant; the aliens (and Reynolds himself) reject both systems.

Perhaps the most interesting story, however, was published in the March 1961 *Analog*: 'Ultima Thule', where revolution – or attempted revolution – is given a rather more positive role in human history. This story is about a young recruit to Section G of the Bureau of Investigation, United Planets. His first task is to find the subversive Tommy Paine, whose activities have been detected on several of the planets – each of which, as a result of the haphazard free-for-all of the colonisation process, has a different socio-economic system, whose right to self-determination free from interference is guaranteed by United Planets. Paine's version of revolution, however, is peculiarly Reynoldsian. To a tribal planet he introduces iron; to a feudal planet, gunpowder; to a slave-owning system, the steam engine and the spinning jenny; in a theocracy, he assassinates the 'immortal' God-King; to the planet Kropotkin (with its capital Bakunin), he introduces high technology items, to make the anarchists unsatisfied with their low-tech lot. Fairly rapidly the new agent realises the truth, which all agents of Section G find out in their probationary period; 'Tommy Paine' is Section G itself, subverting the non-interventionist charter of United Planets from within, in the name of progress.

We aim for changes that will mean an increased scientific progress, a more advanced industrial technology, more and better education, the opening of opportunity for every member of the culture to exert himself to the full of his abilities. The last is particularly important. Too many cultures, even those that think of themselves as particularly advanced, suppress the individual by one means or another.[4]

The *reason* for the necessity of progress is, perhaps, rather specious; it is to prepare mankind for the inevitable conflict with the alien race who is known to exist just beyond the human sphere of activity. This explains the interference with the anarchist utopia: '"And Kropotkin!" Ronny blurted. "Don't you understand, those people were *happy* there. Their lives were simple, uncomplicated, and they had achieved a happiness that − " "Unfortunately the human race can't take the time out for happiness ...".'.'[5] That, as Brian Stableford has pointed out (p. 37) is no more than a rationalisation of a point of view which Reynolds shares with most of his colleagues: that progress is justified as an end in itself − and that it is indeed the only certain purpose of man's existence. In another story, Reynolds has a character say: 'I guess the ultimate goal, Paul, man's ultimate goal, is total understanding of the cosmos.'[6] As Stableford quite rightly says (p. 52), however common an idea this is among SF writers, taking their cue from the ideas of science itself, 'it is not easy to see how it can be expected to stand alone as the focal point of political philosophy, without the addition of extra value judgements about the constituency of the "good life", and hence about the way societies ought to be organised'. Yet this view does lie behind his reworking of Bellamy, *Looking backward from the year* 2000, where limitless energy and total lack of unemployment means that continuing educational and intellectual advancement are what drive and motivate people. In 'Ultima Thule', therefore, Reynolds is expressing a *scientific* view that progress is man's aim, and that revolution (introduced from outside) may be necessary for that progress. Revolution is not necessarily political, or violent here; it may be a scientific revolution that is needed, or an agrarian or industrial one. Reynolds is saying that destruction of particular systems may be necessary − but he is arguing for destruction by natural social or economic laws, rather than by armed revolutionaries.

Rather more relevant to this essay, perhaps, is one of his other alternative views of 2000: *Commune 2000 AD* (1974), which offers a different revolutionary possibility. An academic is detailed to look into what lies behind the increasing drift into communes in the US at the end of the millennium to find whether it is subversive. He visits several communes – including communes of artists, lesbians, gays and nudists – and realises that there is indeed a connection between them, revealed in the secret phrase 'Robert Owen lives' (to which the response is 'And will never die'): the commune underground thus recognises its link with the radical commune movement of the early nineteenth century, and to Owen, the first great socialist in both Britain and the United States. This underground realises that the supposedly utopian society outside is in fact being run for the benefit of a small and wealthy oligarchy. They want to 'carry on to the next level in the evolution of society' (p. 172): eliminate the political sphere, institute economic democracy, and set up an anarchist system – 'we prefer the term "libertarian". Say "anarchist" to most people and they think in terms of bomb-throwing fanatics' (p. 173). The revolution, however, is some way off, and it is obvious that the underground does not know how it is going to happen, unless they think in terms of historical parallels: 'We need some sort of spark. Some overt act on their part, perhaps, to coalesce our somewhat differing groups. Something like the Boston Massacre was to the first American Revolution' (p. 174). *Commune 2000 AD* is far from being great literature, but it is an interesting comment, in the heyday of the modern communal movement in America, on the pluralist possibilities of the revolutionary future. Even Reynolds, however, well-read in socialist theory, and hostile to the conservatism he saw as dominating the SF field, sees revolution in terms of the past – unless here he was simply pandering to his SF audience, already worried by the use of such words as 'anarchism'. Throughout his work he does, however, seem suspicious of the idea of revolution, drawing from the French and Russian Revolutions, perhaps, the conclusion that idealistic emotions are not enough in practice to bring about an ideal system if they have to do it through real politics and real struggle.

In the early 1970s it was not the communal movement, but the feminist movement, which provided some of the clearest ideas of revolution, following the writings of Shulamith Firestone and others. Even with the feminist SF writers, however, the attitude towards revolution is ambiguous. In Joanna Russ's *The female man* (1975), Janet Evason, the representative from the women's utopia, Whileaway, is convinced that her utopia came about because of a plague which wiped out all the males. But at the end of the book she is disabused of this by Jael, who comes (it had appeared) from an alternative time-line.

That plague you talk of is a lie. I know. The world-lines around you are not so different from yours or mine or theirs and there is no plague in any of them, not any of them. Whileaway's plague is a big lie. Your ancestors lied about it. It is I who gave you your 'plague', my dear, about which you can pietize and moralize to your heart's content: I, I, I, I am the plague, Janet Evason. I and the war I fought built your world for you, I and those like me, we gave you a thousand years of peace and love and the Whileawayan flowers nourish themselves on the bones of the men we have slain (p. 211).

But we never know if Jael is speaking the truth (the solid Janet does not think so), or if she is just one viewpoint in this multiple viewpoint novel, reflecting no more than the possibility that women's ultimate liberation can only come about through violent revolution. In other feminist novels, such as Suzy McKee Charnas's *Walk to the end of the world* (1974) and *Motherlines* (1978), it is not revolution which brings about liberation, but separation. As with so many dystopias in American science fiction, the prospect of eliminating a despotic system is beyond the few protagonists in the novel; escape to the frontier, or beyond it, is the only solution. An excellent if totally unwitting parody of this phenomenon is to be found in the film *Logan's run* (1976), where Michael York and Jenny Agutter escape from the Dome, an dystopia which (for no apparent reason) eliminates citizens at the age of thirty. They decide (after meeting Peter Ustinov) that they would rather like to try old age, and they return, not to lead any kind of revolt but simply, and highly implausibly, to persuade the Dome's computer to blow itself up.

Quite separate from the feminist fiction of the 1970s, and indeed quite unique within the modern SF tradition in terms of its attitude to revolution, is Ursual K. Le Guin's *The dispossessed* (1974). It is prefaced by a short story, published separately, called 'The day before the revolution', in which we meet the founder of the revolution, Odo, on the day of her death, and on the eve of the revolution. What sort of revolution it is to be we cannot tell, although the last words she hears before she dies are 'the general strike'. There is to be another great march, from Old Town to Capitol Square: 'another Ninth Month Uprising', someone jokes – referring to an event before his birth. We learn more about Odo: she had written, long before, a book called *Society without government*; she had started strikes, and has been imprisoned; she had founded a House where people lived according to her principles of freedom. She had supporters throughout the planet, who plotted world revolution with her.

The outcome of this revolution is unveiled, gradually, in *The dis-*

possessed, one of the very finest science fiction novels of the last quarter-century. A society founded on Odonian principles has indeed been founded – not on Odo's own fertile planet, Urras, but on the neighbouring desert planet of Anarres. The revolutionaries have been shipped off-planet, to work the mines on behalf of the capitalists on Urras. They have their anarchist society on Anarres, but it is dependent for its survival on the capitalists; and oppression and propertarianism continue to flourish on Urras. The plot of The dispossessed concerns the struggles of an Anarresti physicist, Shevek, to work on his revolutionary new theories of simultaneity, first on Anarres – but a sadly corrupt Anarres, which denies Shevek the freedom to work, seeing his work as unnecessary and potentially damaging to their fragile anarchist society – and then on Urras, where Shevek firstly tries to co-operate with the archist states (both capitalist and, apparently, socialist). In the end Shevek finds himself the figurehead of another revolution on Urras, a revolution of the oppressed workers. But he returns to Anarres to bring renewed revolution there too, in the shape of his theoretical physics (a new form of communication, which will inevitably break down the artificial walls the Anarresti have built to protect their society) and a determination to join with others to rid Anarres of its corruption. Anarchists, he decides, need permanent revolution in order to preserve their ideals intact. Yet that revolution is not necessarily to be violent revolution. In the speech he made to the huge crowd on Urras, Shevek said: 'You cannot take what you have not given, and you must give yourself. You cannot buy the Revolution. You cannot make the Revolution. It is in your spirit, or it is nowhere' [my emphasis] (p. 250).

Le Guin read widely to produce this highly sophisticated musing upon anarchy and revolution – 'years of reading and pondering and muddling, and much assistance from Engels, Marx, Godwin, Goldman, Goodman, and above all Shelley and Kropotkin' (1975, p. 95) – and she might have added, Gandhi. It is the political revolution created by the recognition of personal responsibility to live in a co-operative and sharing way that Le Guin sympathises with; the political revolution created by the changing attitudes of people towards those around them: not the political revolution of the gun, the 'metal object like a deformed penis' (The dispossessed, p. 11). Anarchism inspired her, but 'not the bomb-in-the-pocket stuff, which is terrorism; whatever name it tries to dignify itself with; not the social Darwinist economic "libertarianism" of the far right; but anarchism as prefigured in early

Taoist thought, and expounded by Shelley and Kropotkin, Goldman and Goodman ... the most idealistic of all political theories' (introduction to 'The day before the revolution', p. 121).

The libertarian right is, of course, represented by Robert A. Heinlein — although not consistently. Personal freedom for him is very little to do with sharing, and everything to do with defending the self against others. As one of his characters says: 'The human race has got to keep up its well-earned reputation for ferocity. The price of freedom is the willingness to do sudden battle, anywhere, at any time, and with utter recklessness. If we did not learn that from the slugs [alien invaders], well — "Dinosaurs, move over! We are ready to become extinct!"' (Puppet masters, p. 189). Revolution does figure in Heinlein, but inevitably, it is more the American Revolution than the French Revolution that serves as its model. At one time he had intended, in his Future History series, to write a story about the breaking away of the colonies of Mars and Venus from Earth, in 'Eclipse', a story which 'parallells somewhat both the American Revolution and the break-up of colonialism taking place on this planet today'.[7] As it was, one of the most effective stories of revolution in modern SF, his The moon is a harsh mistress (1966), is deliberately and directly portrayed as a re-run of the American Revolution, although, as we shall see, with a difference. Long before that, however, Heinlein had written other stories of revolution, such as 'if this goes on —' (1940) and Sixth column (1941).

'If this goes on —' is one of the few stories in modern American SF detailing the organisation of a revolt against a despotic but, in constitutional terms, legitimate government of the United States. It is a theocratic government, run by a fundamentalist Christian, the Prophet: a real future possibility, Heinlein thought (postscript to Revolt in 2100, pp. 191-2). The story itself is hardly one of Heinlein's best: melodramatic, and thin on plausibility. But it shows Heinlein, in only the second year of his long writing career, already taking a hard-headed look at the practicalities of politics and revolution. Although that revolution is to be against a home-grown dictator, Heinlein, in his Future History scenarios, refers to it as the Second American Revolution, and the naïve protagonist John Lyle prepares himself by reading Tom Paine, Patrick Henry and Thomas Jefferson. The differences between the late eighteenth and the late twenty-first century are plain to him, however. A modern police-state has far more chance to indoctrinate and to censor: 'I think perhaps of all the things a police state can do to its citizens, distorting history is possibly the most pernicious' (p. 54). And a revolution has to be as modern as its opponent:

Successful revolution is Big Business – make no mistake about that. In a modern, complex and highly industrialized state, revolution is not accomplished by a handful of conspirators whispering around a guttering candle in a deserted ruin. It requires countless personnel, supplies, modern machinery, modern weapons. And to handle these factors successfully there must be loyalty, secrecy, and superlative staff organization (pp. 53-4).

As a result this story of the organisation of an underground army which is eventually launched against the Prophet, and against the majority of US citizens who, misguidedly no doubt, supported him, bears a striking resemblance to those stories by Heinlein which were concerned with the driving out of an alien invader: Sixth column and The puppet masters. The Prophet's methods were unAmerican; an attack on him, followed by the restoration of the old freedoms, was thus a defence of the old Constitution, not an attempt to set up a new political order. In short, in Edmund Burke's terms it is clearly the American, rather than the French, style of revolution. In Sixth column, a.k.a. The day after tomorrow, discussed in this volume in chapter 3, Heinlein replaces George III with the Heavenly Emperor – and adds a dose of racism. The main character is called Jefferson Thomas.

The puppet masters (1951) is more problematical. The parasitic alien slugs, from Titan, who breed very rapidly, attach themselves to the backs of their victims, and thereafter control their personalities and their actions. Only physical examination – or the insistence on topless dress – will determine whether someone is under the control of a puppet master. The plot: how to prevent these aliens from taking over the United States? If this is a story of revolution, it is seen in reverse: the aliens trying to infiltrate, convert (physically, rather then emotionally or intellectually), and subvert the established order. Should it be seen, as Don Siegel's film Invasion of the body snatchers (1956) has been, as an allegory of the subversion of the United States by undercover communism? That film, with people gradually being taken over by pods from outer space, and turned into unfeeling zombies, is, of course, very similar in theme to Heinlein's, though with a downbeat ending, rather than an impending genocide. Siegel himself has denied that his film was intended as an allegory of either communism or fascism: 'Let me repeat that all of us who worked on the film believed in what it said – that the majority of people in the world unfortunately are pods, existing without any intellectual aspirations and incapable of love' (interview with Siegel, quoted in LaValley, p. 159). I know of no definitive statement in Heinlein's case, though certainly Philip E. Smith (p. 149) has argued that the parallel with the threat of communism is made clear by the narrator when he wonders 'why the titans had not attacked Russia first; the place seemed tailor-made for them. On second thought, I wondered if they had. On third thought I wondered what difference it would make' (p. 117). Communists, then, are as good as slug-carriers already. They, or those liable to be swayed by their arguments (which Heinlein time and again, throughout his works, denounces as empty-headed), portrayed as slug-carriers, are devoid of independent thought or initiative, and are unaware of the importance of individual personal freedom; constant vigilance is needed to ensure that they do not win more followers.

If The puppet masters is 'about' a failed Marxist revolution, then it is perfectly clear that The moon is a harsh mistress (1966) is 'about' a libertarian revolution. The Moon colonists, tired of being exploited by the nations of the Earth and denied any type of self-determination or representation, first of all capture the Moon itself from the Warden and his brutal guards. On 3 July 2076 (a day early, because the debate was shorter than predicted) they agree a Declaration of Independence. When independence is not accepted by Earth, they try negotiation. After an abortive attack by Earth they use the convenient gravity-well, bombarding the (relatively unpopulated parts of) Earth with a whole succession of large rocks, causing H-bomb sized explosions, and thus bludgeoning the nations of Earth into permitting their independence. It is an effective and fast-moving novel, once one has got used to the dialect (a clipped English with Russian and Spanish words and phrases added). And it is clear that, despite the parallels with the American Revolution, it has just as much in common with the French Revolution: the Loonies (the colonists of Luna) have in mind not just independence, but a radical change in the structure of government and society. The harshness of their environment, the importance of the conservation of water, air and all essentials, the absolute necessity of co-operation and also of self-responsibility, all push the Loonies towards the Heinleinian view of society. Their motto is his: TANSTAAFL (There Ain't No Such Thing As A Free Lunch). 'Private where private belongs, public where it's needed, and an admission that circumstances alter cases. Nothing doctrinaire' (p. 62), as their theoretician, Professor de la Paz puts it. He calls himself a rational anarchist:

A rational anarchist believes that concepts such as 'state' and 'society' and 'government' have no existence save as physically exemplified in the acts of self-responsible individuals. He believes that it is impossible to shift blame, share blame, distribute blame ... as blame, guilt, responsibility are matters taking place inside human beings single and *nowhere else*. But being rational, he knows that not all individuals hold his evaluations, so he tries to live perfectly in an imperfect world ... aware that his effort will be less than perfect yet undismayed by self-knowledge of self-failure (p. 62: Heinlein's ellipses).

De la Paz offers advice on how to avoid tyranny, and urges a constitution which forbids conscription, and government interference with freedom of press, speech, assembly, travel, religion, education and occupation. But, as the narrator points out at the end, 'Prof underrated yammerheads. They never adopted *any* of his ideas. Seems to be a deep instinct in human beings for making everything compulsory that isn't forbidden' (p. 287). The system set up nevertheless seems to be one where the individual is given greater say, and greater choice over his destiny. (There is no welfare state; fools and the incompetent are not cared for – they tend to die. The Moon is a harsh mistress.) The narrator is nevertheless disappointed at the failure of his own personal revolutionary dreams; he thinks of going off to the asteroids. Heinlein's brand of anarchism tends to operate best at the frontier.

To research this topic thoroughly probably requires a lengthy trawl through SF magazines and novels: as yet, in the absence of any subject indexes to the magazines, a very lengthy process. Sporadic fishing, rather than systematic trawling, on both race and revolution, however, convinces me that whilst the question of race is one that few SF authors have ignored, revolution is an historical and political process that few have investigated. The rash of novels in Britain in the first two or three decades of the century dealing with revolution – either enthusiastically for or against – does not seem to have been present in the United States. Political speculation is, indeed, minimal in most writers: American science fiction these days offers few ways out of the perceived trend towards environmental disaster or political or economic oppression. Near futures are, usually, darker versions of our own world. That a revolutionary change is not seen as the way out of this bind is presumably bound up with the political experience of the United States this century where there is a virtual absence of any political tradition of revolution outside the (normally) conservative image of the American Revolution itself, and where the feeling prevails that the existing political system, despite its imperfections, is better than any alternative. Future dystopias we have in abundance, but few visions of how to dismantle them.

Notes

1 M. Reynolds, Comment on 'Retaliation', in Harry Harrison (ed.), *Backdrop of stars* (New English Library: London 1975), p. 204. He makes similar remarks in his rejoinder to Stableford, 1979, in *Foundation*, 16 May 1979, pp. 54-5.
2 'Sweet Dreams, Sweet Princes', Part 3: *Analog*, December 1964, p. 72: a serial revised and published as *Time gladiator* in 1966.
3 Published in *Astounding/Analog*, May 1960, US edition, but not reprinted in the British edition; I therefore draw from Stableford, 1979, p. 34.
4 Quoted from the British reprint, *Analog*, July 1961, p. 54.
5 Loc.cit., p. 52.
6 In 'The throwaway age', *Worlds of tomorrow*, Winter 1967, p. 158, cited by Stableford, p. 52.
7 'Concerning stories never written: postscript', added to *Revolt in 2100*, 1953, quoted here from the Signet edition (New York, 1955), p. 190.

Bibliography

Bailyn, Bernard, *The ideological origins of the American revolution* (Harvard University Press: Cambridge, Mass., 1967).
Bridge, Carl, 'Burke and the conservative tradition' in Close and Bridge, pp. 79-88.
Close, David, 'The meaning of revolution', in Close and Bridge, pp. 1-14.
Close, David and Carl Bridge (eds.), *Revolution: a history of the idea* (Croom Helm: London, 1985).
Heinlein, Robert A., 'If this goes on –', published in *Astounding*, February and March 1940, and reprinted in the collection *Revolt in 2100*, 1953, quoted here from the Signet edition (New York, 1955).
Heinlein, Robert A., *Sixth column*, serialised in *Astounding*, January–March 1941; published as *Sixth column* in 1949; reprinted as *The day after tomorrow*, and quoted here from the Mayflower edition (London, 1962).
Heinlein, Robert A., *The puppet masters*, 1951, quoted here from the Panther edition (London, 1960).
Heinlein, Robert A., *The moon is a harsh mistress*, 1966, quoted here in the New English Library edition (London, 1969).
Hobsbawm, E. J., 'Revolution' in Porter and Teich, 1986, pp. 5-46.
Howell, P. A., 'Liberal thought about revolution' from Locke to Mazzini' in Close and Bridge, pp. 57-78.
LaValley, Al (ed.), *Invasion of the body snatchers: Don Siegel, director* (Rutgers Films in Print 14) (Rutgers UP: New Brunswick, NJ, 1989).
Le Guin, Ursula K., 'The day before the revolution' in Le Guin, *The wind's twelve quarters*, Vol. 2 (Granada: London, 1978), pp. 121-38; originally published in *Galaxy*, 1974.
Le Guin, Ursula K., *The dispossessed*, 1974, quoted in the Panther edition (London, 1975).
Le Guin, Ursula K., 'Science fiction and Mrs Brown', 1975, reprinted in Le Guin, *The language*

of the night: *Essays in fantasy and science fiction* (Women's Press: London, 1989), ed. Susan Wood.

Morris, William, *News from Nowhere: in Three works by William Morris*, with an introduction by A. L. Morton (Lawrence and Wishart: London; International Publishers: New York, 1968).

Porter, Roy and Mikulá Teich (eds.), *Revolution in history* (Cambridge University Press: Cambridge, 1986).

Reynolds, Mack, *Commune 2000 AD* (Bantam: New York, 1974).

Russ, Joanna, *The female man*, 1975, quoted in the Women's Press edition (London, 1985).

Smith, Philip E., 'The evolution of politics and the politics of evolution: social Darwinism in Heinlein's fiction' in Joseph D. Olander and Martin Harry Greenberg (eds.), *Robert A. Heinlein* (Paul Harris: Edinburgh, 1978), pp. 137-71.

Stableford, Brian, 'The utopian dream revisited: socioeconomic speculation in the SF of Mack Reynolds', *Foundation*, 16 May 1979, pp. 31-54.

8

Vietnam: the War in science fiction

Alasdair Spark

'The future isn't what it used to be.'

Anonymous

In 1987 In the field of fire, edited by Jack Dann and Jeanne Van Buren Dann, was published in the United States. As is now standard, the book was organised on a theme, in this case SF and the Vietnam War. It was an unprecedented choice, and the twenty-two stories were authored both by established talents such as Harlan Ellison, Joe Haldeman, and Brian Aldiss, and newer writers such as Kim Stanley Robinson, Lucius Shepard, and Lewis Shiner. Yet, despite some excellent individual contributions, In the field of fire was a circumscribed view of 'Vietnam SF'. The Danns concluded in the introduction:

The Vietnam War was so psychologically cyclonic and horrific in its effect on individuals that perhaps the dark personal truth of experience can best be reflected through the devices of metaphor and fantasy. Science fiction and fantasy specialize in the creation of worlds and dreams. We think that these dreams ... bring another level of meaning and truth to the war that we have all – in our own ways – experienced. (p. 14)

The notion that the events of the Vietnam War were beyond the power of conventional narrative is now common: Peter MacInerney expressed it best as the 'breakdown and transformation of the historical imagination itself'.[1] The Danns' privileging of SF as a mode for exploring Vietnam was new, though clearly they saw the failure of narrative as resulting from the equally privileged horror of Vietnam. The problem is that by assuming such, the Danns concentrate on contemporary SF, with seventeen of the stories being specially written for the book, presumably to provide purgatives for the individual reader. This assertion of personal experience is part of the dominant paradigm of Vietnam since defeat, which sees the War as a national ordeal for Americans, binding together a 'Vietnam Generation'. This construction aims at collective reconciliation by amalgamating individual experience into a vulgar mass, necessarily omitting, toning down, or most often rendering equivalent all contention. Therefore the Danns' failure to mention in their introduction the controversy generated within the SF community by the War is not surprising, nor their failure to acknowledge the activism of some of their authors – absurd, considering Harlan Ellison's commitment to the anti-War movement. The following essay will attempt to delineate in brief terms the fuller relationship of SF to the Vietnam War which the Danns' contemporary motivation sidesteps: the phenomenon of a genre predicated upon faith in future technology and America, finding itself confronted by futility and perversion in the present.

The Vietnam War was profoundly divisive for America, but, Isaac Asimov claimed, not for SF. While the War had 'divided the microcosm of the science fiction writer, as it has the United States', fears that 'storms and divisions' would cleave the SF community were unfounded, since 'our mutual identification as SF writers persists above and beyond lesser divisions'.[2] SF certainly did not split into overt camps, but the disputes provoked by Vietnam were real, if more covertly expressed in opinion or fiction than Asimov realised. In an interview in a 1969 collection *The new SF*, J. G. Ballard wrote that American SF was no longer

an extrovert, optimistic literature of technology … the new science fiction, that other people apart from myself are now beginning to write, is introverted, possibly pessimistic rather than optimistic, much less certain of its own territory. There's a tremendous confidence that radiates through all of modern American science fiction of the period 1930 to 1960, the certainty that science and technology can solve all problems. This is certainly not the dominant form of science fiction now. (Ballard, p. 59.)

A leader of the British 'New Wave', Ballard correctly noted the parallel shift towards the downbeat, the anti-heroic, and the anti-technological in America. Vietnam was partly responsible, though very little SF dealt with the War explicitly. Nevertheless, after editing *Dangerous visions* in 1967, the first major American anthology of such fiction, Harlan Ellison received a letter from Mrs S. Blittmon of Philadelphia:

Dear Mr Ellison,
    When I picked up your book & read the 2 introductions I thought it was going to be great. I cannot tell you how sick I feel after reading [it]. You say you had a Jewish grandmother (so did I) but I think not; she must have been Viet Cong, otherwise how could you think of such atrocities. Shame, shame on you! Science fiction should be beautiful … (Ellison, vol. 2, p. 10.)

None of the thirty-three stories dealt directly with Vietnam (although Philip K. Dick's 'Faith of my fathers' was set in a post-War Hanoi), yet in a perverse way, Mrs Blittmon's association was correct. Asimov noted that in 1967 an anti-war petition had been passed around writers at American SF conventions, provoking Poul Anderson into organising a hawkish reply. Both were then published in the June 1968 issue of *Galaxy* magazine: on one page, eighty-two American SF writers announced 'We oppose the participation of the United States in the War in Vietnam'; opposite, seventy-two replied 'We the undersigned believe the United States must remain in Vietnam to fulfil its responsibilities to that nation.' The contrasting composition of the two statements is striking. The Hawks were almost exclusively made up of traditionalist writers such as Poul Anderson, Robert Heinlein, John W. Campbell, Edmond Hamilton, Jack Vance, and Jack Williamson, plus a few new 'hard' SF writers such as Larry Niven and Jerry Pournelle. The Doves, while including most of the liberal wing of SF (Bradbury, Del Rey, Sturgeon, Asimov), remarkably included almost all those who described themselves as members of the American 'New Wave', writers such as Norman Spinrad, Samuel R. Delany, Thomas M. Disch, Philip K. Dick, K. M. O'Donnell (Barry Malzberg), Joanna Russ, Judith Merrill, Terry Carr, and Harlan Ellison. Three contributors to *Dangerous visions* - Anderson, Niven, and Joe Hensley – signed the Hawk petition, and sixteen the Dove, although the latter would have been considerably higher if Europeans such as Ballard and Brian Aldiss had been invited to sign.

By 1967 protest at American involvement in Vietnam was considerable: three out of four universities and half the colleges in America saw demonstrations, while marches grew in size, in 1967 culminating in a protest on the steps of the Pentagon. While a minority, protestors were vocal, and concentrated among specific sections of society: Norman Mailer, Allen Ginsberg, Dr Spock, and others, became familiar to the anti-war movement as representatives of the intelligensia. Artists, musicians, writers, poets, even movie stars took sides on Vietnam. SF writers were no exception – indeed, the correspondence of radical and literary politics was central to the New Wave. First used to describe *avant-garde* cinema of the fifties, the term was applied to British SF in association with the magazine *New worlds*, edited from 1964 by Michael Moorcock. While the American New Wave was never as cohesive (Harlan Ellison punningly preferred the term 'nouvelle vague') common tendencies existed: Patrick Parrinder writes of 'knowingness, literary sophistication, [and] almost obligatory commitment to formal experiment'; Robert Scholes and Eric Rabkin of an 'attempt to find a language and social perspective for science fiction that is as adventurous and progressive as its technological vision'; and Samuel Mines an excess concern with 'crude tastes'.[3] Explicit language and sex reflected the dissatisfaction with established SF (and the SF establishment) that was channelled into *Dangerous visions*. In his introduction, Ellison declared the book 'constructed along specific lines of revolution ... intended to shake things up ... conceived out of a need for new horizons, and styles, and forms and challenges' and insisted not just that contributions be original, but that they be the sort of stories that established SF magazines would refuse to publish, given that 'this editor won't allow discussions of politics in his pages, that one shies away from stories exploring sex ... and this one doesn't pay except in red beans and rice' (Vol. 1, p. 26). Frustration at the insulated world of SF led to the desire to expose it to the heat and light of the cultural politics of the sixties, in which Vietnam was integral. The protest articulated by the counter-culture (for that is what it was) was neatly summed up by the deliberate mis-spelling of 'Amerika' suggesting a unity of oppression in which Vietnamese peasant, campus student, and black radical were joined in resistance. Just as the Black Power movement considered the urban struggle and protest against the War as inextricably linked, so many New Wave writers came to believe that radicalism against what Ellison called the SF 'ghetto' and the Vietnam War were part of a general anti-establishment continuum.

Many established writers considered the New Wave a conspiracy to hijack the future of American SF, even James Blish, a Dove signatory. By 1970 Blish (unlike Ballard) did not welcome 'emphasis upon the problems of the present, such as over-population, racism, pollution and the Vietnam War', which he considered 'only slightly disguised by SF trappings'.[4] The New Wave did aim to recast SF as 'speculative fiction' but not simply out of concern for present problems: the issue was far more the failed consensual imagination of the future. In 1961 (as Kennedy stepped up American commitment to South Vietnam), Kingsley Amis claimed in *New maps of hell* that SF was a 'fictional mode in which cultural tendencies can be isolated', hence 'dramatising social inquiry'.[5] This was a common enough legitimation of SF, but as Robert Bloch noted two years before, if so:

Our authors by and large seem to believe wholly in the profit incentive; in the trend to superimpose obedience and conformity by means of forcible conditioning; in the enduring liaison between the government, the military and scientists and technologists; in Anglo-Saxon cultural supremacy, if not outright 'white supremacy'; in the sexual, aesthetic, and religious mores of the day.[6]

Dale Carter argues in *The final frontier* (1988) that this conformity was the result of twin factors: the privileged place of SF, now vindicated by accurate technological predictions, and the resultant demands made by a general audience for prediction about the dawning 'American century'. Taking his cue from Thomas Pynchon's *Gravity's rainbow* (1963), Carter christened this cold war cultural polity the 'Rocket State', a conjunction of technology, authority, and individualism as evident in the space race as in SF. This posed a dual problem. As Sheila Schwartz noted in 1970, 'all a writer need do to qualify as a science fiction writer is record the present with such details as napalm, self-cleaning ovens, pep pills, pollution ...'.[7] But the achievement of a previously imaginary level of technology did not bring social satisfaction to Americans, and worse, the technology was not always American, as Sputnik and Yuri Gagarin proved. Disappointment with the present/future was a keynote of sixties' SF, leading Norman Spinrad to make an interesting observation on Vietnam in *The star spangled future*:

The war had created a lot of European anti-Americanism, which of course was to be expected. But the tenor of it was peculiar. The real gut-feeling had little to do with the plight of the Vietnamese. It was a feeling of sorrow, or loss, of betrayal. Europeans felt diminished by what America was doing ... let down by something they had believed in. (Spinrad, p. 6.)

Spinrad felt similarly diminished by Vietnam, but just as significantly because of the failure of established SF to anticipate such a perverse present. Like most of the New Wave, his reaction was to write of nihilistic near-futures in such as *The men in the jungle* (1967) and *Bug Jack Barron* (1969).

The European New Wave reflected the disillusionment with things American, and at the extremity displaced the Vietnam War to Europe. In Michael Moorcock's *A cure for cancer* (1971), the third Jerry Cornelius novel, Cornelius confronts an invasion of Europe by American forces, although at home things have collapsed and American army units are once again encircled by Red Indians. Moorcock's London is just as subject to bombing, napalming, and defoliation by the US Air Force as Vietnam. Passing Hyde Park, Cornelius smells:

n-butyl ester, iosbutyl ester, tri-isopropanolamine, salt, picloram and other chemicals and he knew that the park had got everything – Orange, Purple, White, and Blue. 'Better safe than sorry.' he pulled up outside Derry and Toms ... A boy and a girl ran out of the smoke, hand in hand, as he entered the store; they were on fire, making for the drinking fountain on Kensington Church Street. (Moorcock, p. 193.)

Kate Wilhelm did much the same for an American small town in 'The village' (1973), but radical displacement occurs in J. G. Ballard's 'The killing ground' (1969), in which the USA is waging a losing war against National Liberation Armies in 'continuous fighting from the Pyrenees to the Bavarian Alps, the Caucasus to Karachi. Thirty years after the original conflict in South East Asia, the globe was now a huge insurrectionary torch, a world Viet Nam' (p. 9). It is as if Ballard took seriously Che Guevara's exhortation to 'create a thousand Vietnams', placing one front on the banks of the Thames. Three American POWs are captured by NLA rebels at the Memorial to President Kennedy at Runnymede, and as impedimenta to the advancing patrol, are shot, ironically counterpointing an elderly grafitto on the memorial's plinth, 'Stop US atrocities in Viet Nam'. Brian Aldiss achieved the same, though more obviously, in 'My country, 'tis not only of thee' (1987), in which at first the War seems to be in Vietnam, but then it becomes clear that terms such as 'gooks' and 'the South' are being applied to England.

Vietnam was an ultra-technological war, a perception intensified by an acronymic language as arcane as the space programme. Two of the agencies charged with wartime research and development were the Defence Advanced Research Products Agency and the Limited War Laboratory, and 'product laboratory' was an apt description: in 1967 the Pentagon's director of research told congress that 'the Vietnam conflict is testing almost all of the tactical military equipment and concepts developed in the last twenty years of R & D'.[8] Defence agencies and military contractors produced an exotic and complex war zone composed of jungle defoliation, troop-detecting 'sensors' and 'people-sniffers', night vision 'look-down' radar, ' psy-war' propaganda, instant satellite communication between the battlefield and the Pentagon, a computerised body count and Hamlet Evaluation System, and even attempts at weather control. More orthodox military technology produced weaponry such as mini-guns capable of firing thousands of rounds per second ('Puff the magic dragon'), laser-guided 'smart' bombs, 'claymore' anti-personnel mines, napalm, riot gas, space-age M-16 rifles (made by Mattel, troops joked), 'fleshette' mortar rounds and – perhaps most transformational of all – fleets of helicopter transports and gunships offering air-mobility, medical evacuation and firepower previously considered fantastic. Yet all this did not bring victory, but instead images of a peasant culture being massacred by a perverted technology.

Social stress was inevitable if the expected future ('the light at the end of the tunnel') did not arrive, but for SF Vietnam was doubly frustrating: for the New Wave, it was a perverted technology focused upon a peasant enemy that had become the object of sympathy; for conservatives, worse still, it was a technology that was losing. The former refused and the latter denied SF the privileged place Carter argued it had won post-World-War-II as a predictive medium, and hence the reaction of Frederik Pohl (as editor) to the June 1968 *Galaxy* statements was interesting: 'There's not a pennyworth of difference between them. To the best of our opinion, if these two groups each constituted a committee for the construction of a World of Twenty-Sixty-Eight and their optimum worlds were compared, they would be essentially the same world. There would be some differences in labels perhaps, little in realities' (p. 7). This was absurd, but Pohl considered the statements indicated the capability of the SF community act as 'time-binders, prepared to consider change'. Pohl asked: 'If it is true that we have this expertise, might not it also be true that we can use it for a productive purpose? Might we not even use it to find some alternative options in this polar debate? Some measures that might replace the opposite imperatives of "Get Out!" or "Win!"?' (p. 8). Pohl proposed a bizarre competition to determine new options for the US in Vietnam - at 100 words maximum. The text read:

What would YOU do about Vietnam? Assume you are being asked for advice. Assume the people who ask you are the President of the United States, the Congress, the State Department, the Joint Chiefs of Staff - anyone and everyone who has any decision-making authority concerning American involvement in Vietnam. Assume they want one suggestion from you ... and assume they will follow it. (p. 11)

The latter was absurd, and what the competition really reflected was the desire of mainstream SF to revalidate itself – the winners would be put to a 'Delphic panel' of intelligent, unbiased, experienced persons, and then perhaps the Government. In the event, a thousand entries were received, and in November 1968 Pohl reported on the five winners, three fans and two SF writers – Poul Anderson and Mack

Reynolds, conveniently one from each pole of opinion. The entries do not seem to have produced much in the way of usable ideas – Pohl concluded that perhaps twenty-five were worthwhile, with 'a fairly large number' being 'clearly impossible', while another 'large group appeared to miss the point of what the war was about' but, Pohl helpfully added, 'admittedly there is some confusion on that question'. Useful replies included the following:

Some suggested new ways of winning the war – a method of interdicting Haiphong harbour without bombing, a guerrilla strategy similar to that used by the British in Malaya. Some suggested ways of disengaging without loss of face – a variation on the tactic of non-violent resistance, a proposal for a plebiscite. Some offered long range plans, including ways of strengthening the UN, or of prejudging 'national liberation' struggles by techniques resembling arbitration. (p. 6)

In the real world, future events led to withdrawal under the cloak of Vietnamisation, the invasion of Cambodia and Laos, the killing of anti-war protestors at Kent State in 1970, the collapse of morale of the United States Army in Vietnam, the Paris Agreement in 1972, Watergate, and the swift capitulation of South Vietnam in 1975 - a total victory for the enemy that not one of Pohl's 'time-binders' predicted. Ultimately, the belief that SF could give privileged advice to the political-military establishment, or some fanciful solution short of victory or defeat, was vanity: the real decision-making authority in Vietnam lay with the Viet Cong and the North Vietnamese Army.

One effect of the authority of the enemy was a lack of pro-war fiction – John Wayne's The Green Berets (1968) is the only movie. Despite the traditional centrality of the military in SF, a similar absence of pro-war SF appears to exist, and one reason may lie in the criticism made by one reviewer that the New Wave was anti-science-fictional by its use of stream of consciousness or other 'techniques which confuse and disrupt the senses', since 'when something strange is afoot, in a strange time or on a strange planet, only a measure of clarity will let us know what is supposed to be going on'.[9] On this planet it took the publication of The Pentagon papers (the Defense Department's secret history of the Vietnam War) to clarify the Kennedy and Johnson Administration's actions to the American people. Attempts such as Poul Anderson's 'I tell you it's true' (1971) to pull a technological rabbit out of the hat read as absurd. By means of 'neuro-induction' – an electric field which renders the subject utterly open to suggestion – insurgents in Thailand, the President of the USSR, black power nationalists, white racists – all are persuaded to drop their demands upon the US. These events are then revealed to be the prognostications of a think-tank, which decides the device will inevitably proliferate, and is therefore too dreadful to use. Five years later, the Chinese bathe America with neuro-induction from satellites, and a Red peace breaks out. Reflecting on McInerney, Vietnam was a war where confusion reigned, and simple stories looked simple. In a war which seemed non-linear, absurdist, and fragmented to much of the public (and to most of the troops), New Wave techniques were more apt.

Barry Malzberg's story 'Final War' (1968) is an interesting example of such. Written in three days in February 1965 (before American combat troops arrived in Vietnam), and rejected by The Atlantic Monthly, Playboy and The Kenyon Review, before being accepted by The magazine of fantasy and science fiction in 1968, 'Final war' concerns a unit of American soldiers in an unspecified war. In a manner reminiscent of Catch 22, the soldiers are bombed by their own aircraft, a sergeant writes his memoirs of four wars and eight limited engagements, and Private Hastings slowly loses his sanity, finally stabbing his new commander in the buttocks with a bayonet. Other elements pre-figure the absurdity many Americans saw in Vietnam: 'On Thursdays, Saturdays, and Tuesdays, the company moved East to capture the forest; on Fridays, Sundays, and Wednesdays, they lost the battles to defend it. Mondays everybody was too tired to fight. The Captain stayed in his tent and sent out messages to headquarters; asked what action to take. Headquarters advised him to continue as previously' (p. 148).

'Final war' struck a chord with SF readers and writers in 1968 (the year of Tet), coming within six votes of winning the Nebula award (given by American SF writers), and was anthologised at least twenty times. Ironically, Malzberg did not consider the story concerned Vietnam at all. In 1979 in Malzberg at large he wrote of 1965:

The evening I finished it, another writer at Syracuse asked me if I'd be interested in attending a Teach-In. 'About what?' I asked, 'and what the hell is a Teach-In?' 'About Vietnam,' she said, 'about what's going on there.' 'Vietnam is an abstraction,' [Malzberg replied], 'I'm interested in getting my work done and not destroying myself in pointless political activism.' (p. 145)

Malzberg was surprised, but grateful for the sale. Gene Wolfe's story 'The Horars of war' (1970), was a product of Damon Knight's Milford Writer's Workshop, which was closely associated with the New Wave, such that there was talk of a so-called 'Milford Mafia'. Wolfe was a Korean War veteran, and details a future jungle war fought not by human soldiers but by HORARS (Homologue ORganisms Army Replacement Simulations), flesh and blood robots, manufactured, not drafted, who fight with programmed enthusiasm, and have no relatives to protest at their death. 2910 may or may not be a human journalist impersonating a Horar: Wolfe leaves the question open, but as Sam Lundwall maintains, 'It is guilt for the Negroes, the Indians, the Jews, the Vietnamese ... and mankind's rape of weaker individuals that comes back in the android'. In contrast to Pohl's competition, sympathy for the victim at times led SF to prescribe strategy for the Viet Cong and North Vietnamese. In John Brunner's story 'Who steals my purse?' (1973) the enemy take the war to America in a terrorist bombing campaign of cities, and in Hank Dempsey's 'The defensive bomber' (1973) a North Vietnamese pilot, infiltrated into the US, and assisted by the Black Panthers and Weathermen, bombs a Navy base from a light aircraft. He intends to surrender, but crash-lands at a nearby airport, whereupon enraged workers and passengers tear him apart as he vainly shouts: 'Prisoner of war! I am in uniform. For ten years you have done this to my country. Five billion dollars in bombs a year. Killed, maimed, women, children' (Harrison, p. 92).

Relations with aliens (so often in SF the enemy) were crucially influenced by Vietnam. One pro-intervention sub-genre that might be called 'Peace Corps SF' was founded on Kennedyesque visions of galactic assistance and advice – though with the same military force behind it which the Peace Corps found in the Green Berets. In Poul Anderson's 'The sharing of flesh' (1969), his second Hugo-winning novelette of the sixties, a clear neo-colonial sentiment is evident: an anthropological survey team from 'the Allied Planets' is studying the inhabitants of the planet Lokon, a backward abandoned Earth colony. The purpose is to determine if a 'civilising mission' is worthwhile, but it is put in jeopardy when one of the team is savagely murdered by the jungle dwellers, and eaten. Revenge seems inevitable, but the resolution is that cannibalism is a necessity, the result of a hormone deficiency, and the victim's wife gives up her right to bring the killer to justice – the white woman's burden. The most obvious example of such was *Star Trek* (1965-80, and the USS Enterprise's mission echoed Kennedy's inaugural call in more than its split infinitive: 'to seek out life and new civilisations, to boldly go where no Man has gone before'. Episodes such as 'A private little war' (broadcast during Tet 1968) confronted issues raised in Vietnam; with the careful ethnic and gender tokenism of the crew, and the 'prime directive' not to interfere, balanced against the quasi-military interventionism of the Federation, Star Trek was perfect Camelot in space. More significant was the reworking found in James Tiptree's (Alice Sheldon) story 'Beam us home' (1969) in which a future Central American insurgency has run to biological warfare. A delirious and dying American pilot, obsessed with Star Trek as a boy, sets out on a final flight – to find himself rescued, beamed up onto the bridge of an alien version of the USS Enterprise.

Tiptree/Sheldon proved the most able architect of the alien contact story in the seventies, but she had earlier inverted neo-colonialism to place the human race in a threatened position. In 'Help' (1968) Earth is contacted by two groups of aliens, competing missionaries who wage war to win the population of Earth for their respective theologies. They are finally driven off, but the hero comments:

'This is all early stage stuff ... like when Tahiti and the Congo were months away from Europe and North America was half wild. The next stage was industrial nation-states got organised into coalitions and went to war for global mastery. What happens to the people in sarongs when something like Admiral Tojo's fleet sails into the lagoon to set up a fortified base? And something like Admiral Nimitz' fleet ... arrives to throw him out?' 'Viet Nam,' murmured Harry. (Tiptree, p. 86.)

By the seventies, the characterisation of aliens, inferior or superior, had been moderated by Vietnam. The familiar galactic empire became endowed with different qualities, either of impotence and collapse, or of benevolence. Ursula K. Le Guin's science fiction most positively embraces the latter tendency, where, as Patrick Parrinder points out, 'the empire-building ideal itself survives in a liberal rather than a libertarian version' (Parrinder, p. 86). Much of Le Guin's seventies' SF concerned the 'Ekumen', a utopian community of worlds, and in novels such as The left hand of darkness (1969) and The dispossessed (1974) Le Guin 'offered an alternative to the technocratic, capitalistic, male dominated ideals of the West that ruled most American science fiction'. Sympathy for the alien – the enemy, the Viet Cong – was best realised in the tellingly titled Nebula-award-winning The word for world is forest, in which Le Guin wrote of the victorious liberation struggle of an alien race against an imperial Earth, aided by a conscience-stricken human doctor. Darko Suvin [10] associated the alien leader with Ho Chi Minh, but Le Guin's sympathy for the Vietnamese is reminiscent of the anti-war romanticism of Susan Sontag or Mary McCarthy. Liberation as a restoration of a primeval stasis had little to do with the changes demanded by Vietnamese Marxism.

E

For all its criticism of established SF, the New Wave broke by the mid-seventies (to the glee of conservatives), and did not become the dominant form of SF, confounding Brian Aldiss's 1973 prediction in *Billion year spree* that SF was becoming far more 'reality-oriented'. In fact, anti-technological sentiments produced post-Vietnam, post-Tolkien novels such as Roger Zelazny's *Amber* series, which Robert Scholes suggested was a return to a cosy 'world in which values are clear (with heroes and heroines, villains and villainesses), and action which is fast and furious, [with] extraordinary appeal for people enmeshed in lives of muddled complexity'.[11] As John Hellmann notes in *American myth and the legacy of Vietnam* (1986) America refused to look at Vietnam full-face in the seventies, and he argues that George Lucas's *Star wars* trilogy (*Star wars* (1977), *The Empire strikes back* (1980) and *The return of the Jedi* (1983) all represent a mythic reworking in SF – the best available medium – of the American experience in Vietnam. Hellmann concluded that the films offered 'a vision of America's opportunity, in the midst of a fallen mythic landscape, to take control of their destiny by taking control of their national consciousness, and thus self-consciously to work out the implications of the Vietnam experience for their larger journey through history'. (Hellmann, p. 220.) The success of other SF films suggests this agenda was fulfilled elsewhere. Steven Spielberg's *Close encounters* (1977) concerns a government conspiracy to conceal from the people of America that 'we are not alone'. Common men, women and children are drawn to the landing site of the mothership, and the benign trustworthy authority of the aliens. Spielberg's later *ET* (1982) and John Carpenter's *Starman* (1984) repeat the point. However, a darker tendency is evident in *Alien* (1980) and its sequel *Aliens* (1986). In the former, a spaceship crew are terrorised by an implacable and apparently invincible enemy lurking in a jungle of pipes and ducts, attacking the crew to implant eggs within their viscera which kill the host upon hatching. The exaggeration of the Viet Cong is clear, and the sequel *Aliens* continues the struggle as a platoon of Colonial Marines fight a Vietnam-style combat with the aliens (during production the film was nicknamed 'Grunts in Space'). The director James Cameron (also scriptwriter of *Rambo II*) commented of the Colonial Marines that their 'training and technology are inappropriate, and ... analogous to the inability of superior American firepower to conquer the unseen enemy in Vietnam. A lot of firepower, too little wisdom, and it doesn't work'.[12] The gruesome battle is resolved only when the aliens are 'nuked' – the ultimate sanction denied America in Vietnam.

The same desire viscerally to shock has always been part of Harlan Ellison's fiction, and is evident in Deathbird stories (1975), a collection of ten years' SF. In 'Basilisk' the eponymous devil enters the world via a corridor provided by the intense pain of a wounded American soldier being tortured by the enemy (by inference Vietnamese). Possessing the soldier, the basilisk wreaks vengeance on the Viet Cong, and then, when the soldier returns home and is shunned, upon the local townspeople. Ellison describes it all in gory detail. 'Bleeding stones' shares the same brutal and violent intention. Pollution brings the gargoyles on St Patrick's Cathedral to life, who then massacre the people of Manhattan. Typically: 'A gargoyle crouches on a mound of bodies, eating hearts and livers it has ripped from the not quite dead casualties. Another sucks the meat off fingers. Another chews eyeballs, savouring the corneal fluid' (p. 198). Ellison aimed to make the reader realise what violence does to the human body, to explain what was already visible in photographs and newsfilm of Vietnam – most notably My Lai. At the mass cultural level the same desire is found in movies of the era, in the slow-motion fountains of blood evident in Bonnie and Clyde (1967), The wild bunch (1969) and Soldier blue (1970), and in underground cinema such as Stan Brakhage's post-mortem film, The art of seeing with one's eyes open (1972).

'Basilisk' concerned a veteran; ironically, few writers served in Vietnam, since the draft favoured with exemptions the typical SF readership of college-educated youth. Veterans include Charles L. Grant, Howard Waldrop, David Drake and Joe Haldeman. Haldeman was drafted after graduation, and in September 1968 he was badly wounded in an explosion which killed several others. In common with many writer-veterans, expression of Vietnam came first in an autobiographical novel, War year (1972), but it was not a success. Haldeman turned to SF, since he felt (prefiguring the Danns) it offered the means to make a statement which war novels could not: 'the only formal plan I had in mind,' he wrote, 'was to address certain aspects of the Vietnam War in science fiction metaphor.'[13] The result was the Hugo and Nebula-award-winning The forever war (1975), but what is striking is that Haldeman did not just write out his Vietnam experiences, but wrote in an explicit reply to SF's classic future war novel, Robert A. Heinlein's Hugo-Award-winning Starship troopers (1959). Haldeman commented: 'I got seventy pages into it before somebody pointed out that I had stolen the plot, all of the characters, all of the hardware from Starship Troopers. It hadn't occurred to me [but it] was my psychological background for the thing, and I subconsciously followed it.'[14] The relationship of the two books is revealing of SF's self-referentiality. Heinlein applauded heroism, revelled in combat, and lauded the organisation of society along military lines (in fact, many readers considered it near-fascist). Haldeman's soldiers are elite draftees, caught in an endless, futile war which strips them of humanity, alienates them from civilian society, and denies them status except in survival. For most this proves impossible, and Haldeman's hero is distinguished by simply living through the war – as was Haldeman.

In the eighties, conscious attempts were made symbolically to reincorporate Vietnam veterans into mainstream society – the Vietnam Memorial in Washington, DC being an obvious example – and Veterans' memoirs and oral history played a major part in the codification of Vietnam into popular culture via texts such as Mark Baker's *Nam* (1982). SF has taken such texts, and woven stories around the detail, placing Vietnam squarely within its regular imaginative repertoire. At times, the crossover is fruitful: several memoirs testify to soldier-tales of ghost helicopters, a theme found in Robert Frazier's 'Across those endless skies' which tells of ghost helicopters that collect soldiers in tune with the war, transporting them to 'a war zone where fighting continued without a break or leave or a discharge, and where death and rebirth were in constant flux, a dark high that he could ride, as he once said in a wishful, yet absurd complaint about the quality of Vietnamese dope, "without ever having to turn off the ignition"' (p. 94). The same motif is found in Jack Chalker's *A jungle of stars* (1976) and Mickey Reichert's *Godslayer* (1987): a soldier dies in Vietnam and is transported to fight as a mercenary in a fantasy landscape. This theme, that after death in Vietnam, or in the half-life of a veteran, Vietnam exists in some fantasy realm, also finds expression in Richard Paul Russo's 'In the season of the rains', in which a soldier escapes the war on a visiting flying saucer, and in the comic book series *The light and darkness war*. Such stories may reflect veterans' current feelings, both in the neurosis that the war never ends, and in the guilty feeling in middle age that perhaps it was the best part of life after all. At the same time, the Reagan Administration was attempting to recast the War as a noble cause in the climate of its new cold war, and the revival of military SF in the 1980s has been striking. Individual novels, series, and multi-volume anthologies such as Jerry Pournelle's *There will be war* (1987) have been published, the latter text implying a relish for the battle not entirely dissipated by Pournelle:

One must wish for peace; it is a religious duty to pray for peace, but if that is all one does, one is not likely to get it. A very long time ago the human race learned a bitter truth: if you would have peace, you must be prepared for war ... If these books need justification, that will serve well enough. (Vol. VII, *Call to battle*, p. 2.)

Pournelle is a scientist with experience in defence, and signed the Hawk statement in 1968. *There will be war* is Kiplingesque in its sentiment for military life – in volume VII two Kipling poems are reprinted, an unlikely first in contemporary SF anthologisation. Factual articles laud the Reagan Administration for its rearmament stance, 'Star Wars' (the Strategic Defence Initiative), and generally chastise the Left as fools or traitors. Perhaps the best example is Peter Collier and David Horowitz's confessional 'Another low and dishonest decade on the left'. Born-again conservatives, the authors write of Vietnam in terms the New Wave would have recognised:

Like most of the movement, we presumed that a Viet Cong victory would mean a peasant utopia in South East Asia. but we were less concerned with what happened in Vietnam, than with making sure that America was defeated. A fundamental tenet of our new Leftism was that America's offenses against Vietnam were only a fraction of its larger imperial sins. (Vol. VII, *Call to battle*, p. 104.)

Kevin Randle and Robert Cornett's *Seeds of war* (1987) and its sequel *The Aldebaran campaign* (1988) revived future war fiction, but the most evident focus in military SF has been the mercenary, in novels such as Pournelle's *The Janissaries* (1979). The peak – or perhaps the trough – is reached in David Drake's *Hammer's Slammers* (1979) and sequels such as *Counting the cost* (1985) and *At any price* (1987), detailing the adventures of Colonel Alois Hammer's mercenaries. As a veteran, Drake finds a message in Vietnam: in 1985, two years after 250 US Marines had died in Beirut, Drake wrote:

I don't want kids joining the marines – or politicians voting to deploy those marines – because at the back of their minds they have the notion that real violence is clean and cute. Violence is sometimes necessary? Maybe; I won't advocate unilateral national disarmament until I'm willing to disarm myself, which at the moment I'm not. But the look and the sound, and smell of people killing one another – that should be clear to everybody. (*At any price*, p. 288.)

But why then praise killing for money? This is not unique to SF: James William Gibson has suggested that the rise of the 'soldier of fortune' and 'paramilitary' heroes such as Rambo, were precise responses to the collapse of institutional morale and military authority in the Vietnam War, promoting alternative private fellowships - such as the Slammers.[15]

In conclusion, Vietnam clearly proved problematic for SF, with its traditional faith in technology and an Americanised future, and its sense of privilege as a predictive medium; for those who sought to escape precisely such a definition, Vietnam was proof of its obsolescence. Post-War, as Gloria Emerson has noted,[16] for Americans 'Vietnam' no longer means a geographical location, but has become part of the imaginative landscape. Certainly contemporary SF has incorporated Vietnam motifs and moods into its repertoire, moulding, codifying, and blunting meaning – for instance, the reprivileged role for SF the Danns promote. Yet, as Lucius Shepard, the most significant contemporary writer to use Vietnam in SF has shown, Vietnam can mean more. Shepard's skill has been to place Vietnam within the imaginative landscape not just of SF and not just of Americans. In stories such as 'Salvador', 'Fire Zone Emerald', and the novel *Life during wartime* (1988), Shepard has constructed a war of the near-future in Central America, its resonance evident from the first line of the novel: 'One of the new Sikorsky gunships, an element of the First Air Cavalry with the words 'Whispering Death' painted on its sides gave Mingolla and Gilbey and Baylor a lift from the ant farm to San Francisco de Jutlican, a small town located inside the green zone, which on the latest maps was designated free Guatemala' (p. 11). In this future 'Vietnam', technology has advanced – soldiers tote M-18 rifles and wear combat suits with computer readouts, but morale problems still exist, staved off by drugs which provide synthetic courage and warrior spirit. They also provide Shepard with the matrix for the hallucinatory world he evokes, as appropriately enough Latin American magic realism meets SF. Such stories come from Shepard's politics:

I get a lot of mail that says 'We like your work, but we wish you'd stop these political stories' ... Nobody complains that another science fiction author has written twenty-five novels about a god-damned glorified military group ... which was the expression of post-war America after WWII ... This is a different time, completely. And if my five or six little stories about Central America make people uncomfortable enough to write a letter, yet still say they like it, even though they're complaining about it, then I'm doing something right.[17]

Shepard brings discussion full circle, and returning to the Danns' desire for purgative SF, it is met by Shepard's two stories set in Vietnam, 'Delta Sly Honey' and 'Shades' (both included in *In the field* of fire.) the latter is a ghost story, set in post-War Vietnam. The hero, a Vietnam veteran speaks of present imaginings:

Miraculous one-man missions to save our honor! Those movies, they make war seem like a mystical opportunity. Well, man it wasn't quite that way. y'know. It was leeches, fungus, the shits ... It was lookin' into the snaky eyes of some whore you were bangin' and feelin' weird shit crawl along your spine, and expectin' her head to do a Linda Blair three-sixty spin ... Stephen King land. Horror. (p. 142)

This is a Vietnam nightmare, but what makes 'Shades' superior is its inclusiveness. It tells of a dead American soldier who now literally haunts Vietnam, and of the veteran who returns to help with an exorcism – not just of the ghost, not just of his own memories, but also symbolically of America from Vietnam. As such, Shepard ironically inverts the structure the Danns considered privileged SF about Vietnam – Vietnam is purged of America - exposing 'Vietnam generation' for the arrogantly exclusive title it is.

Notes

I should very much like to thank David Willson of Green Rover College, Washington State, for his invaluable assistance in locating texts for use in this paper.

1 Peter MacInerney, 'Straight and secret history in Vietnam War literature', in Contemporary literature, 22, 1981, pp. 187-204.
2 Isaac Asimov, Hugo award winners, 1963-1967 (London, 1973), pp. 120-1.
3 Patrick Parrinder, Science fiction: its criticism and teaching (London, 1980), p. 17; Robert Scholes and Eric Rabkin (eds.), Science fiction: history, science, fiction (New York, 1977), p. 88; Samuel Mines, quoted in Sam Lundwall, Science fiction: what's it all about? (New York, 1971), p. 233.
4 Blish, quoted in William Sims Bainbridge, Dimensions of SF (Cambridge, Mass., 1986), p. 87. Sims also provides a statistical analysis of the New Wave, including in relation the Galaxy advertisements.
5 Kingsley Amis, New maps of hell (London, 1961), p. 54.
6 Bloch, quoted in Parrinder, p. 72.
7 Sheila Schwartz, quoted in Damon Knight, '1971: the year in SF', Nebula award stories 7 (London, 1974).
8 Quoted in Gabriel Kolko, Vietnam: anatomy of a war (London, 1988), p. 196.
9 Quoted in Paul Carter, The creation of tomorrow (New York, 1977), p. 283.
10 Darko Suvin, Positions and presuppositions in science fiction (London, 1988), p. 137.
11 Robert Scholes, quoted in Parrinder, p. 31.
12 James Cameron, quoted in Jump cut, 33, 1987.
13 Joe Haldeman (ed.), Body armor 2000 (New York, 1986), p. 4.
14 Haldeman, Body armor, p. 4.
15 James William Gibson, 'American para-military culture and the reconstitution of the Vietnam War' in Jeff Walsh and Jim Aulich, Vietnam after images (London, 1989), pp. 10-43.

16 Gloria Emerson, *Winners and losers* (New York, 1985), p. vii.
17 Interview with Lucius Shepard in *Interzone*, 34, March/April 1990, pp. 34-9.

References

Novels

Chalker, Jack, *A jungle of stars* (New York, 1976).
Drake, David, *Hammer's Slammers* (New York, 1983)
—, *At any price* (New York, 1985).
—, *Counting the cost* (New York, 1987).
Ellison, Harlan, *Deathbird stories* (London, 1975).
Haldeman, Joe, *War year* (New York, 1972).
—, *The forever war* (London, 1976).
Heinlein, Robert, *Starship troopers* (New York, 1959).
Le Guin, Ursula K., *The left hand of darkness* (New York, 1970).
—, *The dispossessed* (New York, 1974).
—, *The word for world is forest* (New York, 1972).
Moorcock, Michael, *A cure for cancer* (London, 1970).
Pournelle, Jerry, *The Janissaries* (New York, 1979).
Randle, Kevin & Robert Cornett, *The seeds of war* (New York, 1987)
—, *The Aldebaran campaign* (New York, 1988).
Reichert, Mickey Z., *Godslayer* (New York, 1987).
Shepard, Lucius, *Life during wartime* (New York, 1988).
Spinrad, Norman, *The men in the jungle* (New York, 1967).
—, *Bug Jack Barron* (London, 1969).
Veitch, Tom, *The light and darkness war* (New York, 1988).

Short stories and editorials

Aldiss, Brian, 'My country, 'tis not only of thee' in Jack Dann and Jeanne Van Buren Dann (eds.), *In the field of fire* (New York, 1987), pp. 370-93.
Anderson Poul, 'The sharing of flesh' in Isaac Asimov (ed.), *The Hugo winners, Volume 2* (London, 1973), pp. 269-308.
—, 'I tell you it's true' in Harry Harrison (ed.), *Nova 2* (London, 1975), pp. 161-82.
Ballard, J. G., 'The killing ground' in *The best SF stories from New Worlds, 6* (New York, 1971), pp. 7-17.
—, 'The new science fiction' in Langdon Jones (ed.), *The new SF* (London, 1970), pp 52-61.
Brunner, John, 'Who steals my purse?' *Analog*, Vol. 91, No. 1, March 1973.
Collier, Peter, and David Horowitz, 'Another low dishonest decade on the left' in Jerry Pournelle, *There will be war*, Vol. 7 (New York, 1988), pp. 100-22.
Dempsey, Hank, 'The defensive bomber' in Harry Harrison (ed.), *Nova 3* (London, 1973), pp. 77-92.
Dick, Philip K., Faith of my fathers' in Harlan Ellison (ed.), *Dangerous visions, Vols. 1, 2, 3*, (London, 1970), pp. 29-71.
Frazier, Robert, 'Across those endless skies' in Jack Dann and Jeanne Van Buren Dan (eds.), *In the field of fire* (New York, 1987), pp. 90-5.
Malzberg, Barry, 'Final War' in *Malzberg at large* (New York, 1979), pp. 143-89.
Pohl, Frederik, editorials in *Galaxy science fiction*, Vol. 26, No. 5, June 1968; Vol. 27, No. 4, November 1968.
Russo, Richard Paul, 'In the season of the rains' in Jack Dann and Jeanne Van Buren Dann

(eds.), In the field of fire (New York, 1987), pp. 107-22.

Shepard, Lucius, 'Fire Zone Emerald', Playboy, February 1986, pp. 162-7.

—, 'Delta Sly Honey' and 'Shades' in Jack Dann and Jeanne Van Buren Dann (eds.), In the field of fire (New York, 1987), pp. 24-44 and 122-58.

—, 'Salvador' in his The jaguar hunter (London, 1988), pp. 81-102.

Spinrad, Norman The star spangled future (New York, 1979).

Tiptree, James, 'Help' and 'Beam us home' in 100,000 light years from home (London, 1975), pp. 65-86 and 242-55.

Wilhelm, Kate, 'The village' (1973) reprinted in Jack Dann and Jeanne Van Buren Dann (eds.), In the field of fire (New York, 1987), pp. 158-69.

Wolfe, Gene, 'The HORARS of war' in Damon Knight (ed.), A pocketful of stars (London, 1974), p. 157-77.

Critical

Aldiss, Brian, Billion year spree (London, 1973).

Bainbridge, William Sims, Dimensions of SF (Harvard, 1986).

Carter, Dale, The final frontier (London, 1988).

Carter, Paul, The creation of tomorrow (New York, 1977).

Gordon, Joan, Joe Haldeman: Starmont reader's guide (Seattle, 1980).

Hellmann, John, American myth and the legacy of Vietnam (Columbia, 1986).

Knight, Damon, '1971: the year in SF', Nebula award stories 7 (London, 1974).

Lundwall, Sam, Science fiction: what's it all about? (New York, 1971).

Parrinder, Patrick, Science fiction, its criticism and teaching (London, 1980).

Scholes, Robert, and Eric Rabkin (eds.), Science fiction: history, science, fiction (New York, 1977).

Sutherland J. A., 'American SF since 1960' in Patrick Parrinder (ed.), SF: a critical guide (London, 1979).

Suvin, Darko, Positions and presuppositions in science fiction (London, 1988).

Walsh, Jeff, and Jim Aulich, Vietnam after images (London, 1989).

9

Nuclear war fiction for young readers: a commentary and annotated bibliography

Paul Brians

I

Until recently, there has been little fiction depicting nuclear war or its aftermath directed at young readers, and almost no attention paid it by critics and scholars. This is perhaps not surprising since adults find it difficult to confront for themselves the dangers posed by the threat of atomic warfare. Explaining the unthinkable to immature minds when one has no ready solutions to offer is a daunting task; yet more and more authors are trying. Recent American interest in the subject was no doubt sparked by the intense public controversy surrounding the 1983 broadcast of The day after, which focused on the effects the movie could be expected to have on children (see, for instance, Palmer). As Barbara Harrison observes (pp. 80-l), adult concerns about the effects of depictions of nuclear war upon children are often masks for adult reluctance to confront the issue squarely. This was undoubtedly the case with The day after. Yet the broadcast did seem to create a breakthrough. Previously it may have been unconsciously assumed that nuclear war was simply an unsuitable subject for young people's fiction. Even in science fiction,where post-holocaust adventure stories set in the waste land have long been a staple of the genre, few examples were oriented specifically toward youth. All that has now changed, with new titles being published each year.

Yet critics and scholars have been slow to note the growth of this literature. Given its early date, it is perhaps not surprising that Margaret Esmonde's 1977 'After Armageddon: the post cataclysmic novel for young readers' lists only one novel depicting the aftermath of a nuclear war: Robert C. O'Brien' s Z for Zachariah. But it is striking that the best known bibliography of books for the young on war and peace issues,

Watermelons not war! A support book for parenting in the nuclear age (1984) does not list a single work of fiction. Similarly, Dennis M. Adams, complaining in 1986 of the lack of coverage of nuclear war issues in school textbooks, made no mention of fiction dealing with the subject.

In more recent times, attention has been focussed on the subject by a spirited exchange in *The Horn Book* (Waters, Fireside, Tolan), a review article in the *New York Times Book Review* (Sutton), another in *Children's Literature* (Cech), and an important article by Joan Glazer in *Children's Literature Association Quarterly*. These articles generally treat together novels which actually depict nuclear war and those which deal only with the fear of nuclear war, such as Judy Blume's *Tiger eyes*, Larry Bograd's *Bad apple*, Virginia Hamilton's *A little love*, Jane Langton's *The fragile flag*, Phyllis Reynolds Naylor's *The dark of the tunnel*, Julian F. Thompson's *A band of angels*, and Stephanie S. Tolan's *Pride of the peacock*.

What has been lacking is a comprehensive list of fiction aimed at young readers which actually depicts nuclear war or its aftermath. The only extensive list so far published, by Eugene La Faille, while distinguishing helpfully among works he recommends for various ages, does not include many books meant specifically for young readers. Two thirds of the items in the present bibliography are omitted by La Faille, who nevertheless includes such obviously adult works as Angela Carter's *Heroes and villains* and Russell Hoban's *Riddley Walker*. In addition, La Faille does not evaluate the novels he lists, blurring the distinction between brilliant works like Daniel F. Galouye's classic *Dark universe* and routine adventure stories like Douglas Hilk's *Huntsman* series and a mindless horror story like James Herbert's *Domain*.

Most other bibliographies have concentrated on nonfictional discussions of war and peace or fictional stories aimed at war prevention rather than focusing on nuclear war itself. In the following discussion and notes, a few of these books are referred to, but they are omitted from the bibliography. Two books intended for younger children – Coerr and Maruki's – although they are based on true stories about victims of the Hiroshima bombing, are included because they are fictionalised. Those seeking a wider spectrum of fiction depicting nuclear war for all ages should consult the bibliography of my book, *Nuclear holocausts: atomic war in fiction 1895-1984*, which lists over 800 items, but which omits many of the titles in the present list either because they were published after 1984 or because I previously overlooked them.

Compiling this list presented several problems, including the familiar one of determining what is and what is not fiction suitable for young readers. Although many clearly adult novels may be read by young people, I have tried to identify those which are specifically aimed at readers ranging from young children to teens. For the purposes of the following discussion distinctions between books aimed at elementary-school children and young adult readers only occasionally proved helpful, so they are generally treated together. Because of widespread disagreement about the appropriateness of these books for various ages, I have not labelled the titles in the bibliography by age category. Readers should make their own judgments based on the annotations.

Another problem may be peculiar to the subject of nuclear war, though it was familiar to me from my work on *Nuclear holocausts*. So haunted are we by the possibility of a nuclear war that we often assume that works depicting the fall of civilisation or the aftermath of any vaguely described catastrophe must portray the result of such a war. Examples of such titles mistakenly suggested to me during the preparation of this article include Terry Nation's *The survivors* (the disaster in question is a plague, not a war), H. M. Hoover's *Children of Morrow* (pollution), Marie Farca's *Earth* (primarily pollution), and G. R. Kestavan's *The pale invaders* and *The awakening water* (both set in a world devastated by civil disorders rather than nuclear bombing).[1]

A notable case is David Macaulay's *BAAA* (Boston, Mass.: Houghton Mifflin, 1985), which was cited by more than one consultant. In fact, *BAAA* very clearly does not depict a nuclear war. The human race has mysteriously disappeared, but no corpses are left behind. There is no evidence of bombing: all buildings are intact and there is no radiation. The foolish sheep which replace humanity and repeat its mistakes do not war on each other. Instead, the themes of the book are the dangers of overpopulation, consumerism, and oppressive government. The idea of the sheep consuming their own dead in the form of the food which gives the book its title is clearly derived from the 1973 film *Soylent Green*, whose subject was overpopulation rather than nuclear war. Yet so obsessed are we with the possibility of atomic Armageddon that numerous readers have read nuclear war into *BAAA*.[2]

Most nuclear war fiction is science fiction. This fact poses special problems for our purposes. Young SF fans often read omnivorously in the field, paying little attention to whether the books that interest them were aimed at them or not. Despite the increasing number of literarily sophisticated SF novels published in recent decades, much of the genre consists of simple, easily digested narratives with wide appeal to fans of all ages. One sign of youth-oriented fiction is, of course, a young protagonist; and young protagonists are very common in SF. But many SF novels, like the pruriently depicted heroine of David R. Palmer's *Emergence*, view their young protagonists with an adult eye. Young adult fiction is more definitively characterised by the presence of a coming-of-age theme, and by the sympathetic depiction of the struggles of the young protagonists with older siblings, parents, and parent figures. There is generally less graphic sex and violence in YA fiction, although the boundaries are constantly being pressed by ever more daring authors. These considerations helped to shape the selection of titles in the present list.

II

Having identified the novels we are discussing, it remains to evaluate them. Those taking part in the current debate over nuclear war fiction for the young often take strikingly different positions from each other. Although it touches only peripherally on our theme, the debate over Dr. Seuss's *Butter battle book* well illustrates the dilemma adults find themselves in. Do we dare to discuss the arms race with children, or will merely raising the issue itself traumatise them? This dilemma was neatly resolved by a recent remarkably obtuse study by a pair of social scientists who pronounced the Seuss book safe reading for youngsters on the grounds that a group of twenty-seven students aged six to eleven were incapable of recognising that the story was in fact an allegory of the arms race (Van Cleaf and Martin). The implication seems to be that we can safely discuss nuclear war with children only so long as we do so in such an obscure fashion that they cannot understand what we are talking about. Yet adults cannot responsibly continue to pretend that children can be shielded from the subject. It is bound to penetrate their awareness at a fairly early age. All we can hope for is to find ways to treat the subject in a manner which will help them to deal with it.

Umberto Eco's recent picture book (strikingly illustrated by Eugenio Carmi), *The bomb and the general*, takes a much more hard-hitting approach but is perhaps even more unsatisfactory than Seuss's. Eco warns his young readers first that all things are made of atoms, then self-contradictorily depicts the atoms in a bomb fleeing it, creating a nonlethal, atomless bomb. The atoms have rejected their role as destroyers because:

> Thanks to them
> there was going to be a huge catastrophe:
> Many children would die,
> many Moms,
> many kittens,
> many calves,
> many birds —
> everybody.
> Whole towns would be destroyed
> where before there had been little white houses
> with red roofs
> and green trees all around...
> ... nothing would be left
> but a horrible black pit.

This terrifying prospect is avoided through whimsy, without human intervention. It is difficult to fathom how such a brilliant writer/artist team can have created such worthless, even dangerous book. With its nonsensical physics and absolute lack of politics, The bomb and the general marks a new low point in trying to say something useful about the danger of nuclear war to children.

There is more of a consensus that nuclear war is a fit subject for teens (as opposed to young children), but no consensus on what sort of approach to the subject is appropriate for young readers of either age group.[3] In her concern to shield tender minds, Stephanie Tolan emphasises the need for authors to provide hope in their stories, even at the expense of realism. The particular case in point is Louise Lawrence's Children of the dust, which, after a naturalistic beginning which provides the most realistic scenes ever written of the probable conditions children would suffer trapped in an ordinary house by radioactive fallout, ends with a fantastic solution to humanity's problems: furry, peace-loving telepathic mutants will inherit the earth. Despite her statement that providing hope in nuclear war fiction is not a simple matter (p. 359), Tolan accepts this extraordinarily simple-minded 'solution': '... I would not speak against anything that offers children an alternative to despair, no matter how unlikely a scientist might find the idea' (p. 361).

Aside from the fact that the evolution of benign telepathic mutants produced by war-related radioactivity is the most clichéd 'alternative to despair' in science fiction (going back to before Hiroshima, in Henry

Kuttner's *Baldy* stories), one can't help wondering why such fantastic escapism is acceptable in nuclear war fiction for young readers when it clearly would not be in fiction dealing with ordinary disease and death. When treated thoughtfully, as in *The chrysalids*, the radioactive teenage mutant theme can be an effective metaphor for the necessity to tolerate diversity, a way of warning against the sort of prejudice that leads to war in the first place. Yet even Wyndham's classic novel seems frivolous placed next to a serious account of a real atomic war, like Masuji Ibuse's adult novel of the Hiroshima bombing, *Black rain*.

Joan Glazer suggests that the pervasiveness of hope in juvenile nuclear war fiction is a function of the fact that 'these are books for children' (p. 87). Yet in fact children's nuclear war fiction differs very little from adult nuclear war fiction in this regard. With rare exceptions, like *On the beach*, most nuclear war novels provide some kind of hope. Besides the extremely common theme of humanity genetically improved by exposure to fallout, we have the rescue by benign aliens, the intervention of a peace-loving super-computer, travel backward in time to prevent the war from having occurred in the first place, and numerous other fantastic pseudo-solutions to the problems posed by the threat of nuclear war.

Bogus hopeful endings which encourage one to feel more comfortable with the idea of nuclear war are not ultimately helpful. Children love the fantasy elements present in Pamela F. Service's *Winter of magic's return* (in my region of Washington State it was one of the most popular books among middle-school readers during 1987); but surely it does nothing to assuage their fears of annihilation. Anyone old enough to read the book knows that an atomic bomb is not really going to blast the top off a mountain in which Merlin has been trapped for centuries and loose magic – complete with unicorns – on the world. Do we really want to encourage children to think of nuclear war as a gateway to a more exciting, adventuresome future? I think not; but many books do just that.

Glazer deals extensively with another form of hopefulness which is also pervasive in adult nuclear war fiction: the way in which most of the novels focus on survivors of the war rather than on victims. Adults, no less than children, do not like to identify with dying protagonists. She does not say so explicitly, but Glazer may be suggesting that hope can be overdone. This is certainly my own position. Most of this fiction, by encouraging us to identify with survivors rather than casualties, breeds a certain callousness about the prospect of the annihilation of the bulk of humanity. Doubtless, reading of the survival of those who experienced the horrors of the past, such as the Nazi death camps, can provide an uplifting affirmation of the indomitability of the human spirit; yet a wilful turning away from the fate of the vast majority of our fellow human beings looks more like escapism than affirmation.

Glazer also notes the persistent failure of the novels she discusses to assign responsibility for the nuclear war. No-one – except perhaps humanity as a whole – is held responsible for the nuclear holocaust: 'Characters remark that they should have been more aware, should have questioned what was going on. Still, all of the protagonists are innocent individuals, trying to cope with a disaster not of their making' (p. 87). Perhaps these authors are trying to avoid overt politics when writing for young children. Yet, although the Russians, the Chinese, or even the Americans are blamed for starting a nuclear war in some adult fiction, the pattern Glazer notes is much more common. No one and everyone is to blame. The war is often an accident. We feel so dwarfed and victimised by our own technology that we create myths of that technology as Nemesis, evading responsibility for attempting to control it.

Roger Sutton hails Judith Vigna's picture book for young children, *Nobody wants a nuclear war*, for laying 'the responsibility right where it belongs', – with the grownups. Vigna is unusual in advocating realistic political action – letter-writing and protesting – as the solution to the problem. It is not enough, Vigna seems to be saying, to reassure children (as does the mother in her book) that we have lived with nuclear weapons for a long time and that nobody really wants to use them. They need the hope provided by adult action to prevent war. A happy ending which is forced and unrealistic is fraudulent.

Whitley Strieber, refusing to provide a facile resolution to *Wolf of shadows*, states in the afterword:

[This] is not the true end of the story. Nobody knows exactly what will happen if someone turns on the nuclear death machine we have installed on our planet.

The true end of the story comes when we decide, as a species, to dismantle the machine and use our great intelligence on behalf of the earth that bears us, instead of against her. (p. 105)

Tolan fears that authors anxious to express their views will lapse from art into propaganda (p. 361); yet not only are the kind of crude polemics she objects to almost entirely absent from children's books, so are reasonable political ideas of any kind, as Sutton notes. Bernard Benson's The peace book is not unhelpful, but absurdly simplistic. Benson advocates political action, but the tactics he depicts as persuading the world's leaders to abandon the arms race are unrealistic.[4] Vigna instead offers hope more realistically, but promises no easy solutions. The only example from the present list of a book which advocates grass-roots political action to prevent nuclear war is James D. Forman's Doomsday plus twelve, in which a plucky young girl leads a peaceful crusade to prevent the citizens of San Diego from taking vengeance on the Japanese who have peacefully and – benignly – occupied the defeated United States. In the more than a thousand nuclear war narratives I have read, this is the only other book besides Vigna's to depict anti-war activism as both rational and hopeful. Yet Forman's book does not provide as useful a model as Vigna's because the success of the peace march is not credibly depicted, it is not directed against a national government (rather against a loosely-organised group of vigilantes), and it takes place after a nuclear war. However, even such hope as these books offer is absent from adult fiction. To my knowledge, no author of adult fiction has yet depicted a peace movement as successfully ending the threat of nuclear war. Our despair runs very deep.

Almost everyone who has written about nuclear war fiction for young people has shown a marked degree of ambiguity on the subject. Tolan, as we have seen, seems to contradict herself, Glazer confines herself to observing patterns without making judgements, and even Sutton, who seems at first glance to be more decisive, is unclear enough to have prompted a rather confused letter of criticism by Austin Tichenor in the 22 March issue of the New York Times Book Review (p. 44). I feel responsible, therefore, to state clearly the standards I have used in judging these books.

III

It goes without saying that nothing can save a poorly written book, so a decently literate style, a responsible and interesting plot, and realistically drawn characters are all prerequisites.

When depicting a nuclear war for the young, one should be reasonably accurate in describing the effects of the bomb. There is no need to dwell at length on gruesome scenes of mass destruction, but the effects of blast and radiation should not be treated only in passing or relegated to deep background. If one is going to treat the subject of nuclear war at all, it makes no sense to try to make it seem less hazardous than it really is. Maruki's Hiroshima no pika and the first part of Lawrence's Children of the dust seem to me exemplary in this regard. The actual details of the effects of nuclear war are surprisingly little known. Most of us prefer to dismiss the subject by referring casually to atomic holocaust as causing 'the end of the world', relegating it quickly to the realm of the unthinkable, like the thought of our own personal deaths. This attitude only pretends to realism: it is actually a form of escapism, and extremely unhelpful when dealing with children.

Radiation in particular should not be used as a sort of magic wand to transform pre-war Kansas into a post-holocaust Oz. It is not fitting that such a serious threat should be treated lightly. All too often, as in Winter of magic's return, and its sequel, Tomorrow's magic, a nuclear war is made palatable by bringing in its wake various transformations and mutations which create a world more attractive than our own. In real life, fallout is very likely to result in leukaemia, persistent sores, excruciating pain, sterility, deformity and stillbirths. It is not at all likely to result in the evolution of an improved version of the human race. Pseudo-Darwinian optimism is entirely out of place. Magical solutions are no solutions at all.

Similarly, young readers should not be encouraged to think of the solution to the problems posed by nuclear war as primarily scientific and technological rather than ethical and political. There is a long-standing tradition in science fiction of defending scientists from accusations that they are responsible for the bomb. Whereas many scientists themselves seem anxious to accept that responsibility, SF authors routinely portray them as unjustly blamed and persecuted in the wake of a nuclear war. Science itself is banned in novels such as Poul Anderson's Vault of the ages and Andre Norton's Star man's son. In such books the tribal taboos against the ancient learning imposed by superstitious elders must be overcome by courageous youngsters eager to restore civilization. Preferable is Leigh Brackett's ambiguity in The long tomorrow, in which the antagonism between faith and science is not facilely resolved in favour of science.[5] The neo-Luddite faith of the masses may be based on wilful ignorance, Brackett seems to be saying; but it may well be the case that scientists cannot undo the effects of nuclear war. The implicit lesson is that such a war must be prevented rather than ameliorated.

Only recently have a few authors begun to challenge the necessity of rebuilding technology and reasserting American power after a nuclear war. Kim Stanley Robinson's fine *The wild shore* treats the fall of American civilisation as partly deserved. The other nations – headed by the Japanese - seek to keep America at a primitive level which will never again threaten world survival; the novel depicts them as being justified in doing so. The young protagonist learns by personal experience that violent rebellion against this regime is worse than useless: it is tragic. When one of his best friends is killed in an ill-conceived raid on a Japanese boarding party, he grieves for months, then learns to accept living in the circumscribed pre-technological village culture left behind by the nuclear war. The young reader can identify satisfactorily with the protagonist who learns love and wisdom in place of empty heroism. Nothing could be further removed from the gleefully successful rebellions so common in traditional science fiction. The pessimism of such works is helpful. It tells us that if we destroy ourselves as a nation, we can expect no second chances.

Politics are not at all inappropriate in this context. Only political action offers reasonable solutions to the nuclear dilemma. Books which present nuclear war as inevitable or self-causing are defeatist. Such fantasies may provide escape for jaded adults, but they can only create feelings of powerlessness and terror in children. They need to know that bombs are built and used by human beings, and that human beings can prevent their use or dismantle them. But politics must be presented reasonably. Governments may often behave foolishly, but the men who run them are rarely idiots or outright villains. In a number of recent nuclear war novels the profound moral dilemmas surrounding nuclear weapons are oversimplified by portraying the President of the United States or other national leaders as fools or traitors, and the military as the enemy of the citizens they are supposed to protect.

In Paul Cook's *Duende meadow* the American military threatens the survival of the human race, and hope is provided by the benign Russian invaders, although it should be noted that this hardly constitutes an endorsement of unilateral disarmament: the invaders are peaceful and friendly non-Communist refugees who have settled depopulated Kansas, and the military constitute an undemocratic elite which has forgotten the ideals it was designed to defend. In *Children of the dust*, a military dictatorship hoards scarce resources in a gigantic government fallout shelter; and in Robert Swindell's *Brother in the land* the British military actually sets up a death camp to rid itself of cumbersome civilians after the war has rendered food and medicine in short supply. In these two latter books, anti-government revolutionaries are presented as role models. Perhaps the sort of regime which emerges after a nuclear war will deserve overthrowing; but is it useful now to present revolution as the sole solution to political problems? A children's crusade or guerilla war is not going to disarm the superpowers. Younger readers cannot be expected to grasp all the complexities of global politics (after all, few adults bother to study them); but we do them a disservice to oversimplify the issues by portraying our leaders without shadings as either heroic or villainous.

Even more out of place are those stories in which the villains are not even human. In Douglas Hill's *Huntsman* trilogy, the precise cause of the holocaust is unclear; but blame is not really assigned even to humanity as a whole because the real terror menacing Hill's protagonists is the dictatorship of some exceedingly old-fashioned alien invaders from another world. By making the villainous Slavers utterly evil, the author removes all moral ambiguity from his tales. The pious hope expressed at the end of the series, that 'humans may never forget that they have to live together in peace and harmony' (*Alien citadel*, p. 120), is quite unjustified by the preceding narrative, since humanity has liberated itself solely by relentless, savage violence.

Even the vogue of post-holocaust survivalist fiction which has produced over a hundred violent pulp novels for men in the past decade has penetrated the young adult market with the appearance of the *Firebrats* novels by Barbara and Scott Siegel, featuring a teenage couple battling villains and beasts in the radioactive wasteland. Although the sex and violence in these books is moderate compared to similar novels aimed at the adult market, they are clearly inspired by works like Jerry Ahern's *Survivalist* series, from their absurd macho cover art to their philosophy that the only hope for the future lies in developing the skills to fight and overcome the menaces which will multiply in the wake of World War III. In comic book shops one can find, in addition to the Judge Dredd comics originally created in England and reprinted in the US by Marvel, independent comics which take the post-holocaust wasteland for granted, with titles like *After apocalypse* (Cliff Biggers, Marietta, Ga: Paragraphics, 1987), and *The shattered earth* (a lengthy series with several linked titles published by Eternity Comics, Newbury Park, Calif.). They are read by youngsters with the same avidity with which they absorb post-nuclear war films like *Mad Max: beyond thunderdome*.

One of the more successful such comic book series to date is *The Terminator*, based on the extremely violent film of the same title. A handful of survivalist humans battle the robots who have destroyed most of humanity in a nuclear war. Typical of readers' responses is one of several letters printed in the August 1989 issue: 'I just finished reading *The Terminator* #'s 7 and 8. The comic book is a whole lot better than the piece of crap movie. The book showed scenes of blood that other comics are afraid to show.' Post-holocaust stories and films, video-games and role-playing games have familiarised a whole generation with the irradiated, bloody landscape of their future, so that almost every American youngster knows the terms 'post-nuke' and 'mutant' as they are used to refer to this projected nightmare.

Susan B. Weston's *Children of the light*, one of the more thoughtful recent novels set after a nuclear holocaust, comments on the vogue for such fiction among young readers:

Welling up beneath responsible national debate was a flood of fantasy books. and science-fiction stories set in post-holocaust landscapes. Now, this happened to suit Jeremy's taste in recreational literature: He actually liked reading about heroes who rode forth on genetic mutations of the horse to do battle with evil monsters called 'leemutes' or 'gamma gorts.' But he was also capable of intuitive leaps, and he knew why these books were so popular. It was the domestication of a society's worst nightmare. Nuclear war as a return to frontier innocence, with an irradiated Huck Finn lighting out for the territories. Wipe the polluted, industrialized slate clean and start over, because it was unimaginable that there wouldn't be somebody to start over. As if, Jeremy thought, to that ultimate horror there might be an arcadian solution, a simplicity, a return to clear moral distinctions (p. 50).

The remainder of the novel is designed to demonstrate how simplistic is this popular view of life after nuclear war.

It is morally indecorous to use nuclear war as the background for adventures which might as well be set in tenth-century France or nineteenth-century Texas. All too often civilisation is destroyed merely to provide a setting for a series of exhilarating battles, captures, and escapes (for instance, Biemiller, Clason, Norton). Nuclear war is too serious a subject to be treated frivolously. The value of dark irony such as that in *Dr Strangelove* is debatable, even for adults; but surely it has no place in young people's fiction.

Finally, decades of fantasising about adventures on a depopulated Earth have numbed us to the prospect of humanity's impending extinction. Fiction which depicts the death of the vast majority of humankind as anything other than an unmitigated disaster is anti-human. By encouraging young readers to think of themselves as survivors possibly benefiting from a holocaust we are actually encouraging them to accept their own annihilation. Nuclear war is not a problem to be adjusted to, like blindness or divorce. Thinking about the unthinkable is crucial. Becoming comfortable with it is suicidal. Young people cannot escape the subject of nuclear war. It pervades our culture now more thoroughly than at any time since the fifties. They deserve books which will confront their fears honestly and present the reasonable but difficult, inescapably political solutions. Let nuclear war not be presented as inevitable or as caused by unknowable forces. If nuclear war brings death and destruction, let the survivors grieve, and not recover so rapidly as to make the war seem merely a passing episode. If they are to have fantasies of life in a post-war world, let them reflect a sense of the losses sustained by humanity in unleashing nuclear weapons.

So far few authors have met these standards. Yet, by and large, the sense of heightened moral obligation common among the authors of children's fiction has led to a larger proportion of good or passable books on the subject than is the case with adult nuclear war fiction, which is preponderantly escapist. Most of these books at least take nuclear war seriously. No author of adult fiction has yet treated nuclear winter as realistically as *Wolf of shadows*. Only Raymond Briggs's *When the wind blows* rivals *Children of the dust* for its presentation of the horrors of trying to survive fallout in an ordinary home. As we noted above, a few children's books are almost unique in treating anti-war activism with respect.

However, the highest achievements of English-speaking authors writing for young people pale in comparison to the most accurate novel about a nuclear war ever published, for young or old: Gudrun Pausewang's *Die letzten Kinder von Schwenborn oder... sieht so unsere Zukunft aus?* (*The last children of Schwenborn or ... does our future look like this?*). Pausewang unsparingly inflicts on a typical middle-class family the sort of suffering which may realistically be expected: radiation disease, typhus, starvation, birth defects and death. As the novel ends, most of the youthful narrator's family has died, and he is showing signs of serious radiation disease. Pausewang's uncompromising book is probably too strong for the tastes of those who find *The butter battle book* alarming; but it would be a pity if it never appeared in English translation. It is simply the best-researched work of its kind, and has a directness and sincerity which is powerfully affecting.

Young readers are at last being offered, on occasion, the serious and thoughtful treatments of this subject that they deserve. As interest in depicting nuclear war for them continues to grow, we may hope to see many more works which may help youngsters grapple with the prospect of World War III in a more realistic and useful way than the majority of their elders have done.

Notes

An abridged version of this chapter appeared previously in The Bulletin of the Atomic Scientists.

1 For some reason, the second novel was published under the name Kesteven rather than Kestavan, but both are pseudonyms of Geoffrey R. Crosher.
2 John Cech suggests that humanity was eliminated by neutron bombing (p. 203). Neutron bombs do not really leave all property intact, as popular imagination supposes; but one might accept his argument even so, given that BAAA is a satire. However, the fact is that there are simply no positive indications that a nuclear war of any kind has taken place. Cech also feels that, like Briggs's When the wind blows, BAAA is not really a children's book. I agree. Their picture book format is reminiscent of children's books, but the content is maturely sophisticated. Similarly, I have excluded from the present bibliography Keiji Nakazawa's comic-book treatment of the Hiroshima bombing, Barefoot gen. Like many Japanese comics, it has an adult audience in mind and is, in addition, shocking in portraying as routine and acceptable extreme violence within the family. It is, however, very helpful in understanding the plight of the ordinary Japanese in World War II.
3 For an excellent study of current opinion on the necessity for an effective nuclear war education for children, see Phyllis La Farge's The Strangelove legacy: children, parents, and teachers in the nuclear age (Harper & Row New York: 1987).
4 The play Peace child, based on Benson's book, is undeniably effective on the stage, particularly when performed, as it often is, by an international cast of children. It can provide a helpful starting point for discussion of disarmament, but only a starting point. Although its sentimental technique moves its audiences, even the youngest viewers need more information than it provides to begin to understand nuclear politics.
5 For an extensive discussion of this theme, see my essay, 'The revival of learning: science after the nuclear holocaust in science fiction' in Phoenix from the ashes: the literature of the remade world, ed. Carl B. Yoke (Greenwood Press Westport, Conn., 1987), pp. 45-53. The same volume contains a good essay by Donna M. DeBlasio entitled 'Future imperfect: Leigh Brackett's The long tomorrow' (pp. 97-103).

References

Adams, Dennis M.,'Literature for children: avoiding controversy and intellectual challenge', Top of the news, 42 (1986), pp. 304-8.
Cech, John, 'Some leading, blurred, and violent edges of the contemporary picture book', Children's literature, 15, 1987, pp. 197-206.

Cloud, Kate, et al., *Watermelons not war! A support book for parenting in the nuclear age* (New Society Publishers: Philadelphia, 1984). ERIC Document Reproduction Service ED 225 876.

Esmonde, Margaret, 'After Armageddon: the post-cataclysmic novel for young readers', *Children's literature*, 6, 1977, pp. 211-20.

Fireside, Bryna J, 'A response to "Members of the last generation"', *The horn book*, 62, 1986, pp. 89-92.

Glazer, Joan I, 'Nuclear holocaust in contemporary children's fiction: a surprising amount of agreement', *Children's literature association quarterly*, 11, 1986, pp. 85-8.

Harrison, Barbara, 'Howl like the wolves', *Children's literature*, 15, 1987, pp. 67-90.

La Faille, Eugene, 'Nuclear war: visions of the Apocalypse in books and films', *VOYA*, 9, no. 1, April 1986, pp. 15-21, 56.

La Farge, Phyllis, *The Strangelove legacy: children, parents, and teachers in the nuclear age* (Harper & Row: New York, 1987).

Palmer, Edward L, 'The flower and the mushroom: young children encounter *The Day After*', *Marriage and family review*, 10, no. 2, June 1986, pp. 51-8.

Sutton, Roger, 'Yooks, zooks and the bomb', *New York Times Book Review*, 22 February 1987, p. 21.

Tichenor, Austin, 'Children and the bomb' (letter), *New York Times Book Review*, 22 March 1987.

Tolan, Stephanie S., 'A writer's response to "Members of the Last Generation"', *The horn book*, 62, 1986, pp. 358-62.

Van Cleaf, David W. and Rita J. Martin, 'Seuss's *Butter Battle Book*: is there a hidden harm?' *Childhood education*, 62,1985/6, pp. 191-4.

Waters, Kate, 'For members of the "Last Generation"?', *The horn book*, 61, 1985, pp. 339-41.

Annotated bibliography

Note: Many of these titles are also available in paperback reprints.

Anderson, Poul, *Vault of the ages* (Winston: Philadelphia,1952).

The tribal elders of the future ban the ancient knowledge which they blame for the nuclear holocaust. A young boy successfully defies the ban by showing them how gunpowder can help defend them against their enemies. A typical SF novel justifying war even in the wake of a war which has destroyed civilisation.

Biemiller, Carl L., *The, hydronaut adventures* (Doubleday: Garden City, NY, 1981).

Originally published separately by Doubleday as *The hydronauts* (1970), *Follow the whales: the hydronauts meet the otter people* (1973), and *Escape from the crater: more adventures of the hydronauts* (1974).

Plucky youngsters explore the aquatic world created by the melting of the polar icecaps by a nuclear war. They encounter various mutants and a cryogenically preserved survivor. The young people are pacific and environmentally-minded, while their elders are belligerent and prejudiced. Occasionally thoughtful about nuclear war, but essentially frivolous.

Brackett, Leigh, *The long tomorrow* (Doubleday: Garden City, NY, 1955: Mayflower: London, 1962).

In the wake of a nuclear war, the New Mennonite religion bars the rebuilding of cities and the use of pre-war technology. Rebellious youths seek out the underground research centre which has preserved the old knowledge, but find it almost as repressive as the villages they fled.

Clason, Clyde B., *Ark of Venus* (Knopf: New York,1955).

A juvenile adventure story of an expedition to Venus 180 years after the atomic wars have altered the political complexion of Earth. Little reference to the wars themselves.

Coerr, Eleanor, *Sadako and the thousand paper cranes* (Putnam: New York, 1977).
The lightly fictionalised story of a real twelve-year-old girl who died of leukaemia caused by her exposure to the atomic bomb in Hiroshima when she was two. Finely combines political intelligence and realism.

Cook, Paul, *Duende meadow* (Bantam: New York, 1985).
After 600 years of life deep underground, survivors of the holocaust explore the surface, to find it occupied by the descendants of Russian refugees. Unusual in emphasising the importance of international understanding and rejecting military solutions to problems.

Eco, Umberto and Eugenio Carmi, *The bomb and the general*, trans. William Weaver (Harcourt Brace Jovanovich: New York, 1989).
Beautiful but trivial picture book telling an anti-nuclear arms fable.

Forman, James D., *Call back yesterday* (Scribner's: New York, 1981).
Saudi Arabian nationalists seize the American embassy, creating a crisis which precipitates a nuclear war. The heroine is the centre of a romantic rivalry which helps trigger the war. Written in the wake of the Iranian hostage crisis, the novel bears little relevance to our theme.

—, *Doomsday plus twelve* (Scribner's: New York, 1984).
A courageous young woman leads a powerful crusade against an enclave of military survivors of a nuclear war who want to destroy Japan, which has become the world's greatest power after the fall of Russia and the US. This novel is unique in portraying the effective use of Gandhian techniques. A sequel of sorts to *Call back yesterday*, but only very distantly related to it.

Godfrey, Martyn, *The last war* (Collier Macmillan Canada: Ontario, 1986; Collier Macmillan: New York,1989).
Young adult 'easy reading' post-holocaust novella.

Halacy, D. S., Jr, *Return from Luna* (Norton: New York,1969).
A young man stranded on the moon when a nuclear war on Earth occurs helps his comrades survive. A mad antinuclear scientist sabotages their power plant. Finally they join forces with similarly stranded Russians at a nearby Soviet lunar base, demonstrating that in the wake of nuclear war, the old enmities make no sense. Not a distinguished story, but earnest in its way.

Hamilton, Virginia, The Justice Cycle: *Justice and her brothers*,(1978); *Dustland* (1981) and *The gathering* (1981) (all Greenwillow: New York). (*The gathering* was also published in London by MacRae, 1981).
A sensitively told three-volume story of telepathic children exploring the future, where a supercomputer is trying to restore the Earth, which has been laid waste by pollution and warfare. Only in the third volume is it suggested that a nuclear war may have happened in the future the children travel to.

Heinlein, Robert A., *Starship troopers* (Putnam's: New York,1959; Four Square: London,1961).
In this notorious work glorifying the military and combat against evil aliens, soldiers carry and use personal H-bombs. Dangerously simplistic.

Hill, Douglas, *Alien citadel* (Atheneum: New York,1984).
Third volume of the Huntsman trilogy. The aliens leave Earth, having found an uninhabited, less troublesome planet to exploit. Hill's books are routine adventure stories of no particular merit.

—, *The huntsman* (Atheneum: New York, 1982).
First volume of the Huntsman trilogy. In a post-holocaust world, humans are plagued primarily by evil conquering invaders from space who have enslaved them. The only allusion to nuclear weapons is indirect: misshapen plants and creatures are bred in contaminated areas.

—, *Warriors of the wasteland* (Atheneum: New York, 1983).
Second volume of the Huntsman trilogy. Adventures in the radioactive wasteland. In this

volume it is clearly stated that a nuclear war of unknown origin involving seventy-one bombs occurred.

Johnson, Annabel and Edgar, The danger quotient (Harper & Row: New York, 1984).
A time-travelling youth from the post-holocaust future seeks in the twentieth century clues which will help him solve the problems of his own time. By dealing in far more detail with World Wars I and II than with the nuclear holocaust, the novel seems to justify war in general: the protagonist learns to doubt his scorn for the militarism of the past. Although the authors refrain from the usual SF cliché of having the protagonist use time travel to prevent the nuclear war from ever having taken place, the solution to Earth's problems is fantastic and irrelevant to problems of our own time.

Lawrence, Louise, Children of the dust (Harper & Row: New York, 1985; Bodley Head: London, 1985).
The first third of this novel is a uniquely detailed and powerful account of a young mother struggling to keep her children alive in an improvised fallout shelter after a catastrophic nuclear attack on England. The second third describes the search of long-term military shelter-dwellers for other life. The final third deals with the evolution of pacific telepathic mutants who will inherit the Earth, rendered unfit for ordinary human habitation by the destruction of the ozone layer.

Lightner, A.M.The day of the drones (Norton: New York,1969).
Post-holocaust Africa is portrayed as technologically advanced, Britain as primitive in this entertaining book dealing with the dangers of both racism and war. It belongs to the 'revival of learning' category which depicts the ignorant suppression of science in the wake of a nuclear war as an evil to be overcome, but is more thoughtful than average. The young black female protagonist is a strong, independent-minded figure.

Martel, Suzanne,The city underground, trans. Norah Smaridge (Viking: New York,1964).
In the year 3000 courageous young boys who live in a sterile utopia far beneath the ruins of Montreal discover that the surface is now safe, and help to bring together their own English-speaking race with a race of French-speaking surface-dwellers. A parable of tolerance only indirectly bearing on the dangers of nuclear war.

Maruki, Toshi, Hiroshima no pika, trans. Anon. (Lothrop, Lee & Shepard: New York, 1982).
Translation of a picture book first published in Japan in 1980, telling the experiences of one family caught in the blast of the atomic bomb which hit Hiroshima. Based on the recollections of one woman, it blends together the experiences of many survivors. Illustrated with powerful watercolours by the author, who with her husband Iri created a series of frescos depicting the atomic bombing, this may be too frightening for the young children who would be attracted by the book's format, but precisely because of that format may not be read by the older children who could absorb its message.

Mayhar, Ardath, The world ends in hickory hollow (Doubleday: Garden City, N.Y, 1985).
A family survives World War III in east Texas through a combination of courage, love, resourcefulness, and good luck. Although the novel begins promisingly, by focusing on a remote rural area, it obscures the full impact of the war.

Miklowitz, Gloria D., After the bomb. (Scholastic: New York ,1985).
A young boy proves his mettle when his mother is gravely wounded and his older brother becomes sick in the wake of an accidental nuclear strike on his city. Contains a good deal of information about radiation sickness, but is more a coming-of-age story than a serious treatment of nuclear war. Because the bomb is an isolated fluke, aid is available from outside, which would not be the case in a real attack.

Norton, André, Star man's son (Harcourt Brace: New York, 1952).
A young mutant earns his tribe's respect and tolerance in a war-wasted world. A simple adventure story.

Nourse, Alan E., Raiders from the rings (McKay: New York,1962; Faber and Faber: London, 1965).
Russian and American space crews refused to participate in a nuclear war, at the

prompting of aliens who seek to protect life and intelligence. Their descendants have turned to raiding Earth for supplies and women. Although this is mostly a simple adventure story, it ends in reconciliation between enemies.

O'Brien, Robert C., Z for Zachariah (Atheneum: New York, 1974; Armada: London,1976).
A resourceful young girl who may be the last human female left on Earth cares for and then must protect herself from a ruthless scientist bent on rape and domination. Moving and effective, although the author's death prevented him from creating a really satisfying conclusion.

Pausewang, Gudrun, Die letzten Kinder von Schwenborn, oder ... sieht so unsere Zukunft aus? (Otto Maier: Ravensburg, 1983).
A remarkably well-researched account of the effects of a nuclear war on a typical German family, told from the point of view of a boy who is almost thirteen when the bombs hit. Most of the family dies in the course of the novel. Many of the victims display heroic qualities, including generosity and compassion; but in the end the plague of radiation and the effects of nuclear winter nullify all they can do.

Robinson, Kim Stanley, The wild shore (Ace: New York,1984; Orbit: London,1985).
A moving and intelligent tale of a young man's coming to understand the tragedy of the war which has created his world through the death of a friend. One of the best recent science fiction novels.

Service, Pamela F., Tomorrow's magic (Atheneum: New York,: 1987).
Tolkienesque sequel to Winter of magic's return. Arthur and his allies use magic powers to battle the forces of evil led by Morgan Le Fay. The latter hurls Merlin and the heroine back in time to London, just before the nuclear war breaks out; but the magician is able to redirect the energy of the bombs to defeat Morgan.

—, Winter of magic's return (Atheneum: New York,.1985).
After five hundred years of nuclear winter, King Arthur returns. Pure escapism.

Siegel, Barbara and Scott, Firebrats: #1, the burning land (Archway: New York, 1987).
A pair of teenagers survive the nuclear destruction of their hometown in an improvised shelter and battle their way out into the countryside, in quest of his family, which was visiting the West Coast when the war broke out.

—, Firebrats: #2, survivors (Archway: New York,1987).
The protagonists learn how to deal with bandits from a kindly old survivalist.

—, Firebrats: #3, thunder mountain (Archway: New York, 1987).
The protagonists deal with wild animals escaped from a game park and a horde of strange insects, aided by a friendly veterinarian.

—, Firebrats #4, shockwave (Archway: New York, 1988; Teens: London,1988).
As nuclear autumn persists the protagonists foil a band of slave-trading bikers and save Denver from flooding caused by a lake which was formed by the bombing.

Strieber, Whitley, Wolf of shadows (Knopf: New York, 1985; Hodder & Stoughton: London, 1986).
A naturalist and her young daughter struggle through a world transformed by nuclear winter with the aid of a pack of wolves she has befriended. One of the best treatments of our theme.

Swindells, Robert, Brother in the land (Oxford Univ. Press: Oxford, 1984; Holiday: New York,1985).
After nuclear war devastates Britain, a local military unit turns vicious, murdering the survivors and monopolising supplies. They are overthrown by a resistance movement, but since the environment has been severely damaged, there is little hope for the future. The most pessimistic of youth-oriented nuclear war novels.

Weston, Susan B., Children of the light (St Martin's Press: New York, 1985).
The nineteen-year-old son of an activist mother finds himself mysteriously transported into a period long after a nuclear holocaust called 'the time of the light'. A few descendants of survivors struggle on in isolated communities, producing mentally and

physically handicapped offspring. He struggles to redevelop certain aspects of technology with limited success, but his main contribution to the community is as a fertile male in a world where such men are rare, begetting offspring on an eager group of young women. The novel is considerably more thoughtful than most, developing in some detail the protagonist's reluctance to become a mere stud, reflecting on the difficulties of rebuilding civilisation once it has been destroyed.

Wyndham, John, *The chrysalids* (Michael Joseph: London,1955). Rpt. as *Re-birth* (Ballantine: New York, 1955).

An excellent story of an emerging race with extrasensory perception, hunted by 'normals' trying to hang on to traditional values, ruthlessly exterminating all deviation. Despite the essentially escapist nature of its theme, this is the best and most well-known if the many novels depicting the creation of a super-race by war-caused atomic radiation.

Scholarly books dealing generally with nuclear war in fiction

Bartter, Martha, *The way to ground zero: the atomic bomb in American science fiction* (Greenwood Press: Westport, Con, 1988).

Brians, Paul, *Nuclear holocausts: atomic war in fiction 1895-1984* (Kent State Univ. Press: Kent, Ohio, 1987).

Sowling, David, *Fictions of nuclear disaster* (Univ. of Iowa Press: Iowa City, 1987).

Note: Millicent Lenz is at work on a book tentatively entitled *Mushroom clouds over Gaia: imagination in a nuclear age*, which will deal with a number of books for young readers not covered in this chapter.

10

Eternally safe for democracy: the final solution of American science fiction

H. Bruce Franklin

For almost two centuries, Americans have led the world in fantasising about some ultimate weapon that would make war obsolete.[1] Usually appearing first as science fiction, these fantasies reveal crucial aspects of American culture. More important, they have helped to determine the history of both the United States and the world. Indeed, the conditions of human existence on this planet have been transformed – and threaten to transform once more – because of superweapons conceived in American science fiction and delivered by what has come to be known as the American military – industrial complex. Even the vision of America as a capitalist weapons-making wonderland was itself first imagined by American science fiction.

Modern technological warfare was introduced to the world by the US Civil War (1861-5) and the Franco-German War (1870-1), in which immense armies were transported by railroad, co-ordinated by telegraph, and equipped with an ever-evolving arsenal of mass-produced weapons designed by scientists and engineers. This advent of technowar brought forth in the 1870s a new genre: fiction imagining future wars.[2] From that moment in history right through to the present, this form of fantasy has in turn stimulated and accelerated the development of technowar itself. The typical early European fiction was militaristic propaganda designed to terrify its newly-emerging mass reading audience with a spectre of their ill-prepared homeland invaded by some likely enemy, often armed with a deadly new weapon. But American authors churned out hundreds of novels and stories imagining future wars from a peculiarly American perspective. In this fantasy, the emergent faith in American technological genius wedded the older faith in America's messianic destiny, engendering ecstatic visions of made-in-America superweapons that would allow America to defeat all evil empires, wage war to end all wars, and make the world eternally safe for democracy.

In the decades leading to World War I, this fiction was a main dish in the cultural diet of what is now called middle America. Before being published in bound volumes, many of the future-war novels were serialised in popular magazines and nationwide Sunday inserts in major newspapers. Here they not only expressed but deeply influenced America's conception of its Manifest Destiny, its transformation from a republic repudiating standing armies into a global military colossus, and its ever-more-frenetic quest for the ultimate superweapon.

A most revealing example is Frank Stockton's 1889 novel The great war syndicate, which appeared first as a serial in the popular Collier's Weekly. At the time, America's nascent imperialist ambitions were beginning to challenge Britain, the dominant world empire, and the two countries were frequently on the verge of war. Like dozens of other American science fiction novels of the period, The great war syndicate offers a vision of what such a war might be. As soon as the imagined war between Britain and the United States breaks out, twenty-three 'great capitalists' form a 'Syndicate, with the object of taking entire charge of the war' (p. 12). Their objectives: a decisive military victory for the nation and enormous profits for themselves. The Great War Syndicate speedily develops several miraculous new weapons, including the 'Motor Bomb', with the explosive force of an atomic bomb. Merely demonstrating the dreadful weapon brings victory. England is then allowed to enlist as a junior partner in what now becomes the 'Anglo-American Syndicate of War' (p. 180), and the world submits to the Syndicate's benevolent rule. In the novel's final words: '... all the nations of the world began to teach English in their schools, and the Spirit of Civilization raised her head with a confident smile.'

It would be hard to imagine a more striking display of characteristic American fantasies about the superweapon and American destiny than Edison's conquest of Mars. This 1898 novel was offered as the happy ending sequel to H. G. Wells's The war of the worlds.

The war of the worlds appeared in 1897, in the midst of the most aggressive expansion of the British Empire, as it led the colonial powers in their final cut-throat division of the non-white world, which was to culminate in the First World War. Wells's novel was an assault on imperialism, on the gospel of progress, and on faith in the manifest destiny of the British nation and the human species. Wells asks his readers to confront their own imperialist outlook by imagining more technologically advanced civilisations that also might have expansionist aims and as much regard for humans as the white nations have shown for peoples of colour. Before judging the Martian invaders too harshly, he cautions, 'we must remember what ruthless and utter destruction' Europeans have wrought upon non-white peoples such as the Tasmanians, who 'were entirely swept out of existence in a war of extermination waged by European immigrants in the space of fifty years. Are we such apostles of mercy as to complain if the Martians warred in the same spirit?' (pp. 125-6).

This leads to the second great theme of *The war of the worlds*. Wells foresees the rapid advance of weapons technology, yoked to the ideology of the genocidal warfare waged by Europeans on non-whites, potentially leading to a similar 'war of extermination' waged by Europeans against other Europeans. Although in the novel it is extraterrestrial invaders who conduct 'the rout of civilization, the massacre of mankind' (p. 224), Wells here suggests how that post-1870 European future-war fiction, with its propaganda for superweapons, could lead to the catastrophic global conflict he was later to predict in *The war in the air, The world set free* and *Things to come*.[3] When he compares the invaders' form of war with previous human wars, he hints of the future: 'Never before in the history of warfare had destruction been so indiscriminate and so universal' (p. 173). Viewed in this light, the Martians, with their armoured war machines, poison gas, flying machines, and heat beams, are invaders not so much from the neighbouring planet as from the approaching century.

Within a month of the final instalment of *The war of the worlds* in the December 1897 *Cosmopolitan* and other American periodicals, the first instalment of the American sequel appeared, *Edison's conquest of Mars*. Written by Garrett P. Serviss, astronomer, journalist, and populariser of science, this marvellous expression of the American imagination ran in the *New York Evening Journal* in January and February 1898, that decisive year for American imperialism, when the United States went to war to seize overseas colonies in both hemispheres. *Edison's conquest of Mars* converts Wells's jeremiad against imperialism and technowar into an effervescent advertisement for imperial aspirations, superweapons, and warfare of extermination.

By 1898, Thomas Alva Edison – now known as 'The Wizard of Menlo Park' – had become a towering mythic figure in American culture, the living embodiment of American technological genius, all-conquering optimism, and boundless destiny. Within two decades, this myth would lead to his becoming a founding father of the military-industrial complex, a role foreshadowed in Serviss's fantasy.[4]

The American novel opens just after Wells's concludes. Even more dreadful than the terrible physical devastation left by 'the merciless invaders from space' is 'the profound mental and moral depression' produced by the encounter with our technological superiors. This 'universal despair' becomes 'tenfold blacker' when strange lights on the surface of Mars signal the imminence of a new invasion. But then the saviour arises: 'Suddenly from Mr Edison's laboratory at Orange flashed the startling intelligence that he had not only discovered the manner in which the invaders had been able to produce the mighty energies which they employed with such terrible effect, but that, going further, he had found a way to overcome them' (p. 5). This is 'a proud day for America':

> Even while the Martians had been upon earth, carrying everything before them, demonstrating to the confusion of the most optimistic that there was no possibility of standing against them, a feeling — a confidence had manifested itself in France, to a minor extent in England, and particularly in Russia, that the Americans might discover means to meet and master the invaders.
>
> Now, it seemed this hope and expectation was to be realized. (p. 5)

But this is only the beginning of the miraculous powers of Mr Edison, the incarnation of America's genius.

Edison now discovers an electrical force that can overcome gravity, and uses it to design and build a space ship. Faster and more manoeuverable than the Martian space vehicles, Edison's ship in one quick jump leapfrogs the aeons of Martian science and technology. Not content with this single-handed feat, Edison also invents (again all by himself) a weapon more potent than the deadly heat beam used by the Martians — a disintegrator beam capable at vast distances of reducing any substance into its constituent atoms.

In *The war of the worlds*, Wells puts his readers in the position of those being colonised by the industrial capitalist nations; the most modern British firearms are mere 'bows and arrows' compared to the beam weapons of the Martians (p. 177). Echoing this passage, *Edison's conquest of Mars* reminds its readers that the Martians, having many more epochs than humans in which to develop their science and technology, had used against us weapons 'as much stronger than gunpowder as the latter was superior to the bows and arrows that preceded it'. The moral of this American story, however, is precisely the opposite of Wells's tale: 'But the genius of one man had suddenly put us on the level of our enemies in regard to fighting capacity' (p. 102).

Upon learning of the American genius's inventions, the heads of all the nations and peoples on Earth convene, in Washington of course, to arrange financing for total war against Mars. Edison is put in charge of an interplanetary war fleet of one hundred of his electrical anti-gravity spaceships, each manned by a crew of twenty intermingled male citizens of various nations. Since these two thousand men include all the world's great scientists, Earth will be entirely defenceless should they fail (p. 104). Needless to say, they don't. 'The Wizard' proves to be as brilliant at leading an invasion of an alien planet as he is in tinkering around in his New Jersey laboratory.

The message of *Edison's conquest of Mars* must have been clear to those who read it as a *New York Evening Journal* serial in early 1898. Sensationalist news about a possible attack on the United States by Spain or about American naval preparations to carry the war to the enemy preceded each day's new instalment. The departure of Edison's war fleet came in the 15 January issue as an instalment entitled 'To Conquer Another World'. On the front page of this issue, under a giant 'EXTRA', ran a banner headline: 'MAINE MAY SAIL FOR HAVANA AT ANY MOMENT'.

At first, the sheer numbers of Martian spaceships defending their home world stalemate the superweapons of the humans. Unfazed, Edison speedily devises a means to annihilate their whole civilisation by flooding the planet. Leading a raiding party to the fortified building that controls the main floodgates, Edison is not even stymied by the alien technology. 'Don't touch anything,' he shouts, 'until we have found the right lever':

But to find that seemed to most of us now utterly beyond the power of man.

It was at this critical moment that the wonderful depth and reach of Mr Edison's mechanical genius displayed itself. He stepped back, ran his eyes quickly over the immense mass of wheels, handles, bolts, bars and levers, paused for an instant, as if making up his mind, then said decidedly, 'There it is ... ' (p. 157).

Compared to this mythic Edison, the technological supermen who single-handedly achieve global peace in many other American future-war novels are neighbourhood handymen. *Edison's conquest of Mars* extrapolates into gigantic fantasy the boundless optimism and self-aggrandisement characteristic of the bumptious upstart American empire in 1898. In place of Wells's sombre reflections on the limits of ethnocentrism and anthropocentrism appears a pep rally for American nationalism. Well's warnings to industrial society are transformed into mindless glorification of the cults of progress, empire, individualism, and technology. The sense of a world plunging into the arms race that may lead to wars of extinction yields to cheerleading for superweapons and hurrahs for the planetary annihilation of intelligent life.

Of course this genocidal war takes place against an alien species on another planet, and Edison's conquest of Mars does envision a league of united nations fighting against these aliens rather than each other. But the rapturous descriptions of victorious combat, with atomic disintegrators blasting enemies out of existence and an American conqueror unleashing total war, appeared within a particular historical context. The nation was whipping itself up into a war fever, convincing itself that its manifest destiny was not merely continental, but global. Within two months of the final instalment of Edison's conquest of Mars, the United States would begin its conflict with Spain for imperial possessions in the Caribbean and Pacific.

While apologetics for the genocide of non-white peoples is merely a major subtext of Edison's conquest of Mars, it was the main theme of many other works of American science fiction. Whereas The great war syndicate was typical of the fiction that imagined wars against other white people, who were customarily vanquished by a mere harmless display of Americas superweapons, no such mercy was meted out to non-whites. Many of the future-war novels and stories projected as a precondition for perpetual peace and prosperity the utter extermination of the Black, Red, or Yellow race. 'Yellow Peril' literature was especially ferocious.

For example, Jack London's 1910 short story 'The Unparalleled Invasion' predicts that in 1975, when the world seems doomed to be overrun by hordes of Chinese, it is saved by a secret weapon developed by an American scientist. Fleets of airships shower China with 'missiles' loaded with 'every virulent form of infectious death', exterminating the entire Chinese population with 'bacteria, and germs, and microbes, and bacilli, cultured in the laboratories of the West'. This is, as London so aptly says, 'ultra modern war, twentieth-century war, the war of the scientist and the laboratory'. Once the Yellow Peril is entirely expunged – 'All survivors were put to death wherever found' – the world becomes a virtual utopia for the victorious forces of progress, led by America.

Millions of young Americans in their formative years were avidly devouring such science fiction. For example, 'The unparalleled invasion' was published in McClure's, a magazine whose subscribers included a young Missouri farmer named Harry S. Truman. As he wrote to his sweetheart Bess in 1913, 'I suppose I'll have to renew my subscription to McClure's now so I won't miss a number.'[5] In 1910, the very year that London's story appeared, Truman was profoundly impressed by another, earlier, version of airships fighting the final dreadful war to end all wars and thus bringing about a prosperous, unified world.

Indeed, he was so inspired by this science fiction poem that he carefully copied down ten lines from it and placed them in his wallet. The lines depict ultimate aerial superweapons of the future, waging a terrible climactic war in the skies:

> ... there rain'd a ghastly dew
> From the nations' airy navies grappling in the central blue ...

The horrors of this scientific warfare bring about universal peace and world government:

> ... the war-drum throbb'd no longer, and the battle-flags were furl'd
> In the Parliament of man, the Federation of the world.

In July 1945, Harry Truman, believing that he was about to gain control over the ultimate aerial superweapon, pulled that now-faded slip of paper from his wallet, where he had been carrying it for thirty-five years, and recited those lines from Tennyson's 'Locksley Hall' to a reporter (Smith, p. 286).

As I have argued in more detail elsewhere, Truman's decision to explode atomic bombs on the cities of Hiroshima and Nagasaki was evidently influenced by his belief that this demonstration of the ultimate superweapon might indeed bring an end to war.[6] If so, his thinking was typical of millions of Americans of his generation, who had grown up in a cultural matrix bubbling with fantasies of ultimate weapons. These fantasies were to shape the nation's conceptions of nuclear weapons and responses to them, decades before they materialised.

The situation in which the President saw himself in August 1945 is forecast by the first novel to imagine radioactivity used as a weapon of war: Roy Norton's 1907 The vanishing fleets, which was serialised in the Associated Sunday Magazines, a Sunday insert carried by most leading American newspapers (the Parade of its day). Japan launches a sneak attack. But American scientists invent 'the greatest engine of war that science has ever known' (p. 223), giant 'radioplanes' powered by radioactivity and capable of sweeping off the seas entire fleets of enemy warships. The President, 'his Americanism exceeded only by his humanitarianism' (p. 237), decides that his solemn duty to humanity is to use this weapon in war – in order to end war. He explains why secrecy is imperative: 'If our secret becomes known', the Japanese might not continue the war, thereby depriving the US of the opportunity to actually use this 'most deadly machine ever conceived ... thereby ending wars for all time'. 'Let us bear with fortitude whatever reproaches may be heaped upon us, for we are the instruments of God', he declares (p. 237). After American fliers win 'the last great battle in history', the President announces: 'The United States, having faith in the Anglo-Saxon race as ... the most peaceful and conservative, has formed an ... alliance with Great Britain' (p. 341). Thus comes the end of the war. The fantasy of *The great war syndicate* is here updated to incorporate the airplane and radioactivity. Indeed, American-Anglo hegemony and perpetual peace are guaranteed by the eternal American monopoly on the superweapon produced in secret by American ingenuity and merging air power with radioactivity.

The first truly nuclear weapon of war appeared in Godfrey Hollis's 1908 novel, *The man who ended war*. An American scientific mastermind invents a focused beam of 'radio-active waves' which instantly disintegrates the atoms of all metals into subatomic particles. When the big powers fail to comply with his ultimatum demanding immediate universal disarmament, he begins annihilating their fleets with his radioactive beam weapon. The nations capitulate and disarm. 'The man who stopped all war' then destroys his machine, his plans, and himself – so that no-one will obtain the 'secret' of the weapon and the world will therefore be permanently at peace. This characteristically American fantasy presents a striking contrast to H. G. Wells's 1913-14 novel *The world set free*, which imagines 'atomic bombs' not as peacemakers but as the instruments of global armageddon. Unlike Wells, who was to recognise that the scientific knowledge required to produce atomic energy or weapons could never be kept private or monopolised, *The man who ended war* promulgates the myth of the atomic 'secret', which would have a critical influence on American politics and culture beginning, as we shall see, in 1940 and extending through the Rosenberg case and beyond.

The American mode of atomic fantasy evolved further in *The man who rocked the earth*, by Arthur Train and Robert Wood, which was serialised in 1914-15 by the *Saturday Evening Post*, another magazine whose fiction was read eagerly by young Truman. It opens with the World War stalemated, as a torrent of innovative weapons merely enlarges the scale of the slaughter. Then appears an American scientific wizard who calls himself 'PAX'. PAX's ultimate weapon is a radioactive beam which can annihilate mountain ranges or armies. He fires this atomic weapon from an airship powered by 'atomic energy' (p. 100) generated by uranium forced into rapid disintegration. His atomic attacks produce scenes interchangeable with descriptions recorded by survivors of Hiroshima, including detailed accounts of death from radiation sickness (pp. 68, 134-5). Armed with atomic weapons, PAX declares that that 'either war or the human race must pass away forever' (p. 142). In the fantasy, of course, it is war that is doomed. Confronted by the peacemaker's atomic threats, the nations destroy their arsenals, abolish armies, and form a world government to ensure perpetual peace.

Atomic energy and weapons remained a popular subject of fiction through 1940. Science, politics, and the mass media were not too far behind. By the end of 1939, World War II had begun in Europe and physicists in Germany, Great Britain, the United States, the Soviet Union, Japan and other nations were working on atomic energy. That year, scientists published almost a hundred articles on nuclear fission. By 1940, American newspapers and magazines – from *Popular mechanics* to *Time* and *Newsweek* – were thrilling their readers with fantasies about the wonders to come from splitting the atom.[7] The public was told that the nuclear chain reaction needed for atomic energy, and possibly even atomic bombs, now depended mainly on developing practical means for producing significant quantities of the unstable isotope Uranium-235.

Simultaneously, a serialised science fiction novel read by millions of Americans developed both the doctrine of US global supremacy through nuclear weapons and a proposal for institutionalising this hegemony later to be presented as the Baruch Plan. This was *Lightning in the night*, which ran in weekly instalments during the pivotal months of August to November 1940 in *Liberty*, one of America's top three magazines.[8]

The action begins five years in the future, after Germany and its allies have conquered Britain and France. Japan and the Soviet Union carry out a sneak attack on Hawaii. Fleets of Soviet, Japanese and Nazi bombers devastate American cities. Hordes of Reds, Japanese, Mexicans and Germans invade on three fronts, inflicting on an unprepared United States the 'macabre nightmare of modern warfare' (19 October instalment).

The Nazis now demand a meeting with the American President. Hitler begins by outlining the theory of atomic energy and summarising the history of atomic research. The Nazi leader recalls that 'by the year 1939 the physicists of the Reich, of Denmark, and of America were frantically at work attempting to free and harness atomic energy' (9 November).

'The secret of world mastery', Hitler continues, of course would go to the nation that 'first could produce great quantities of pure U-235', the uranium isotope sufficiently unstable to sustain an explosive chain reaction. The Reich, he announces, has discovered this 'key to atomic energy', and has begun production of pure U-235, with its 'power to blow entire cities off the face of the earth'. 'Within one month, that devastating power can be unleashed against your cities', Hitler boasts, so 'further resistance becomes utterly foolhardy'. After this 'month of grace' he will unleash 'literal and total annihilation'.

The President concedes that a nation without atomic weapons would be helpless to resist a nation with them. And so this 9 November instalment concludes with the United States apparently ready to capitulate to the Nazis, forcing the millions of readers of *Liberty* in 1940 to confront a picture of their future if America were to lose a nuclear arms race with the Nazis.

But the final instalment reveals that the United States had secretly been conducting a crash programme to develop its own atomic weapons. Great cyclotrons and other marvellous equipment had been put at the disposal of the nation's 'most ingenious and resourceful scientists'. The President expounds America's vision of atomic energy, a vision like that of 1940 articles in *Harpers, Collier's* and the *Saturday Evening Post*,[9] a fantasy that would reappear after Hiroshima and Nagasaki under the slogan 'Atoms for Peace'. The story goes on:

We saw its potentialities as a weapon of war, but even more clearly as an unlimited source of heat, of light, of power for peaceful production and transportation - all this at an almost incredibly low cost. ... poverty would vanish from the earth. So would war itself; for the economic causes of war would no longer exist ... that Utopia, if you like – was what we envisioned: a free world of free peoples living in peace and prosperity, facing a future of unlimited richness. (16 November.)

Although the Nazis now have 'the secret' of the ultimate weapon, they are too late. At this very moment, '50,000 feet over the Atlantic, great United States stratospheric bombers', specially modified for intercontinental flight and carrying atomic bombs, are 'heading for every great city in Germany'.

So now the President turns the tables and presents the American proposal for peace and atomic disarmament. Its terms will later prove to be identical with those of the only proposal for nuclear disarmament ever actually offered by the United States, the Baruch Plan of 1946: a body dominated by American scientists would control both the world's supply of uranium and the licensing of nuclear energy facilities to other nations; the United States would maintain its monopoly on nuclear weaponry until some unspecified date in the future when it would be turned over to an international agency. '"We have no wish," the President said, "to assume for long the task of policing the world. When the world is restored and made free, a Council of Nations shall take over the task we inaugurate now."'

Germany surrenders. Japan and the Soviet Union capitulate a day later, after an American bomber drops one nuclear bomb on 'the deserted Russian steppes'. The American atomic bomb has brought the blessed Pax Americana to the planet.

The nation's motives for developing atomic weapons in the novel are precisely those of the Manhattan Project: to forestall Nazi use and to achieve a lasting peace. Like those who later were to make the decision to use atomic bombs, Lightning in the night assumes that the first nation to deploy atomic weapons wins and ends the arms race. The fictional President, like his actual counterpart in 1945-6, fails to realise that this might just accelerate the race for nuclear superweapons and open an epoch ever more dominated by them.

In late 1940 the US government began to wrap atomic research in a shroud of secrecy. Even the secrecy itself was secret. Newspapers, magazines, news services and radio broadcasters were soon ordered not to mention atomic power, cyclotrons, betatrons, fission, uranium, deuterium or thorium. Army Intelligence later even attempted to block access to back issues containing popular articles on atomic energy in order 'to wipe the whole subject from memory'.[10]

Thus ended the free exchange of knowledge that had symbolised the international community of science, to be replaced by one of the more grotesque features of our times: the attempt to transform vital parts of human knowledge into secrets whose existence is to be classified by the state and kept inviolate by the secret police. When the seventeenth-century church authorities forced Galileo to stop promulgating Copernicanism, at least they claimed they were prohibiting the dissemination of *false* belief. The US government, however, was consciously outlawing scientific truth about the fundamental nature of the universe. As early as 1941, John J. O'Neill, president of the National Association of Science Writers, charged that this censorship on atomic research amounted to 'a totalitarian revolution against the American people'. Pointing to the devastating potential of an atomic bomb utilising Uranium-235, O'Neill asked a fateful question: 'Can we trust our politicians and war makers with a weapon like that?'[11]

So for the crucial years 1941-5, public discussion of atomic weapons was banished from the nation that claimed to be leading the fight for democracy and freedom, while a handful of men secretly spent two billion dollars of public funds to develop these weapons. During these years, the only Americans exposed to public thoughts about atomic weapons were readers of science fiction. At first the government disregarded atomic weapons in science fiction, which was considered a subliterary ghetto inhabited by kids and kooks. But then it became alarmed by every science fiction atomic bomb. So even though there already had been widespread public discussion of the two main technical problems of atomic bombs – isolating sufficient quantities of the fissionable isotope Uranium-235 from Uranium-238 and achieving critical mass suddenly enough to set off an explosive chain reaction – government censorship clamped down on the imagination of fiction writers. When Philip Wylie submitted his novella *The paradise crater* in early 1945, he was placed under house arrest; an Army Intelligence major informed him that he was personally prepared to kill the author if necessary to keep the weapon secret (Moskowitz, pp. 292-3). Even science fiction comic strips were censored. On 14 April, the McClure Newspaper Syndicate ran strip one of 'Atom Smasher', a new Superman series pitting America's favourite superhero against a cyclotron. The Office of Censorship promptly forced the running of a substitute series (in which Superman played a baseball game singlehanded).[12]

The only citizens left to contemplate the consequences of atomic weapons were the readers of *Astounding science-fiction*, which stirred up a major security investigation when it published Cleve Cartmill's 'Deadline' in the March 1944 issue.[13] The story suggested that the anti-fascist Allies would never use an atomic bomb because they realise that nuclear weapons could eventually threaten the existence of 'the entire race', leaving nothing but 'dust and rocks'. This was not the view of the men who did decide to drop the bombs.

The decision to explode atomic bombs on two Japanese cities, one of the most fateful in history, has been the subject of one of the greatest historical debates. Today few serious historians accept the original public position, still widely shared, that the atomic bombs significantly shortened the war, eliminated the need to invade Japan, and thus saved hundreds of thousands of American lives. The debate has tended instead to focus on the motives of the decision-makers, principally President Truman himself. Since he was aware of the Japanese peace feelers and had been guaranteed that a huge Soviet army was poised for an all-out assault on the main surviving Japanese forces, to be launched between 8 and 15 August, and since he believed that the Soviet attack would end the war ('Fini Japs when that comes about,' he secretly recorded),[14] did he have other motives?

The debate has tended to polarise views along an axis defined by two opposing positions. One suggests that Truman and his advisers intended the atomic bombs on Japan as what many believe they turned out to be – the opening shots in the cold war against the Soviet Union. The other argues that the decision was made by default, through bureaucratic inertia and myopia, that there was just never any doubt that the bomb would be used. But the President may have had another incentive as well. For Harry Truman and his key advisers evidently believed that destroying cities with atomic bombs might bring an end to war itself.

Defending his part in the decision to use atomic weapons, Secretary of War Stimson explained that he was persuaded 'that the bomb must be used' because 'that was the only way to awaken the world to the necessity of abolishing war altogether. No technological demonstration ... could take the place of the actual use with its horrible results' (Sherwin, p. 44). Edward Teller argued that the bomb was so horrible that it might actually help 'get rid of wars', so '[f]or this purpose actual combat-use might even be the best thing' (Szilard, p. 209). And so President Truman re-enacted the role of the president in *The vanishing fleets*, the novel that first imagined the United States wielding a weapon based on radioactivity, who decides that only by using this 'most deadly machine ever conceived' can he end 'wars for all time'.

It was on his way to Potsdam that President Truman recited those lines from Tennyson prophesying that 'ghastly' combat waged by airships would still 'the war-drum' and bring about 'the Federation of the world'. Given details of the Alamogordo test, Truman recorded in his diary his thoughts about the atomic bomb: 'It seems to be the most terrible thing ever discovered, but it can be made the most useful.' When he learned of the devastation of Hiroshima, he proclaimed: 'This is the greatest thing in history.' Echoing the President in *The vanishing fleets*, who declared that America must 'bear with fortitude whatever reproaches may be heaped upon us, for we are the instruments of God', President Truman called the atomic bomb 'an awful responsibility which has come to us', and told the nation: 'We thank God that it has come to us, instead of to our enemies; and we pray that He may guide us to use it in His ways and for His purposes.'[15] Did the President believe that he now possessed what Americans had long fantasised, the absolute weapon that would achieve perpetual peace under the global hegemony of the United States?

Within months of Hiroshima came the Baruch Plan, which some see as merely 'an ultimatum' to the Soviets 'to forswear nuclear weapons or be destroyed' (Herken, p. 171). But the Baruch Plan – virtually identical to the atomic ultimatum issued by the President in the 1940 novel *Lightning in the night* – may be comprehended more deeply as an expression of the treacherous mirage of the ultimate weapon endemic in American culture.

On 14 June 1946, the United States, represented by Bernard Baruch, dramatically announced that the only way the nations of the world could choose 'World Peace' rather than 'World Destruction' would be by submitting to a new international agency, not subject to veto, to be staffed by personnel 'with proven competence' in atomic science (in other words, by those who had created America's atomic bombs), and empowered to evoke the 'immediate, swift, and sure punishment' of any nation violating its orders. They must do so, Baruch declared, because America is now in possession of 'the absolute weapon'. No nation would be allowed to have nuclear weapons except for the United States, which would keep producing them until it had 'a guarantee of safety, not only against the offenders in the atomic area but against the illegal users of other weapons – bacteriological, biological, gas – perhaps – why not? – against war itself.'[16] Here is the culmination of that great fantasy, from the motor bomb of *The great war syndicate* in 1889 through the atomic bomb of *Lightning in the night* in 1940: by wielding the ultimate weapon, the United States forces the world to end war for all time.

The future didn't work out quite the way it appeared in the fantasy. The atomic bomb turned out to be neither the ultimate weapon nor a guarantee of peace for either the world or the United States, which has been at war more continually since dropping the bomb than at any previous time in its history. The government of the United States has kept accelerating the race for the true ultimate – and of course purely defensive – weapon, chasing faster and faster after this hallucinatory mechanical rabbit, leading the human species closer and closer to the brink of extinction.

But if the cult of the superweapon sometimes seems like an irresistible force, within American culture it has always faced an immovable object in the form of a deep desire for peace not contingent upon militarism and military hardware. I do not have space in this essay to explore the magnificent cultural manifestations of this nemesis of the quick technological fix, but its presence in the popular will has surfaced again and again in American history, as evidenced by the mighty movement against the Vietnam War. How has the battle between these two forces shaped the American people's views of the race for nuclear supremacy?

Only once in history has any major portion of the people of the United States had an opportunity to register their views on the nuclear arms race at the ballot box. The result was a stunning mandate.

In 1982, responding to the Reagan Administration's frantic escalation of the arms race and the massive European protest against it, there arose a tremendous American movement calling for a bilateral, verifiable freeze on the production, testing and deployment of more nuclear weapons. Despite formidable legal obstacles, the freeze organisers managed to get the issue directly on the ballot in cities, counties and states across the country. Hundreds of towns and cities backed the freeze by vote of the populace or city council. In the early fall of 1982, the freeze won in Alaska and Wisconsin, where it enjoyed a better than three-to-one landslide. On national election day that November, the electorate in nine states had an opportunity to vote on the issue. The freeze won in eight states and several major cities which together included a quarter of the country's population. Its only defeat, by a tiny margin, was in sparsely-populated Arizona, the one state where it has ever lost. It carried California despite lavishly financed opposition from the aerospace industry and the Reagan Administration, and it passed by two-or three-to-one margins in Massachusetts, Montana, North Dakota, Rhode Island, Michigan, Oregon and New

Jersey. By February 1983, the state legislatures of Maine, Connecticut, Minnesota, Oregon, Massachusetts, Vermont, Kansas, New York, Wisconsin and Iowa had called upon Congress to support the nuclear freeze.

Ronald Reagan's counter-response to this popular groundswell against nuclear weapons shows how closely attuned the President's mind was with the cultural forces I have been sketching in this essay. On 23 March 1983, in a television address to the American people, he announced that the way to escape from the nuclear doomsday machine that we had built to defend ourselves was to build a new ultimate defensive superweapon, which would make the world eternally safe for democracy. The climax was his famous declaration of a new course for the future: '... I call upon the scientific community in our country, those who gave us nuclear weapons, to turn their great talents now to the cause of mankind and world peace, to give us the means of rendering these nuclear weapons impotent and obsolete.'

The miraculous beam and other antimissile weapons of Ronald Reagan's Star Wars fantasy, designed to make America invulnerable and thus to secure eternal peace, had long been familiar features of American science fiction, dating back even before Edison's disintegrator beam in *Edison's conquest of Mars*. By the late 1930s, they had become standard features in comic books and Hollywood movies.

Take, as an especially revealing example, the 1940 Warner Bros.' film *Murder in the air*, featuring 'a new super-weapon': the 'inertia projector', a ray machine destined to 'make America invincible' and thus to become 'the greatest force for world peace ever discovered'. Some dastardly foreign spies steal the plans for this ultimate defensive superweapon, and are making their escape in an aeroplane. There is only one hope left for the world: heroic Secret Service agent Brass Bancroft, who uses the miraculous beam to blast the spies' plane out of the skies. the young actor who thus saved America with its ultimate superweapon for peace was named Ronald Reagan.

If we comprehend the potency of these fantasies in American culture we can understand some beliefs and behaviour of American leaders that may otherwise seem rather baffling: dropping atomic bombs on cities in the belief that this might establish the United States as the bringer of peace to the planet; proposing that all the other nations of the world, including the Soviet Union, accept a US monopoly on nuclear weapons until such time as a US-dominated international agency with almost unrestricted power would declare that the day had arrived for nuclear disarmament; militarising space as the way to ensure peace.

Advocates of Star Wars – the latest technological fix that is supposed to make the world eternally safe for democracy – look upon the people who seek to get rid of our superweapons before they destroy us as mushy-headed dreamers with no sense of practical reality. The practical men are those who are building a new superweapon, purely defensive of course, that can make us more secure by vanquishing in combat the previous generation of ultimate weapons. According to this vision, it is far more practical and realistic to try to shoot down ten thousand nuclear warheads after they are launched than to try to dismantle them before they are launched. So, once again, the human species may be forced to confront the disparity between the fantasy of an ultimate weapon in American science fiction and its dreadful reality.

Notes

Parts of this essay are adapted from the author's *War stars: the superweapon and the American imagination* (Oxford University Press: New York, 1988).

1 The eighteenth-century American versions of the ultimate purely defensive superweapon, including the submarine and the airship, are explored in my *War stars: the superweapon and the American imagination*.

2 The ground-breaking study of this genre, and still the leading work on the British and European literature, is I. F. Clarke's *Voices prophesying war: 1763-1984*.

3 This relationship was pointed out by Clarke, pp. 98-9.

4 *Edison's conquest of Mars* was serialised in the *New York Evening Journal*, 12 January-10 February 1898. The edition cited here is a reprint, with an informative introduction by A. Langley Searles. for a discussion of Edison as high priest of the cult of the superweapon and his role in establishing the military-industrial complex, see 'Thomas Edison and the industrialization of war', Chapter 3 of *War stars*.

5 This note to Bess and other evidence of young Truman's insatiable appetite for the fiction in *McClure's*, the *Saturday Evening Post*, and other magazines can be found in Ferrell, *Dear Bess*, pp. 78-9, 126, 157, 161.

6 See *War stars*, Chapter 9, 'Atomic decision'.

7 See, for example: A. G. Ingalls, 'Incomparable promise or awful threat', *Scientific American*, 161, July 1939, p. 2; 'Vast power source in atomic energy opened by science', *New York Times*, 5 May 1940, p. 1; 'Vast atomic power possible if enough uranium is isolated', *Newsweek*, 15, 13 May 1940, p. 41; 'Atomic power in ten years?, *Time*, 35, 27 May 1940, p. 44; 'Harnessing the atom', *Popular mechanics*, 74, September 1940, pp. 402-5. Also see Note 9.

8 According to *Liberty* 24 August, the novel was written by Fred Allhoff with 'the advice and counsel of General Robert Lee Bullard, Rear Admiral Yates Stirling, George E. Sokolosky, and many others'. I am currently tracing direct connections between the men who prepared this novel and atomic decision-making.

9 John J. O'Neill, 'Enter atomic power', *Harpers*, 181, June 1940, pp. 1-10; R. M. Langer,

168

'Fast new world', Collier's, 106, 6 July 1940, pp. 18-19, 54-5; William L. Laurence, 'The atom gives up', Saturday Evening Post, 213, 7 September 1940, pp. 12-13, 60-3. Also see Note 7.

10 John W. Campbell, Jr, The atomic story (New York, 1947), p. 123; Leslie R. Groves, Now it can be told: the story of the Manhattan project (New York, 1962), pp. 146-8, 325; Paul Brians, Nuclear holocausts (Kent, Ohio, 1987), p. 7; Anthony Cave Brown and Charles B. MacDonald (eds.), The secret history of the atomic bomb (New York, 1977), pp. 203-9; 'Drop that Post!', Saturday Evening Post, 8 September 1945, p. 4.

11 'Writer charges US with curb on science', New York Times, 14 August 1941.

12 Newsweek, 20 August 1945, p. 68.

13 Albert I. Berger, 'The Astounding investigation: the Manhattan project's confrontation with science fiction', Analog, September 1984, pp. 125-37.

14 Robert H. Ferrell (ed.), Off the record: the private papers of Harry S. Truman (Harper & Row: New York, 1980), p. 53.

15 Ferrell, Off the record, p. 56; Truman, Year of decision, p. 421; radio report to the American people, 9 August 1945, Public papers of the presidents of the United States: Harry S. Truman (US Government Printing Office: Washington D. C., 1961), p. 213.

16 All citations are to the text of The international control of atomic energy: growth of a policy (US Government Printing Office: Washington, D.C., n.d.).

References

Allhoff, Fred, Lightning in the night, Liberty, 24, 31 August; 7, 14, 21, 28 September; 5, 12, 19, 26 October; 2, 9, 16 November 1940.

Cartmill, Cleve 'Deadline', Astounding science-fiction, March 1944.

Clarke, I. F., Voices prophesying war: 1763-1984 (London and New York, 1966).

Ferrell, Robert H. (ed.), Dear Bess: the letters from Harry to Bess Truman, 1910-1959 (New York, 1983).

—, Off the record: the private papers of Harry S. Truman (New York, 1980).

Franklin, H. Bruce, War stars: the superweapon and the American imagination (New York, 1988).

Herken, Gregg, The winning weapon: the atomic bomb in the cold war 1945-50 (New York, 1982).

Hollis, Godfrey, The man who ended war (Boston, 1908).

London, Jack, 'The unparalleled invasion', McClure's magazine, July 1910.

Moskowitz, Sam, Explorers of the infinite (Cleveland, 1963).

Norton,Roy, The vanishing fleets (New York, 1908).

Serviss, Garrett P., Edison's conquest of Mars, ed. A. Langley Searles (Carcosa House: Los Angeles, 1947).

Sherwin, Martin J., 'Old issues in new editions', Bulletin of the atomic scientists, 41, December 1985, p. 44.

Smith, A. Merriman, Thank you, Mr President (New York, 1946).

Stockton, Frank, The great war syndicate (New York, 1889).

Szilard, Leo, Leo Szilard: his version of the facts, ed. Spencer R. Weart and Gertrud Weiss Szilard (Cambridge, Mass., 1978).

Train, Arthur and Robert Wood, The man who rocked the earth (Garden City, NY, 1915).

Truman, Harry S., Year of decision (Garden City, NY, 1955).

Wells, H. G., The war of the worlds in The time machine and the war of the worlds, ed. Frank D. McConnell (New York, 1977).

11

Normative fiction

Martha A. Bartter

Few doubt that fiction has a normative effect on society; we assume that fiction and culture interconnect. (The mere existence of this volume evidences that assumption.) Even fewer agree on the process by which this interconnection takes place, or its locus. Most of us who write on the topic deal with such uncertainties by ignoring them. We tacitly assume that interconnections are either too obvious to need explanation or too complicated to explain, and, in either event, that what we do not say cannot be held against us. The apparent complications usually arise during attempts to describe what fiction 'is'. Let us instead discuss what literature *does*; or, to speak more accurately, what *we do* with literature.

We can begin by looking at specific problems. One such problem comes from the popular belief that the term 'normative fiction' means that fiction can somehow make people behave in ways they otherwise would not. Such a belief in the power of fiction often forms either the tacit justification for propaganda, or the reverse, the explicit justification for censorship. We, on the other hand, claim only that fiction can represent possibilities for action to a large number of people in such a way that they can more clearly perceive possible choices and the various socio-cultural sanctions attached to those choices. The very act of considering choices irrevocably alters our assumptions about ways we may act, and since actions derive from assumptions (in the sense that both doing and choosing not to do must be considered actions), fiction can indeed endanger the *status quo*. The censors are right – for the wrong reasons.

These considerations demonstrate the inherent ambiguity of the term 'normative fiction'. On the one hand, every fiction arises from a particular culture in a particular time and place; it demonstrates to its hearers/readers a tacit consensus regarding cultural norms. On the other hand, and *at the same time*, it can introduce to its readers possibilities that they previously did not know or had not considered, and make these possibilities vividly 'real' by fictional devices such as plot, character, setting, etc. Through a 'willing suspension of disbelief', readers conduct socio-cultural *gedankenexperimente*:[1] they test how such ideas might work out in reality and what effects they might produce, and consider the possibility of a new consensus. Through creatively imagining such new possibilities, and contrasting the results to our familiar world, we may begin to identify assumptions underlying our current culture; we may choose some different assumptions to live from. Since both definitions of 'normative fiction' – that which reinforces and that which revises the *status quo* – require a reader, we shall discuss what 'fiction' does while keeping in mind that it is a process that humans *do*.

Critics have long tried to define 'literature', usually hoping to select objective criteria that will sort the 'worthwhile' from the textual 'everything else' without excluding anything they wish to include.[2] This provides an engrossing task for the critic, but not a harmless one. While focusing upon 'literature' we have ignored much 'text' with normative influence on all of us, critics included. Moreover, in order to seek such a definition we must assume that literary standards exist as discoverable, extra-textual *objects*. By making this assumption, we tacitly eliminate ourselves from the evaluation.[3] By omitting ourselves, denying our own influence as well as most of the influences acting upon us, we reduce the problem to manageable size at the price of falsifying it. Like fiction, criticism is a process that humans do; and the doing necessarily affects us as writer and reader.

Let us, for the sake of argument, redefine both 'text' and 'reader'. Let us consider as 'text' any communication preserved in repeatable form, oral (if recorded or replayed, as in the theatre) or written; and 'reader' as anyone who assimilates and responds to such a text.[4] Thus, an EXIT sign constitutes 'text'; going out of the exit (or choosing not to) constitutes a response; and following a 'This Way to the Egress' sign may constitute a response we designate a 'misreading', one based on assumptions drawn from previous experience with (apparently) similar text.[5] We have thus defined 'text' as artefact, 'thing made', and 'reader' as human dealing with that artefact. In order to construct a workable metafictional system, a fiction for and about fiction, we also need to make two other points about human behaviour: first, that we humans *assume*, that we cannot *not-assume*, and that we always act from these assumptions, most of which we are not consciously aware of; and second, that we *transact* with ourselves and with our environment.

The term *transacting* requires its own definition.[6] We use it in preference to 'interact' or 'react' because the 'trans-' reminds us that all actions performed by humans also operate upon the operator. The necessity of such a reminder becomes obvious when we note that our primary cultural tool, our language, makes that two-way relationship hard to remember. In a vast majority of our utterances we speak as though an (unchanging) subject *does something* to an object. We thus model one-way causality in our speech, whether we 'believe' the world works that way or not.[7] (We speak of 'rereading' a book, for instance, as though the 'I' who reads 'again' is the same 'I' who read before.) This tacit assumption affects our dealings with ourselves, with text, and with the 'others' who constitute our environment, from whom we have assimilated our culture.

Rigorously to account for the normative process of fiction requires dealing with multiple transactings, none of them one-way. Although literary theories began as frankly normative (Plato, for instance, refused poets admission into his *Republic* lest their fictions pervert his people), later critics reduced the interaction of text and reader. Mimesis defined text as a (limited) imitation of an objective 'reality'; romantic theory valued literature for its ability to inspire appropriate emotions in the reader; the New Criticism set out evaluative criteria applicable to the text alone, eliminating readers, authors and context from consideration. Gradually such reductionism has given way to a number of critical theories, many of them more willing to admit limited transactions of reader and text.[8] But no contemporary theory of criticism fully accounts for the normative power of fiction; indeed a theory capable of doing so threatens to become a mass of uncontrolled variables. The critic must consider the following transactions:

reader with self
reader with text
writer with self
writer with text
writer/reader with society.

As critics, we must locate ourselves and the writer/reader in historical time and in cultural experience. Nor can we consider our criticism as 'metatext'; we must include it in the transaction. We must see ourselves as critical writers/readers, and all writers/readers as *de facto* critics. Our initial observation – that we humans do transact with literature in normative ways – logically compels us to assume that we actually do all this. Now we need to find ways to talk about it.

I

Humans make sensory contact with their environment. This contact is not a simple, one-way process of 'gathering information', however. It always involves transacting, changing both the 'actor' (the self) and the 'acted upon' (the environment). For instance, as I write this chapter, both I and the projected work change. the act of writing (including gathering information) has revised some of my own assumptions about atomic war, which naturally show up in the text; it has changed the way I read nuclear war stories, and made me more aware of the difference I find in rereading a story after writing about it; it has changed the way I organise and emphasise items in the chapter as I work on it. My doing the work, my process of learning, uncovering and checking assumptions, of organising them and writing them down, changes the work, the way I work, and the pattern of assumptions that I work from at the same time. This change is inevitable and irreversible.

The process is simultaneously personal and cultural. I transact not only with my external environment, but also with my internal one: my feelings, my memories, the kinds of 'sense' I have made of my sensory experience. Since daily living gives us all more experience than we can handle, we 'make sense' of it by selecting the details we pay attention to and organising them into plots, many of them borrowed from fiction. This process both depends upon and alters the pattern of assumptions from which we act. When I change my assumptions, I find myself doing things differently, and doing different things. When I act from these changes, others necessarily act – transact – differently with me. My change cannot remain mine alone; nor can I determine where the effect of the new transacting disappears.

We encounter a major problem when we try to discuss the most important of the assumptions we live by: we usually don't know what they are. We construct our assumptions on a pre-verbal, sensory-motor level, through contacting our environment, though we can express them only in language.[9] Our most powerful assumptions remain unconscious and unnoticed; they seem to us simply to reflect the way things 'really are'. But since what we do is the outward and visible sign of what we assume, we can disclose at least some of our assumptions by studying actions. To disclose what I assume, I must examine what I do; to explain what I do, I must enquire into what I assume; and to do differently, I must assume differently. This sounds like a closed circle, but in fact it is not, since the very act of disclosing assumptions opens them to change. And fiction is one of the our best vehicles for disclosing assumptions.

To identify an unconscious assumption, we can look at 'perfectly logical' actions that produce unexpected results. For example, a large part of the world currently operates from the logical assumption that nuclear devices, though admittedly dangerous, form our only defence against invasion, or worse. Given that assumption, any request to reduce our nuclear arsenal seems like a polite invitation to suicide, even though failing to do so leads to nuclear escalation, which reinforces our feelings of danger. But not everyone holds that nuclear devices provide defence, and the conversation between those who do and those who do not often degenerates into a political shouting match, or (worse yet), into apparent agreement where neither side really knows what the other side meant. Such 'agreements' rapidly deteriorate, with charges of bad faith and trickery. Only in fiction can we bring our assumptions into the open, and try other assumptions out without having to deal with the consequences in fact. Yet, by trying out these assumptions in fiction, we have in fact irrevocably altered our transactions with our socio-cultural environment as surely (though differently) as if we had put them into 'realtime' operation.

We can thus argue that a transaction of 'text', 'reader' and 'culture' takes place through the powerful but ambiguous consensus-building process of fiction; and that critics can properly study this process. To demonstrate this I shall examine a single genre, American science fiction; a single issue, nuclear war; and a single image; that of the nuclear scientist. Science fiction has established itself as the literature most awarely transacting with its readers, and the nuclear scientist symbolises both national salvation and world destruction. I shall show how this problematic image achieved cultural consensus, how that consensus transacted in an historical context, and how that culture and that history has subsequently transacted with the consensus-text.

II

In American fiction, the image of the research scientist is frequently conflated with that of the technologist, the 'lone inventor', first epitomised by Robert Fulton, and later by Thomas Alva Edison.[10] The 'lone inventor' is capable of meeting any danger; he has only to devise appropriate technology. It can be argued that the image of heroic scientist-as-lone-inventor was constructed to express the American fascination with scientific progress, while countering its older sibling from Frankenstein (1818). Mary Shelley portrays Dr Victor Frankenstein both as a scientist and as a misguided alchemist, a brilliant researcher who violates the laws of God and man, and whose reach far exceeds his grasp. American science fiction generally avoids theoretical science and stresses technology, often applied by attractive heroes whose secret weapons always work as they are supposed to, with no harmful side-effects. Later, as Superman, the lone inventor becomes the secret weapon, while remaining boyish, charming, and psychosexually safe (Bartter, 1988, pp. 1-3).

But as the hero conquers every fictional dilemma, writers face an authorial one: what threat, simple enough to be represented in the unsubtle prose of the scientific romance, would call forth the 'lone inventor's' full capability? As the rising star of the western world, America could believe herself worthy of attack by a foreign power, while such a threat tacitly validated her position in the world. A sneak attack makes marvellous plot material; countering such an attack requires a superweapon powerful enough to end such threats forever, leaving a 'pure' America as world peacemaker. Moreover, since the plot would focus on the weapon, the scientist-inventor could be safely ignored. Thus, the 'instantaneous motor-bomb' is the hero of Frank Stockton's The great war syndicate (1889). Controlled by the War Syndicate, a group of capitalists who have taken charge of a conflict between the United States and Great Britain (presumably on a cost-plus basis), scientists must be creating 'inventions and improvements in the art of war' (p. 17), but readers never see them. The motor-bomb does all the work and gets all the glory.

Roy Norton's The vanishing fleets (1908) also pays more attention to the invention than to the inventor. Since war with Japan seems inevitable, a young Englishman tries to convince Norma Roberts to marry him and flee the inevitable conflict. Instead, she vanishes with her eccentric inventor father just as war is declared. The American President attempts to coerce all nations into a world war in the name of peace, to justify his confiscation of their battle fleets using the airship that Roberts invents with Norma's help, and that Norma herself pilots. This book repeats three pernicious beliefs about technological warfare: first, that scientific discovery comes by lucky accident; second, that discoveries can be kept secret; and third, that the use of a superweapon to stop war forever is both practical and morally acceptable.

The scientist as Frankenstein surfaces briefly in Hollis Godfrey's *The man who ended war* (1908) in the person of John King, whose campaign against war leads him to sink ships of every nation and to kill nearly as many men as might have died had war actually been declared. King never offers to share his invention, a lethal radioactive ray, even with the US government; at the end of the book, he sinks his own ship before dying himself, taking his secret with him. But King is not the focus of the story; the book is about the invention, not the inventor. Science is personified by Dorothy Haldane and her brother Tom: wealthy, well-educated, competent amateurs who work unremittingly (and successfully) to disclose the identity of the destroyer of fleets. Although the emphasis throughout the book rests on stopping the 'Man', King's attempt to prevent (undeclared) war seems in the end to excuse the appalling loss of life he has caused.

These works celebrate a national confidence in technological progress, an optimism amounting to euphoria (Boyer, p. 271). Their superweapons feature the newly discovered, 'magical' element, radium; they also feature strong, attractive, scientifically trained young women, reflecting popular admiration for Marie S. Curie. This marks the first, and – with few exceptions – the last time science fiction gives positive roles to women as scientists, although an increased number of women were then taking scientific degrees at American universities.

As World War I rolled over Europe, the fictional scientist-inventor remained virtually invisible. In J. U. Giesy's *All for his country* (1914), the young inventor is intimidated by a corrupt Senator, vanishes with his superweapon, and must be ferreted out to save America from Japanese invasion. In *The man who rocked the earth* by Arthur Train and Robert Williams Wood (1915), the anonymous inventor of the Ray, with which he has stopped World War I, accidentally kills himself just as he is about to be discovered. Like the earlier works, these stories not only reiterate the belief that scientific discoveries can be kept secret; they also reinforce the image of the scientists as an asocial, eccentric but effective magician. They then place this image in a familiar scenario: an inevitable war won with superweapons so deadly that no-one could challenge America's right to impose *pax Americana* on the world. Fiction both invented and validated the 'war to end war'.

American soldiers entered World War I under that slogan. In fighting 'a war to end war', Americans tacitly assumed the right to impose peace by force on everyone *except ourselves*, and the United States Senate acted upon that assumption when they rejected the League of Nations treaty. Then, since the 'war to end war' failed to accomplish its task, while stimulating the development of ever-more-powerful weapons, we also assumed that the (inevitable) next war would be even worse – and that, in large measure, scientists and their inventions were to blame.

This shows up in a number of 'awful warning' stories published between the wars. In Pierrepont B. Noyes's *The pallid giant* (1927), the prehistoric Sra have a nuclear superweapon. Through their fear of their own weapon, they destroy themselves and their world as well as their 'enemies'. Noyes then informs his readers that German scientists are working on a similar weapon.

Atomic war stories in the science fiction magazines often showed the scientist as Frankenstein, or worse. In S. P. Meek's 'The red peril' (1929), a brilliant scientist's brain tumour causes him to coerce Russia into attacking the rest of the world. In Carl Spohr's 'The final war' (1932), a scientist drafted after the sneak attack invents an atomic weapon, hoping the threat of its existence will stop war. Instead, it gets used in combat, ending the war by virtually ending the world. Stories like John Taine's 'Seeds of life' (1931), Stephen G. Hale's 'The laughing death' (1931) and 'Worlds adrift' (1932), Isaac R. Nathanson's 'The world aflame' (1935), and Willard Hawkins's 'The dwindling sphere' (1940) variously portray the scientist as criminally careless, as uncaring, or – as in Spohr's 'the final war' and Robert A. Heinlein's 'Solution unsatisfactory' (1941) – as helpless to control the applications of atomic science.

Officially claiming to present 'Extravagant Fiction Today - Cold Fact Tomorrow!' Hugo Gernsback had in 1926 created a genre apparently featuring science, but actually featuring the technology derived from science. In 'Space operas' like E. E. 'Doc' Smith's *The skylark of space* (1928), the 'lone inventor' hero follows the romantic model that would become Superman in 1939. John Campbell's 'Uncertainty' (1936) shows this 'lone inventor' at war: a wealthy, handsome young genius-hero who serves in the galactic equivalent of the border patrol out of sheer altruism, and who saves the world from alien invasion by turning Heisenberg's probability theorem into a solid superweapon. Contrasted to the Frankenstein image of the scientist as world-wrecker, the Superman as living superweapon seemed perfectly safe.

The atomic bomb had been named by H. G. Wells in a scientific romance. The world set free (1914), in which a scientist plays an important (and misguided) role. We know that Leo Szilard read this novel; he has recorded how it influenced his understanding of nuclear war, and his determination to keep his work on nuclear energy from Nazi hands. In a very real sense, through Szilard, Wells designed the Manhattan Project.[11] One of its most important aspects was the application of assembly-line techniques to scientific research. By dividing the scientists into teams, each doing a small portion of the research, a high level of secrecy could be imposed on a discipline officially dedicated to the free exchange of information.

Many young scientists were eager to join the Project because it gave them a chance to do 'cutting edge' work while serving their country. Few argued against the stifling secrecy; even fewer felt they could properly direct how their work should be used.[12] That these assumptions are somewhat self-contradictory does not make them less powerful, merely less conscious. Scientists themselves read science fiction; many publicly admitted that such reading led them to their careers in science (Barron, pp. 63-4). Science fiction tacitly assumes that the role of scientist included that of alchemist as well; it seems that some Manhattan Project scientists were influenced by these assumptions.

In 'Solution unsatisfactory', Heinlein repeats the belief that scientists, unlike technicians, deal with things that man 'was not meant to know', and may be unequal to the task of using their own inventions. The scientist commits suicide when she finds that her discovery will be used as an atomic weapon, while the war (and the peace) is won by the 'practical' engineer. The disastrous result of the scientist's attempt to prevent another nuclear war in Theodore Sturgeon's 'Memorial' (1946) reflects the frustration of scientists who had tried to play a responsible role in determining the way the atomic bomb would be used in World War II through the Franck Report.[13] In contrast to the real world, however, fictional scientists are often shown as terribly, even terrifyingly effective; Raymond Jones's 'A stone and a spear' (1950) and Philip K. Dick's 'Jon's world' (1954) are merely two examples.[14]

Following Hiroshima and Nagasaki, popular admiration of nuclear scientists changed to suspicion. Not only did these scientists have secret knowledge, but they disagreed with each other about the uses to which that knowledge should be put. Worse yet, in the years immediately following World War II, many of them even proposed sharing 'atomic secrets' with the world. That most scientists agreed that 'atomic secrecy' was impossible (even without the intervention of spies) when the basic research had been published for years was disregarded by many politicians, who seemed astonished at the speed with which Russia developed its own bomb. These politicians, many of whom had themselves been influenced by science fiction, found themselves in a serious dilemma: they had to depend upon scientists for guidance on atomic research and development, but they saw those same scientists as dangerous, suspiciously naïve and unreliably international (Hall, 284-7). Scientists were not given the opportunity to control the uses of their invention in post-war America. Nor was the general public encouraged to take an active role in their own future, when it included the development and testing of atomic weapons.

Immediately after Hiroshima, America began to fear retaliatory attack (Boyer, pp. 4-5). Long a given in science fiction, this assumption has shaped post-war policy to this day. Two major plots, each reflecting popular assumptions, emerged immediately. The most common anticipated a sneak nuclear attack on America, as in Rog Phillips's 'Atom war' and Will F. Jenkins's *The murder of the USA* (both 1946). Many of these stories also assumed the end of civilisation as we know it: Theodore Sturgeon's 'Thunder and roses' and Will F. Jenkins's *Fight for life* (both 1947) represent the emotional extremes for this assumption. The alternate plot showed scientists either as responsible for the inevitable war, as in Louis N. Ridenour's 'Pilot lights of the Apocalypse' (1946), in which nuclear war is started by technological accident, or as already responsible for irrevocable damage to the biosphere. In either case, though humanity might survive, it would be irreversibly altered, probably through genetic mutation, as in Poul Anderson and F. N. Waldrop in 'Tomorrow's children' (1947), and Rog Phillips's *'So shall ye reap!'* (1947). Phillips's mutants are so deformed that they live only to the age of twelve or thirteen. The editorial introduction to this story suggests that atomic bomb tests then under way in the Pacific might already have created the necessary preconditions for this disaster.

Unlike Theodore Sturgeon in 'Memorial' (1946), few writers assume that nuclear destruction of civilisation will end humanity forever. Few stories give up all hope of a future. Some expect scientists to follow the atomic bomb with an equally effective defence, as Murray Leinster had done in 'The power plant' (1931, reprinted in 1947). In 'Atom war', Phillips has scientists produce a defence so miraculous that ordinary civilians could build and use it. Many writers, like Francis

Flagg in 'After Armageddon' (1932) and Ray Bradbury in 'The million-year picnic' (1946) imply that driving humanity back to the wilderness would be a very good thing, especially since atomic war would leave only a 'sacred remnant' to rebuild a (presumably better) society (Bartter, 1986). Some later stories, like Philip Wylie's *Tomorrow!* (1954) advise that relative safety lay in adequate civil defence. (In'erestingly, in none of these stories does the author name the attacking nation; Leinster perhaps because none was established, and the others probably because its identity was established beyond question.)

The public image of the scientist remained confused, especially because some writers, best represented by the immensely popular team of Henry Kuttner and C. L. Moore, presumed a 'bright side'. Writing as 'Lewis Padgett', they suggest in 'The fairy chessmen' (1946) and 'Tomorrow and tomorrow' (1947) that nuclear war is positively good for humanity because it stimulates scientific research and weeds out the weak. As 'Lewis Padgett', Kuttner and Moore also sought a bright side to genetic mutation. In the 'Baldy' stories (1945; collected in *Mutant*, 1953), nuclear war creates a race of benevolent mind readers. A 'sacred remnant' could even escape to another planet from a world irrevocably damaged by atomic radiation, as they do in 'Clash by night' (1943) by Kuttner and More, writing as 'Lawrence O'Donnell'.

This ambivalent attitude toward scientists was well represented in science fiction. Some repeated that scientific secrets could be kept, as Charles Willard Diffin had suggested in 'The power and the glory' (1930). C. M. Kornbluth brought the belief up to date in 'Gomez' (1955), implying that scientific knowledge is both too dangerous for ordinary mortals, and too arcane, beyond their ability to comprehend. Few stories emphasised the normal scientific need to publish. This left the scientist in the position of unilateral censor, having to make the decision whether to hide or destroy his work or to claim privileged knowledge, disregard popular opinion and continue despite the danger, as in Leigh Brackett's *The long tomorrow* (1955). Other stories suggested that scientists could somehow prove the rightness of their cause, as in Kornbluth's 'Two dooms' (1958, one of the few stories to represent the Manhattan Project accurately), or would pursue their scientific interests regardless of consequences, as in Fredric Brown's 'The weapon' (1951). Walter M. Miller, Jr.'s *A canticle for Leibowitz* (1959) masterfully and tragically connects all of these themes.

Immediately following Hiroshima, popular opinion of science –

which had been almost embarrassingly laudatory – turned to suspicion and dread (Boyer, 269-72). Post-war control of nuclear devices was not permitted to nuclear scientists; Robert Oppenheimer was subjected to a 'loyalty' trial and refused further contact with nuclear research; other scientists, who frequently failed to agree on the applications of their work, were brought under political suspicion.[15] Women had long been denied a positive role in science fiction (Le Guin, p. 208); in the laboratory, they lost the gains they had made before the war. While we do not claim that reading science fiction *caused* these things to happen, we can show that science fiction offered stories based on assumptions that logically lead to these actions, and had done so very persuasively over a considerable period before the actions were taken. Since readers of science fiction inevitably transact with society, their assumptions would necessarily affect the larger group.

Can we trace any results of such assumptions to the present day? For one thing, women are not the only people currently 'included out' of science. In 'Blowups happen' (1940), Robert A. Heinlein's Dr Lentz arrogantly remarks, 'You are none of you atomic physicists; you are not entitled to hold opinions in this matter' (p. 260). This has been taken to heart by the reading public. Science, presented either as dangerous (atomic research), morally questionable (genetic engineering), or romantic (manned space flight), seems out of reach of 'ordinary mortals'. This leads to a popular ignorance of science and the scientific method. All scientific research dealing with superweapons has remained highly classified, unless the government have wanted people to support it. Alfred Bester addressed this problem in *Tiger! Tiger!* (1956). When his hero finally understands the peril of the superweapon PyrE, he arranges for full public disclosure as a measure of protection, if not a solution. But despite the wishes of a number of scientists, a policy of full disclosure has not been followed.

Lacking a broad public knowledge base, support of public policy must occur in a climate of public ignorance. The current controversy over 'Star Wars', a science-fictional concept if there ever was one, certainly feeds on this ignorance. The uninformed expect simple answers. Scientists who try to remain intellectually honest appear merely undecided; those with a personal stake in the outcome make unsupportable claims; and 'ordinary people' don't know enough about scientific method, much less about science, to evaluate the situation.

III

Accurately to discuss what humans do with fiction requires a fully transactional literary theory. We have already indicated the major transactions this theory must account for: writer/reader with self, with text, and with society. Clearly, the example given here does not deal with all these transactions; it may be that no single theoretical approach can do so. Looking at or focusing on what humans do in one area naturally requires us to look away from, or 'background', what they do in other areas. the important aspect (and the only new aspect) of our proposal comes in clarifying the scope of the transaction, requiring that we hold each type of criticism as part of this whole rather than as a whole in itself. A brief normative study like the one presented here allows us to connect reader to text and to diachronic context,[16] but it does not discuss the reader's transaction with self, and leaves the readers' transaction with society more or less open.

Studying the process of transacting with (reading) literature illuminates certain aspects that have become problematic for critics who focus on other aspects of the literary transaction. Many do not recognise the importance of this process. For instance, reader response criticism aims to 'refocus criticism on the reader', showing the 'role actual readers play in the determination of literary meaning, the relation of reading conventions to textual interpretation, and the status of the reader's self' (Tompkins, p. ix). Nevertheless, although these critics shift 'the locus of meaning from text to reader', they have not broken 'out of the mold into which critical writing was cast by the formalist identification of criticism with explication' (Tompkins, p. 225). Contemporary critics who deny 'the existence of any reality prior to language and claim[s] for [all] discourse the same relation to the real – namely, that of socially constructed versions of it' (Tompkins, p. 224), often lament their inability to avoid the interpretation of text. They see this as a failure to stick to their own position.

But all criticism must begin with the transacting of self-and-text that we call 'reading'. This necessarily involves negotiating 'meaning', or 'interpreting'. In the example above, I had to 'interpret' the stories before I could 'read' them as examples of 'the image of the scientist'. That I did not discuss (that is, I backgrounded) this negotiation of meaning – this transacting – does not make it a less important preliminary to the normative process. Critics who have disclosed the role of language in the construction of 'reality' have not only backgrounded the transacting of reader with self and the necessary (re)construction of (often pre-verbal) assumptions this process entails, they have failed to notice their own change as they 'interpret' text. Interpretation deserves to retain an honoured place in criticism as long as we recognise what we do when we do it: that we simultaneously pattern the text to fit our assumptions *and* our assumptions to fit the text.

To deal more adequately with fiction – with its normative functions, as well as with the plethora of critical literary theories in general – we might consider that the transactings of reader/writer with self, with text and with culture forms a multi-dimensional matrix roughly defined at least by temporal locus, textual experience,[17] and socio-cultural contact. To place a 'reading' in such a matrix, we need to ask what the experiencer (the reader/writer) does with the text rather than what the text is; and what the experiencer does with that doing, and when and how. The analysis of normative fiction presented here lies along a brief segment of the temporal plane, assuming that a particular type of textual experience crosses a much broader socio-cultural connection than the individual reader (especially since science fiction has always had a limited readership). This analysis assumes that reader and society transact in certain ways, but does not attempt to explain that transacting in detail. It omits discussion of myth, symbolism, psychology, reader-response, gender, socioeconomics, etc. It is, in short, a narrowly focused, limited study.

Contemporary literary study must be interdisciplinary in the widest sense; it must include the sensory-motor behaviour of humans as they transact with themselves, their living and non-living environment, and the patterns they have drawn from these transactings that they call fiction. All critical endeavours lie on some point in the transactional matrix. Each must focus on some aspect of that transaction, and by so doing, must fail to focus (background) some other aspect. Each has greater value when its assumptions are properly considered. Our problem lies in constructing the matrix, in locating our textual transacting on it (though not in some final, 'objective' sense), thus disclosing the relationships among textual acts, and in remembering that we change it as we change ourselves by using it. As reader/writers, we need to acknowledge that even as criticism has itself altered over time, we should never hope to establish a final 'right' or complete reading so long as we contextualised, mutable humans engage – transact with – the text.

Notes

1 German for 'thought experiments', *gedankenexperimente*, became familiar to scientists as Einstein's most creative tactic. John W. Campbell, Jr suggested that science fiction provided unparalleled opportunity for socio-cultural thought experiments; others have agreed (Bartter, 1988, pp. 238-9).

2 Hazard Adams introduces the problem of literary study with the question, 'What is literature?' He then advises the 'serious student of literature' to 'understand the relation of literature to the life around him', acknowledging that 'this is a complex matter' (1969, p. 1). In their introduction to *Critical theory since 1965*, Adams and Searle call for 'criticism and interpretation, which, in order to do its cultural work, must be different from what it interprets' (1986, p. 21).

3 On the other hand, critics who admit that they cannot demonstrate 'objective' standards of literature, but 'know it when they see it', tacitly acknowledge the importance of *transacting* with the text, of including the reader in the evaluation.

4 The insistence on *recorded* text should not encourage us to neglect the importance of the ephemeral, but it limits us to consideration of the *recoverable*.

5 Barnum's infamous method of moving loitering spectators through his indoor side-show involved tricking those who interpreted the 'egress' as yet another fantastic exhibit.

6 I follow C. A. Hilgartner in this use, which he derived from Dewey and Bentley (1978, p. 178).

7 By speaking as though we believed something, we make it harder to believe otherwise. We should not forget that speaking is an action, and that it both follows from and alters assumptions.

8 Summarised from Tompkins, pp. 201-25.

9 In contacting the environment, we form our first and simplest reality. From that contact we *abstract* or construct various levels of assumptions.

10 See H. Bruce Franklin's *War stars*, especially Chapters 1 and 12, for a discussion of the roles of Fulton and Edison, respectively, in the American 'love affair' with superweapons.

11 The story of Leo Szilard and *The world set free* has been widely reported. An extended discussion occurs in Rhodes, pp. 13-28.

12 Among those who knew what was going on, some – including I. I. Rabi and Enrico Fermi - did protest. See Rhodes, pp. 452-68.

13 'The Franck Report, initiated by James Franck and signed by six other scientists, was sent to Washington in June 1945. It urged that the bomb be used only as a demonstration and not to take human life.' If it was received in Washington, it was not acted upon. (Bartter, 1988, p. 111-12. n. 5.)

14 For a more complete listing of nuclear war stories, see Paul Brians's fine bibliography, *Nuclear holocausts*.

15 For example, Rhodes quotes J. Robert Oppenheimer as bluntly demanding, in a speech to other scientists in November 1945, public control of atomic weapons in 'a world that is united, and a world in which war will not occur' (pp. 761-2). Although Oppenheimer helped Edward Teller develop the H-bomb, he was eventually declared a security risk and removed from further contact with atomic research.

16 Any substantive criticism must take generic conditions into consideration. In science fiction, these include understanding that most of the early writers came from fandom, knew each other, and shared ideas and criticisms; that the readership shared an invented language and set of assumptions that created a new, coherent context; that input from readers was institutionalised in SF; and, of course, understanding the economic, cultural and historical context. Text influences writer influences text.

17 In the term 'textual experience' I subsume such variables as the reader/writer's

experience with the text at hand and with other texts; with the contemporary textual tradition; and with the socio-cultural assumptions surrounding 'reading' and the interpretation of text.

References

Fiction

Anderson, Poul and F. N. Waldrop, 'Tomorrow's children', *Astounding science-fiction*, March 1947.

Bester, Alfred, *Tiger! Tiger!* (London, 1956). American title, *The stars my destination* (New York, 1957).

Bradbury, Ray, 'The million-year picnic', *Planet stories*, Summer 1946.

Brackett, Leigh, *The long tomorrow* (New York, 1955).

Brown, Fredric, 'The Weapon', *Astounding science-fiction*, April 1951.

Campbell, John W. Jr, 'Uncertainty', *Amazing stories*, October-November 1936.

Dick, Philip K., 'Jon's world' in *Time to come*, ed. August Derleth (New York, 1954).

Diffin, Charles Willard, 'The power and the glory', *Astounding stories of super science*, July 1930.

Flagg, Francis, 'After Armageddon', *Wonder stories*, September 1932.

Giesy, J. U., *All for his country*, 1914. (Rpt. New York, 1915).

Godfrey, Hollis, *The man who ended war* (Boston, Mass., 1908).

Hale, Stephen G., 'The laughing death', *Amazing stories*, April 1931.

—, 'Worlds adrift', *Amazing stories*, May 1932.

Hawkins, Willard, 'The dwindling sphere', *Astounding science-fiction*, March 1040.

Heinlein, Robert A., 'Blowups happen', *Astounding science-fiction*, September 1940.

—, as 'Anson MacDonald', 'Solution unsatisfactory', *Astounding science-fiction*, May 1941.

Jenkins, Will F., *Fight for life: a complete novel of the atomic age* (New York, 1947).

—, *The murder of the USA* (New York, 1946).

Jones, Raymond F. 'A stone and a spear', *Galaxy science fiction*, December 1950.

Kornbluth, C. M., 'Gomez', *New worlds*, February 1955.

—, 'Two dooms', *Venture science-fiction*, July 1958.

Kuttner, Henry, *Mutant* (New York, 1953). Collection of stories originally printed in *Astounding science-fiction*, 1945-53.

Kuttner, Henry and C. L. Moore as 'Lawrence O'Donnell', 'Clash by night', *Astounding science-fiction*, March 1943.

—, as 'Lewis Padgett', 'The fairy chessmen', *Astounding science-fiction*, January 1946, pp. 7-45; February 1946, pp. 122-76.

—, 'Tomorrow and tomorrow', *Astounding science-fiction*, January 1947, pp. 6-56; February 1947, pp. 140-77.

Leinster, Murray, 'The power planet', *Amazing stories*, June 1931. Reprinted in *Avon fantasy reader* no. 1 (February 1947), pp. 7-44.

Meek, Captain S. P., 'The Red peril', *Amazing stories*, September 1929.

Miller, Walter M., Jr, *A canticle for Leibowitz* (New York, 1959). Collection of stories published in *The magazine of fantasy and science fiction*, 1955-7.

Nathanson, Isaac R., 'The world aflame', *Amazing stories*, January 1935.

Norton, Roy, *The vanishing fleets* (New York, 1908).

Noyes, Pierrepont B., *The pallid giant: a tale of yesterday and tomorrow* (Old Tappan, NJ, 1927). Reprinted as *Gentlemen, you are mad!* (New York, 1946).

Phillips, Rog, 'Atom war', *Amazing stories*, May 1946.

—, 'So shall ye reap!', *Amazing Stories*, August 1947.

Ridenour, Louis N., 'Pilot lights of the apocalypse', *Fortune magazine*, January 1946.

Shelley, Mary, *Frankenstein, or, the modern Prometheus*, 1818.

Smith, E. E., Ph.D., *The skylark of space*, Amazing stories, August-October 1928.
Spohr, Carl, 'The final war', *Wonder stories*, March 1932.
Stockton, Frank, *The great war syndicate* (New York, 1889).
Sturgeon, Theodore, 'Memorial', *Astounding science-fiction*, April 1946.
—, 'Thunder and roses', *Astounding science-fiction*, November 1947.
Taine, John, 'Seeds of life', *Amazing stories quarterly*, Fall 1931.
Train, Arthur and Robert Williams Wood, *The man who rocked the earth* (Garden City, NY, 1915).
Van Vogt, A. E., *Empire of the atom* (Chicago, IL, 1957). Collection of stories from *Astounding science-fiction*, 1946-7.
Wells, H. G., *The world set free* (London and New York, 1914).
Wylie, Philip, *Tomorrow!* (New York, 1954).

Non-fiction

Adams, Hazard, *The interests of criticism: and introduction to literary theory* (New York, 1969).
Adams, Hazard and Leroy Searle (eds.), *Critical theory since 1965* (Tallahassee, FL, 1986).
Barron, Arthur S., 'Why do scientists read science fiction?', *Bulletin of the atomic scientists* 13, no. 2, February 1957, pp. 82-5, 70.
Bartter, Martha A., 'Nuclear holocaust as urban renewal', *Science fiction studies* 39, 1986, pp. 148-58.
—, *The way to ground zero: the atomic bomb in American science Fiction* (London and Westport, CT, 1988).
Boyer, Paul, *By the bomb's early light: American thought and culture at the dawn of the atomic age* (New York, 1985).
Brians, Paul, *Nuclear holocausts: atomic war in fiction, 1895-1984* (Kent, Ohio and London, 1987).
Franklin, H. Bruce, *War stars: the superweapon and the American imagination* (New York and Oxford, 1988).
Hall, Harry S., 'Scientists and politicians', *Bulletin of the atomic scientists*, February 1956. Reprinted in Bernard Barber and Walter Hirsch (eds.), *The sociology of science* (New York, 1962), pp. 269-87.
Hilgartner, C. A., 'The method in the madness of western man', *Communication*, 3, 1978, pp. 143-242.
Le Guin, Ursula K., 'American SF and the other', *Science fiction studies*, 7, November 1975, pp. 208-10.
Rhodes, Richard, *The making of the atomic bomb* (New York, 1986).
Tompkins, Jane P. (ed.), *Reader-response criticism: from formalism to post-structuralism* (Baltimore and London, 1980).

Notes on contributors

Martha A. Bartter is Assistant Professor of English at the Ohio State University, Marion, Ohio. A member of the Science Fiction Writers of America, she is the author of stories as well as critical essays on SF. Her book *The way to ground zero: the atomic bomb in American science fiction* was published by Greenwood Press in 1988

Paul Brians is Professor of English at Washington State University, Pullman, Washington. He is editor of *Nuclear texts and contexts*, the newsletter of the International Society for the Study of Nuclear Texts and Contexts. He has published numerous articles on nuclear war in fiction. His book *Nuclear holocausts: atomic war in fiction 1895-1984* was published by Kent State University Press in 1987.

Philip John Davies teaches in the Department of American Studies at the University of Manchester. He has written on many aspects of American society, including, for Manchester University Press, *Cinema, politics and society in America* (edited with Brian Neve) and *Political issues in America today* (edited with Fredric Waldstein).

Antony Easthope is Senior Lecturer in English at the Polytechnic of Manchester. His publications include *Poetry as discourse* (Methuen, 1983), *British post-structuralism* (Routledge, 1988) and *Poetry and phantasy* (Cambridge University Press, 1989).

H. Bruce Franklin, author or editor of fifteen books and a hundred articles on culture and society, is the John Cotton Dana Professor of English and American Studies at Rutgers University, Newark, New Jersey. His concern about superweapons and militarism dates from his experience as a US Strategic Air Command navigator and intelligence officer in the 1950s.

Edward James teaches in the Department of History at the University of York. He is the author of several books on the early medieval history and archaeology of France, and is editor of *Foundation*, Europe's leading critical journal of science fiction.

Jacqueline Pearson teaches in the Department of English at the University of Manchester. She has published mostly on Renaissance and Restoration topics most recently in her book *The Prostituted muse: Images of women and women dramatists 1642-1737* (Harvester, 1988). She is currently writing a book on feminism and fantasy

Christopher Pike teaches Russian language and literature in the Department of Modern Languages at the University of Keele, Stafford-shire.

Alasdair Spark lectures in American Studies at King Alfred's College, Winchester. The interest in the war in Vietnam and its representation in American culture that prompted his essay in this volume is also the foundation for his recent essays i *Vietnam after images* (eds. J. Walsh and J. Aulich, Macmillan, 1989) and *Essays ar studies* (ed. T. Shippey, Oxford University Press, 1990).

Carl Tighe, a free-lance lecturer and writer, can on occasion be foun teaching in the Extra-Mural Department at the University of Manchester.